LEADERSHIP AND WISDOM

Leadership and Wisdom: Narrating the Future Responsibly gives business students and practitioners the opportunity to re-read tales, poems, myths and fables that have been interpreted by leading management scholars in order to translate the world's folk wisdom into insightful and actionable lessons for a more responsible leadership practice.

Most, if not all, cultures generate narratives that teach people how to make sense of the world and how to respond to challenges with wisdom. These sources provide a medium for character, as well as a guide for decision-making in ambiguous and uncertain circumstances. Management and organization scholars increasingly focus on what narrative wisdom traditions can teach us about leadership and organizational practices, and this book is designed to bring it to students and practitioners. Statler and Küpers have assembled a world-class team of contributors, who reflect on narratives near and dear to them and draw out the lessons for leaders.

With consistency throughout and end-of-chapter questions, this book enables all readers – including undergraduate and postgraduate students of leadership, management and organization studies, as well as interested researchers and practitioners – to reflect on the contents and implications of folk wisdom.

Wendelin Küpers is Professor of Leadership and Organization Studies at Karlshochschule International University, Germany and affiliated Professor at ARTEM ICN Business School Paris, Nancy, Berlin.

Matt Statler is the Richman Family Director of Business Ethics and Social Impact Programming and a Clinical Associate Professor of Business and Society at NYU Stern School of Business, USA.

LEADERSHIP AND WISDOM

Narrating the Future Responsibly

Edited by
Wendelin Küpers and Matt Statler

NEW YORK AND LONDON

First published 2020
by Routledge
52 Vanderbilt Avenue, New York, NY 10017

and by Routledge
2 Park Square, Milton Park, Abingdon, Oxon, OX14 4RN

Routledge is an imprint of the Taylor & Francis Group, an informa business

© 2020 Taylor & Francis

The right of Wendelin Küpers and Matt Statler to be identified as the authors of the editorial material, and of the authors for their individual chapters, has been asserted in accordance with sections 77 and 78 of the Copyright, Designs and Patents Act 1988.

All rights reserved. No part of this book may be reprinted or reproduced or utilised in any form or by any electronic, mechanical, or other means, now known or hereafter invented, including photocopying and recording, or in any information storage or retrieval system, without permission in writing from the publishers.

Trademark notice: Product or corporate names may be trademarks or registered trademarks, and are used only for identification and explanation without intent to infringe.

Library of Congress Cataloging-in-Publication Data
Names: Küpers, Wendelin, editor. | Statler, Matthew, editor.
Title: Leadership and wisdom : narrating the future responsibly /
edited by Wendelin Küpers and Matt Statler.
Description: 1 Edition. | New York : Routledge, 2020. |
Includes bibliographical references and index.
Identifiers: LCCN 2019051054 | ISBN 9781138292338 (hardback) |
ISBN 9781138292345 (paperback) | ISBN 9781315232997 (ebook)
Subjects: LCSH: Leadership. | Management.
Classification: LCC HD57.7 .L43733 2020 | DDC 658.4/092–dc23
LC record available at https://lccn.loc.gov/2019051054

ISBN: 978-1-138-29233-8 (hbk)
ISBN: 978-1-138-29234-5 (pbk)
ISBN: 978-1-315-23299-7 (ebk)

Typeset in Sabon
by Newgen Publishing UK

CONTENTS

List of Figures	vii
List of Photos	viii
Acknowledgements and Dedication	ix
List of Contributors	x

	Editors' Introduction: Overview of Chapters	1
	WENDELIN KÜPERS AND MATT STATLER	
	Prometheus, Humbled: Leadership and Hope in the Anthropocene Age	11
	WENDELIN KÜPERS AND MATT STATLER	
1	The Sandpiper and the Clam Struggle	36
	CHRISTOPHER MICHAELSON	
2	"Don't Fly Too Close to the Sun": Using Myth to Understand the Hazards of Hubristic Leadership	44
	EUGENE SADLER-SMITH	
3	Choosing Our Cross with Wisdom: A Folktale for Living and Leading	62
	ELENA P. ANTONACOPOULOU AND REGINA BENTO	
4	King Popiel, the Killer Mice and the Story of the Post-Lie Leadership	83
	MICHAŁ IZAK AND MONIKA KOSTERA	
5	The Wisdom of Others: Cultural Acclimatization and Engaged Leadership	98
	TIM GILMAN-ŠEVČÍK	
6	A Tale from the Ah-Ah Country	116
	ELEN RIOT	

CONTENTS

7 Laocoön, Leadership and Wisdom 136
ROBIN HOLT

8 How You Wanna Go? Learning from the Unfortunate
Rake 161
MATT STATLER

9 The Story of Merlin as a Tale of Wisdom 178
WENDELIN KÜPERS

Index 231

LIST OF FIGURES

9.1	Merlin as Wild Man of the Forest	203
9.2	Nautilus, fern and Celtic knot and spiral patterns	207

LIST OF PHOTOS

5.1	Boots in New York	99
5.2	Control Room	107
5.3	Facade	110
5.4	Russia Access Hatch	114
7.1	*Laocoön and his sons,* or *Laocoön Group*	148
7.2	William Blake Laocoön 1826	152

ACKNOWLEDGEMENTS AND DEDICATION

We, the editors, are particularly grateful to Sharon Golan for her patience and editorial guidance from the beginning of this project. Furthermore, we would like to thank Alston Slatton and Meredith Norwich for helping us to publish this book.

Moreover, we would also like to thank all the participants in the 2017 EGOS stream "The Moral of the Story: Ethics and Aesthetics in Organizations" in Copenhagen, where this project was born and took its current shape.

Overall, we dedicate this book to our past, current and future students and readers, who engage together with us and others in an ongoing dialogue that spirals across generations.

LIST OF CONTRIBUTORS

Elena P. Antonacopoulou is Professor of Organizational Behaviour at the University of Liverpool Management School, UK, where she leads the GNOSIS research initiative. Her principal research expertise lies in the areas of Organisational Change, Learning and Knowledge Management with a focus on the Leadership implications. Since 2003 as one of only 16 Senior Fellows appointed to lead the prestigious Advanced Institute of Management Research, she has fostered the development of innovative, international, interdisciplinary and interactive modes of research. She is published widely in leading international journals and has held several leadership roles in the top international professional bodies in her field.

Regina Bento is the BGE Distinguished Chair of Business and Professor of Management at the University of Baltimore, US. Born and raised in Brazil, Regina did her doctoral studies at Harvard and MIT (PhD Sloan School of Management, MIT, 1990). At UB since 1991, she has taken sabbaticals and leaves-of-absence to serve as Visiting Professor at MIT's Sloan School (1999, 2007) and as Associate Director of the Christensen Center at Harvard Business School (2006–2009). She has served in leadership roles at the Academy of Management, and Organizational Behavior Teaching Society. Her full biography is available at http://home.ubalt.edu/rbento.

A conceptual artist and writer, **Tim Gilman-Ševčík** is interested in the strategic reimagining of institutions of all kinds to help them adapt to the momentous changes brought about by technology, climate change and social responsibility. With a background in conceptual art, he has created and curated exhibitions and served as artist-in-residence extensively at museums and galleries throughout the US and abroad including the Irish Museum of Modern Art, the Brooklyn Museum, Prague Biennial and many others. He was the founding Artistic Director for Gulliver's Gate, the miniature world museum in Times Square. His writing and art criticism has appeared in a wide range of publications including the *Village Voice*, *The Guardian*, *Art in America* and *Flash Art*, among others. *Cover*, a monograph on his collaborative art practice with Františka Gilman, was published by Triga in 2009, and his book, *The Academy of Forgetting*, was published by Atropos Press in 2016. He serves as Executive Director of the Resilience, Education, Training and Innovation (RETI) Center, a New York City nonprofit focused on urban resilience that was founded in response to Super Storm Sandy. His work as a copywriter and Creative Director for advertising clients such as the Israel Ministry of Tourism, the National Education Association, Transamerica and many more has won numerous industry awards. He was a co-founder of the Peabody-winning Studio 360 for WNYC and the interdisciplinary academic journal *continent*. Professor Gilman-Ševčík also teaches Social Impact at New York University, incorporating contemporary art, critical thinking, experiential learning, visual thinking, design and interdisciplinary studies. He has also been a visiting lecturer at Columbia University Graduate School of Architecture, Planning and Preservation; Parsons School of Design, School of the Visual Arts, and others.

Robin Holt is Professor at the Department of Management, Philosophy and Politics at Copenhagen Business School, Denmark. He is the author of *Judgment and Strategy* and co-author (with Robert Chia) of *Strategy Without Design*. rh.mpp@cbs.dk

Michał Izak is a Reader in Management and Business at the University of Roehampton, UK. His research interests include Critical Management Studies, fiction as a reflection of organizational dynamics, and organizational storytelling. Most recently he researches the neoliberal organizational flexibility discourses. He publishes regularly in peer-reviewed journals and is a member of the editorial boards as well as co-organizer of many international conferences.

Monika Kostera is Professor Ordinaria and Chair of Management at the Jagiellonian University in Kraków, Poland, and at Linnaeus University, Sweden. She holds several visiting professorships. She has authored and edited over 40 books in Polish and English, including her last book, *Management in a Liquid Modern World* with Zygmunt Bauman, Irena Bauman and Jerzy Kociatkiewicz (2015), as well as a number of articles published in journals including *Organization Studies*, *Journal of Organizational Behavior Management* and *British Journal of Management*. Her current research interests include organizational imagination, disalienated work, ethnography and critical organization studies.

LIST OF CONTRIBUTORS

Wendelin Küpers is Professor of Leadership and Organization Studies at Karlshochschule – International University in Karlsruhe, Germany, and Affilated Professor ARTEM ICN, Paris, Nancy, Berlin. Previously, he has pursued a research project in India and taught and researched with various universities in Europe (including St. Gallen University) and in New Zealand. Combining a phenomenological and cross-disciplinary orientation, his research focuses on embodied, emotional and creative, as well as transformational dimensions in relation to more responsible, and wise forms of organizing and managing. Furthermore, his research focuses on integrating artful and aesthetic dimensions of practical wisdom into organization and leadership. Research outputs by him have appeared in a number of leading academic journals and edited volumes. He is also an editor of a book series on "Practical Wisdom, Leadership, Organization and Integral Business Practice" with Ashgate Gower/Routledge and at the moment is working on a book on the nexus of Praxis, Practices and Phronesis in relation to sustainable actions in organization and leadership.

Christopher Michaelson is David A. and Barbara Koch (pronounced "coach") Distinguished Professor of Business Ethics and Social Responsibility at the University of St. Thomas, Opus College of Business, US. As a scholar and business advisor, he explores how meaning and purpose in life and at work can improve our own and others' lives. Throughout his career, Christopher has built bridges between scholarship and practice. After earning his PhD in philosophical ethics and aesthetics from the University of Minnesota in 1997, he helped launch a business ethics advisory practice, which became part of a global risk consulting network, in the New York office of a Big Four firm. He served on the editorial boards of ten CEO surveys and as the firm's Strategy Officer to the World Economic Forum on projects examining the role of business in society. A few years into his consulting career, Christopher took a full-time lectureship at the Wharton School of the University of Pennsylvania while keeping a foot in practice. In 2005, he joined the Business and Society faculty of the New York University Stern School of Business, on which he has remained since moving home to Minneapolis in 2006. He went to St. Thomas in 2008 and is also an affiliate faculty member of the University of Minnesota's Center for Bioethics. He is the Humanities and Business Ethics Section Editor of the *Journal of Business Ethics*, on the editorial board of the *Academy of Management Learning & Education* and on the Executive Committee of the International Society of Business, Economics, and Ethics.

Elen Riot is an Assistant Professor of Strategy in the Laboratoire REGARDS (Economics and Management) of the University of Reims

LIST OF CONTRIBUTORS

Champagne Ardenne, France. She defended her PhD in 2009 at Hautes études commerciales (HEC) and is a graduate from HEC and from the ENS of Lyon (Literature and Social Sciences). She initially studied political economy, comparative literature and anthropology and she is, more than ever, plowing the field.

Eugene Sadler-Smith is Professor of Organizational Behaviour, Surrey Business School, University of Surrey, UK. His current research interests are intuition (in organizational decision making) and hubris in business and political leadership. He is the author of a number of books, including *Inside Intuition* (2008) and *The Intuitive Mind* (2010). His latest book, *Hubristic Leadership*, was published in 2018. He has delivered hubris workshops to organizations including the CIPD, ICSA, AcademiWales and the Home Office.

Matt Statler is the Richman Family Director of Business Ethics and Social Impact Programming and a Clinical Associate Professor of Management and Organizations at NYU Stern School of Business, US. Previously, Matt served NYU's Center for Catastrophe Preparedness and Response as the Director of Research and as Associate Director of the International Center for Enterprise Preparedness. He worked as the Director of Research and as a Research Fellow at the Imagination Lab Foundation in Lausanne, Switzerland, following several years as a management consultant in New York City. His research on ethics, leadership and strategy has been published in dozens of peer-reviewed journal articles and book chapters. He completed a PhD in Philosophy from Vanderbilt University, US; spent a year in Germany as a Fulbright Scholar at the University of Heidelberg; and obtained undergraduate degrees in Spanish and Philosophy from the University of Missouri, US. He lives in Brooklyn with his wife Roxanna, daughter Roya, and son Cyrus.

EDITORS' INTRODUCTION
Overview of Chapters

Wendelin Küpers and Matt Statler

A Story about Stories: Key Themes and Questions from the Chapters

The purpose of this book is to give readers the occasion to develop themselves as wise leaders by reflecting on narratives. Toward that end, we the editors contacted potential contributors, described the nature of the volume and invited them to select a primary text that has particular significance for them and interpret its significance for leadership study and practice. The following briefly interprets these chapters, raising additional questions for students and scholars of leadership.

In "The Sandpiper and the Clam Struggle" (Chapter 1), Christopher Michaelson retells an ancient folktale as an allegory for (Darwinian) zero-sum business competition where predators and prey, fixated on their adversarial relationship, all lose when they do no learn to collaborate. It is a tale of greed that warns us not to try to accomplish goals in one fell swoop or to believe in one single stroke of luck, but to work persistently and with patience. Corresponding to the Prisoner's Dilemma it conveys the need for trust, the limitations of controlling individualism and values of a collectivist understanding of shared intelligence and wisdom as well as institutions that yield more mutual benefits. The quality of this tale is that it uses animal metaphors and allegory, and also shows the value of animals' capacity for reciprocity and other apparently virtuous behaviours, suggesting that also in nature, "there is room for cooperation for the common good".

When we try to interpret Christopher Michaelson's fable, he appears to be referring to the common good as a convivial state of nature that we can reflect on and learn from. With this example, he makes an argument that leaders should not be blinded by competition. In terms of simulating and emulating, the story invites leaders to act not in a hyper-competitive mode, but with humility and a sense of collaboration. By enacting such conviviality, leaders can cultivate the types of mutually beneficial relationships that mitigate the risks and damages associated with the Anthropocene. Additionally, because this narrative involves animals, it sensitizes contemporary readers to the ancient traditions of viewing humans alongside other animals involved in similar struggles to survive and thrive. As we address the challenges of the Anthropocene, leaders will surely have to consider the needs as well as the insights of other living beings throughout the planetary ecosystem.

Questions that can guide further reflection, discussion and interpretation include:

- How do narratives shape what we consider to be 'fair' as competition?
- How are collective actions and problems moulded by narratives?
- How do narratives influence and contour dynamics of power and competition?
- What narratives have driven the industrial and organizational developments that have contributed to the Anthropocene?
- What narratives provide possibilities to address collective problems and unintended consequences of what is associated with the Anthropocene, including pollution, carbon usage, etc.?
- How can leadership be a catalyst for an imaginary and practical change of affective dispositions, attitudes and perception as well as habits and practices of collaboration and conviviality in organization, individually and collectively?
- Why is the use of a fable with animals as protagonist helpful for thinking about sustainable leadership in an 'Eco-cene' thus an era beyond Anthropocene?

Eugene Sadler-Smith, in his chapter titled "'Don't Fly Too Close to the Sun': Using Myth to Understand the Hazards of Hubristic Leadership" offers us profound insights about hubris; specifically, characteristics, causes and (unintended) consequences of hubristic leadership that exerts over-confident and over-ambitious judgement and behaviour. Taking from Ovid's *Metamorphoses* the story of Dædalus and Icarus, the dream of god-like power of flight that led to Icarus' downfall are retold and interpreted. He is offering an interpretative sense-making and re-storying of this myth of modern-day organization and leadership. Following the hubris-followed-by-nemesis archetypal pattern, such destructive leadership is that while it implicates volitional, systematic and repeated leader behaviours that violate legitimate interests of organizations and their members through a misuse of power or position, it also generates negative unintended consequences. Furthermore, he suggests possibilities for mitigating hubristic leadership through moderating practical wisdom and its prudential judgement.

INTRODUCTION

Interpreting this story, we see that here the author is problematizing the implications of a self-centred, hyper-ambition, pride and hubris. The story sensitizes leaders to simulate/emulate courage and compassion as well as moderating practical wisdom and its prudential judgement. Overall, this tale demonstrates the need to decentre and question the high-flying 'anthropos' for overcoming hubristic Anthropocene for moving toward 'eco-scenic' practices, toward more prudent sense-makings, wise imaginaries and collaborative actions, and corresponding forms of leadership.

Questions that can guide further reflection, discussion and interpretation include:

- Why is hubristic leadership dangerous? Why has it been referred to as the 'tragic flaw'? In the proverbial phrase, why does 'pride go before destruction', a haughty spirit before a fall?
- What could you do to avoid hubris in your life?
- What tragic figures of hubris can you find in the contemporary business landscape?
- How would those leaders' narratives be different if they had exercised more humility?
- How has hubris contributed to the Anthropocene?
- Recalling the fate of Prometheus from above, how can contemporary leaders approach the Anthropocene with humility?
- How can stories like this one offer the potential to transform leadership practices?

Elena Antonacopoulou and Regina Bento offer a chapter called "Choosing Our Cross with Wisdom: A Folktale for Living and Leading". This chapter is inspired by the folktale about a man who constantly complained about the weight of his 'cross', but then, in a dream, was given the opportunity of choosing his own cross. In this folktale, we come to appreciate suffering as an inescapable part of life. Yet, the wisdom of our choices influences our ability to deal with suffering and allows it to become a source of personal growth. Such choices can influence not only the cause of our suffering (for example, when the suffering relates to something that is conceivably under our control), but, more importantly, those choices can influence the effect that suffering has on us, even when we cannot do anything about the suffering itself. But how can we 'pick' (choose) our cross with wisdom, so that we can also 'pick up' and carry it through life, in a sustainable way, that opens us to joy, and helps us greet both happiness and suffering with equanimity?

Here we draw from various religious, spiritual and philosophical traditions to examine the wisdom of picking up a cross in a way that involves assessing both the burden (the weight to be borne) and the bearer (our capacity to bear that weight) in a lifelong search for meaning. We then explore the challenges and opportunities this entails for leaders, as those who can influence the burdens of others, and their capacity to bear burdens. And then this chapter concludes by reflecting about the role of leadership education and development in helping prepare future leaders to pick up individual and collective crosses with wisdom.

By recognizing the limits of the self, and finding courage to continue in 'crossed circumstances', this story encourages leaders-as-learners to simulate/emulate a Stoic attitude toward suffering while cultivating the courage, commitment, confidence and curiosity to continue. Along the way, the story suggests that leaders can discover and enact compassion through the practice of dialogue and the development of trusting relationships. This story additionally calls for us to carry the cross and 'cross over' the anthropogenically induced suffering in the Anthropocene.

Questions that can guide further reflection, discussion and interpretation include:

- What does 'suffering' and 'picking a cross' mean and imply for leadership today?
- How could you as a leader stand your ground, firm and strong for your convictions, virtues and values while facing challenges in your professional life?
- What role does giving up control as well as empathy and compassion for becoming a (joyful) wiser leader?
- How can leaders influence the burdens of others, and their capacity to bear those burdens in the everyday lives of organizations?
- How can leadership contribute to deal with collective crosses with practical wisdom?
- How would you transform breakdowns into breakthroughs as a leader-as-learner?
- Find or create a short poem about implications for the development of more responsible and sustainable leadership practices based on the ideas of this chapter!

Chapter 4 by Michał Izak and Monika Kostera titled "King Popiel, the Killer Mice and the Story of the Post-Lie Leadership" retells the legend of old king Popiel and the killer mice, reveals the problems of consequences of disconnecting leadership from the people and the land, while also showing a way out of the seemingly desperate situation this kind of leadership produces. They situate and relate their story to our current context as a time of uncertainty and turbulence, placed in a 'Baumanian' interregnum (eroding Capitalism, disintegration of democratic and economic institutions, and the eco-crisis).

INTRODUCTION

What they show is the importance of using imagination in order to point to natural and social roots and consequences of leadership inviting us to a creative journey to find ways of reclaiming the missing roots, or what we regard as the truth (and practice) of leadership. The morale of their story emphasizes that leadership needs to be in contact with land and people, as otherwise it and its power lose legitimization (turning into usurpation in need of constructed justifications to persevere as their retelling demonstrates revealingly).

This story shows the impacts of monstrous lies, even in a post-lie world, and the lack of being in contact, while encouraging simulating/emulating to engage in dialogue and cultivating a trust culture. With regard to the Anthropocene, not only are there also monstrous lies like climate changer deniers, one fundamental problem is that of being disconnected from what is going on, also in relation to nature, in need for reintegration.

Questions that can guide further reflection, discussion and interpretation include:

- Why is Popiel's and Gerda's self-centred and short-termist leadership problematic?
- What qualities and influencing forces of leadership processes and actions or agencies allowed transformations in the story?
- What does an 'honest, truthful and sustainable leadership' mean for you personally?
- Please see additional 'Questions for Reflection and Discussion' in the chapter itself on pages 93–94.

Tim Gilman-Ševčík offers us a chapter called "The Wisdom of Others – Cultural Acclimatization and Engaged Leadership" in which he presents and interprets a passage from Jonathan Swift's famous satire, *Gulliver's Travels*, where the narrator offers his opinions about the qualities of travel writing. This passage deals with truth and falsehood, and with the troubling fact that 'falsehood flies, while truth comes limping along afterward'. Swift's narrator claims to be offering nothing but truth, yet the fable itself appears as an intense satire of the political and economic realities of Swift's time. Gilman-Ševčík's interpretation of these dynamics appears even more ambiguous because he himself worked as the creative director of a re-telling of the fable *Gulliver's Gate*, that has been staged as a huge tourist destination in Times Square in New York City.

This chapter asks us to simulate/emulate an attitude of openness to cultural diversity, a willingness to experience and assimilate to different cultures, going far beyond learning the language or creating some new representation of the cultural 'other'. It helps us to critique any claim to perfect rationality, arguing that the means and the ends of human action remain inevitably bound up with the cultural context. Ultimately, the chapter provides yet another warning against hubris, arguing that our interpretation of the text cannot be considered static or closed in some final way. Rather, we remain wise, argues Gilman-Ševčík, as we resist closure and remain attuned and open to new experiences and interpretations of the world around us.

Questions that can guide further reflection, discussion and interpretation include:

- Who are the Lilliputians, Brobdingnagians, Houyhnhnms and Yahoos in your life?
- Who are the Lilliputians, Brobdingnagians, Houyhnhnms and Yahoos in the contemporary business and political landscape?
- What stories do you find yourself repeatedly telling about your experiences struggling with cultural understanding or integration?
- How have you been able to gain understanding that has helped you to reconcile cultural differences?
- In what ways might pride about your cultural identity prevent you from gaining greater understanding of others?
- How have colonialist travel narratives contributed to the Anthropocene Age?
- How do narratives about cultural identity shape or constrain our capacity to respond to the challenges associated with the Anthropocene?

In Chapter 6, titled "A Tale from the Ah-Ah Country", Elen Riot presents the figure of the trickster, who problematizes the relationship between truth and falsehood, making it difficult to distinguish what appears from what disappears. Like Gilman-Ševčík, Riot here builds on her own artistic practices, including the publication of short fiction as well as the creation of immersive gallery shows presenting an imaginary Himalayan tribe. This chapter imagines a folk literature in which that tribe, the Ah-Ah's, come into being, exist and struggle for a period time, and then disappear following an encounter with explorers. Through these episodes, the tribe resists simple binary distinctions and the pride that inspires them, remaining wise as they cultivate a beginner's mind in which many new things are possible.

This chapter invites readers to simulate/emulate that attitude of openness to the reality of experience, without closing ourselves off to possibilities by clinging to simple differentiations of truth from falsehood. It counsels wise leaders to recognize that even sources of hope remain ever subject to failure, and that culture as such does not provide any security against future calamity. The layers of ambiguity associated with the folk narrative as such – imagined and articulated by Riot, drawing on and playing with our own assumptions about the 'naturalist' wisdom of Himalayan tribes who can listen to the river rapids and learn

INTRODUCTION

from them – ask us to reconsider the narratives associated with the Anthropocene Age.

Questions that can guide further reflection, discussion and interpretation include:

- How has the history of humanity as such been crafted or constructed as a narrative within the academic disciplines of anthropology, biology, psychology, etc.?
- How have those narratives contributed to the differentiation of the 'human' from the 'animal' or 'natural' world?
- How do narratives of progress shape the differentiation of modern from pre-modern humanity?
- What would it mean for you to practice 'impression management'?
- Discuss the following statement: 'you must fake it until you make it!' critically.
- How can you creatively narrate new possibilities for humanity in the Anthropocene?
- How can leaders motivate and organize people through the creation of new stories?
- How do certain narratives enable particular tribes (i.e., organizations) to survive, thrive or perish?

In Chapter 7, titled "Laocoön, Leadership and Wisdom", Robin Holt focuses on the figure of the Trojan priest, who, suspecting an Athenian trick in the Trojan Horse, tried to proclaim the truth to his fellow Trojans. However, the priest was dragged into the sea along with his two sons by sea serpents sent by Athena to silence him and maintain the ruse. Holt presents and interprets three different versions of this tale, the first from Virgil's Aeneid, the second from Lessing's interpretation of a classic sculpture depicting the story, and the third from Blake's verbal and visual montage. Through these illustrations, Holt raises a series of fundamental questions about time and space, representation and knowledge, and the exercise of political power through narratives and images as well as imagination.

We interpret this chapter as a call, similar to Gilman-Ševčík's, to resist closure when it comes to claims to knowledge or legitimacy. The chapter invites us to simulate/emulate the activity of speaking 'truth to power', yet cautions us that we cannot so easily differentiate or make distinctions between concerning what is true or false, good or bad, beautiful or ugly. Similarly, the chapter reminds us that we should not be lulled into accepting a particular medium or form of communication or expression as true. Instead, we should remain 'on the ground', wisely seeking as many different perspectives as possible about anything that matters to us. As we engage in such practices of pragmatic inquiry, we may then find ourselves riding along with the flow of events in the world.

Questions that can guide further reflection, discussion and interpretation include:

- What truth am I afraid to tell?
- What sort of truth will unfold through me?
- How will I respond when confronted with unethical or unsustainable business practices?
- What is the role of a revived power of imagination in the sense of Blake for leadership?
- How can I cultivate myself as someone who imagines possible futures?
- Through what narratives and representations is political power exercised in our world today?
- What forms of representation do you think will most effectively enable us to thrive collectively in the Anthropocene Age?

Matt Statler's chapter, "How You Wanna Go? Learning from the Unfortunate Rake", introduces folk music as one of the possible media for presenting narrative accounts of wisdom. Focusing on the 'Ballad of the Unfortunate Rake', a cycle of songs originating in Ireland and England, and continuing in the New Orleans jazz and American folk musical traditions, the chapter considers the question of how we should live when faced with death. Integrating considerations from ancient Greek and Roman philosophy with Montaigne and Nietzsche, the chapter encourages leaders to adopt stoic equanimity in the face of death while cultivating the affirmation of life while it lasts. The implications of this lesson for leaders include re-framing leadership as an aesthetic phenomenon, exploring the potential of aesthetic phenomena to enable collective action, and shifting the ontology of action toward an engaged or active passivity, playing along with the world.

This chapter invites readers to simulate/emulate active non-doing, indicating that such a mode of engagement with the world can be joyful and productive even though it involves layers of multiplicity and ambivalence. From one perspective, the Rake presents a figure of Stoic ethics combined with Epicurean epistemology: sensitive and aware of the vicissitudes of experience, affirming them even as they may pass. This story suggests that the dystopian and apocalyptic stories associated with the Anthropocene are in some sense not as new and as unique as they appear. Rather throughout history, people have struggled in the face of crisis and catastrophes, while still taking time to appreciate and even cultivate the qualities of experience while it lasts.

Questions that can guide further reflection, discussion and interpretation include:

INTRODUCTION

- What narratives shape your understanding and attitude toward death?
- How do your narratives about death shape your understanding of the meaning and purpose of life?
- What narratives shape our understanding of the past, present and future of the earth?
- What forms of life should be affirmed in view of the Anthropocene?
- What organizational practices and activities should be affirmed in view of the Anthropocene?
- What could an affirmative joyful Amor Fati mean for you as a leader?
- What aspects of wise leadership might be uniquely cultivated through music and songs?

Chapter 9 by Wendelin Küpers, "The Story of Merlin as a Tale of Wisdom", takes the figure and stories about Merlin as a tale for learning about wisdom. Reinterpreting various narrated messages and inspirations evoked by this archetypical character are linked to leadership and organizations as well as their stakeholders. In particular, insights and learnings are explored with regard to envisioning futures, mentoring and counselling of political leadership (King Arthur, Camelot) and institutionalized forms of governance (Round Table). Furthermore, adventurous quests for integration (Holy Grail, Wild Man, Love Spell) as well as the role of an engaged but placid letting-go are discussed. Parts of this retelling are also ambiguities, challenges and perspectives that emerge by reconstructing and reinterpreting the stories of Merlin as a source for what wisdom of leadership was, is and could be.

Inspired by the incarnated arche-type of Merlin, this tale encourages leaders to play multiple creative roles for experimenting and enacting wisdom in meaningful ways. It invites readers to simulate/emulate serenely and equanimous practices of visionaries, mentors or counsellors, but also strategist or 'institutionalizer' of governance and integrator. In this way, Merlin's wisdom and especially his retreat into the wilderness can be read as a critique in relation to the Anthropocene and for cultivating a different relationship to oneself, others and 'nature–culture' and thus an integral living in an 'Eco-scene'.

Questions that can guide further reflections, discussions and interpretations may include:

- What role does the capacity of embodied imagination and envisioning with in-, hind-, and foresight mean and imply for 'possibilizing' and sense-making in leadership?

9

- Why do strategic visions of the future need to permeate decisions and actions, as well as energizing, and empowering all organizational members to be enacted effectively?
- What can be learned from the transformative tales of Merlin, especially when they are related and used for transformational leadership in contemporary organizations?
- What characteristics would an excellent mentor(ing) in your professional life demonstrate?
- If you would become a mentor, what would you convey or impart, and in what way, to your protégé?
- Why is a 'Round Table' a symbol and medium for an integral leadership and for instituting governance today?
- Who would you invite, and for which reasons, to a Round Table for discussing issues of Corporate Social Responsibility (CSR) and sustainability?
- What does a 'Quest', for what kind of 'Grail', mean in your professional and personal life?
- What happens if leaders on their virtuous quests connect their search with practical wisdom in today's world?
- Can a wise Merlinian leadership practice accomplish the right ends using the right means at the right time, and include making prudent decisions and enacting them in relation to everyone and everything? What would 'right' mean and constraints or conflicts imply in the neoliberal age and for a more sustainable and flourishing future to come?
- Give reasons why business and civic society can only ignore at their peril the cultivation of the art of wisdom in relation to sustainable and flourishing living.
- What would you do if you were playing the role of a Trickster?
- Why is it meaningful for leaders to retreat sometimes?
- Find some interpretation of the statement "Kinship instead of Kingship"!
- What shadows would leaders in general and you in particular need to learn to integrate for developing genuine forms of responsive and responsible practices that are more sustainable?
- What would 'letting-go' mean for you in your leadership practice and your art of living?

PROMETHEUS, HUMBLED
Leadership and Hope in the Anthropocene Age

Wendelin Küpers and Matt Statler

This book contributes to the education of practically wise leaders capable of sustaining life today and in the future. Reaching across various narrative traditions and genres, it brings different stories about wisdom into dialogue with each other and relates them to leadership. By presenting these storied forms of wisdom, the contributing authors respond to the emerging social, political, economic, organizational and environmental challenges that we face in our contemporary world.

Living in this so-called Anthropocene Age, we are increasingly learning about and experiencing the dramatic impacts that humanity has on the planet. Gloomy, dystopian and apocalyptic stories of disaster, decline, demise and extinction are increasingly told as part of an eco-eschatological 'dark ecology' (Morton, 2016).[1] The ongoing use of nature as a resource for instrumentalist progress- and growth-oriented economic practices has reached a level that makes Anthropocene even more adequate to be called 'capitalocene' (Moore, 2016). Yet we can understand how we have arrived at this crisis and its junctures in history by recalling the ancient Greek myth of Prometheus, who tried to steal fire from heaven in order to gain mastery over nature.

Zeus took vengeance on Prometheus by giving him a cursed box containing all kinds of evils and plagues – including greed, envy, hatred, mistrust, sorrow, anger, revenge despair, sickness and death – that were released and scattered across the world for humans to torment when Pandora opened the box. When Pandora realized what she had done, she quickly shut the lid to the box, and only one thing was left inside, '*Elpis*', the personification of hope as the potentially mitigating, though ambivalent force. For Hesiod, whose account of the Prometheus myth we recall here, hope rests on the notion that by experiencing trouble, a fool may become wise. Erasmus later cast the figure of hope as "he whom mistakes made wise" (Barker, 2001: 32). So then, can we who have sought to control and master nature by using it as a 'resource' to be 'exploited'

11

to produce 'economic growth' and 'progress' learn from the Prometheus myth and become wise before our foolishness gets the better of us all? Or rather, failing fully to master nature, can we nevertheless save our skins through technological innovation, and thereby redeem the hopes of neoliberal, pro-growth optimists? It seems that only by endangering and almost despoiling the planet do we realize just how much a part of it we are, and always have been. Waking up to our entanglement with the world and all its beings that we are destroying requires us to re-imagine our relationship to it.

We cannot do this except through the creation and sharing of stories. But how, then, exactly? Instead of Promethean mastery *of* nature (Gehmann, 2004), playing now the role of 'God with the Climate' (Hamilton, 2013), how can we develop and share stories that emphasize a wiser 'mastery' as an embodied art of a convivial relationship *with* nature (Baskin, 2015: 16)? How can we learn to tell 'better', i.e., non-totalizing and non-normative, or even non-moralizing stories about life in and of the planet (Zylinska, 2014: 46)? How would stories appear that leave behind human(ist) ascension and exceptionalism as well as its masculinist rationality, binary systems and hierarchizing dualisms? How might we move even beyond the hubristic '*anthropos*' as world-maker or destroyer, and develop narratives that include non-human or more-than-human beings existing more sustainably in 'nature–culture' (Haraway, 2003) connections with each other?

This book responds to these questions, helping students and scholars to develop new forms of wise leadership as they share and interpret narratives. While facing the limit-character of the current auto-destructive situation of the Anthropocene with its impending global catastrophe or possible dead-end futures, rehabilitating and retelling tales of wisdom and its learning (Küpers & Gunnlaugson, 2017) becomes even more important. We think a critical discussion of the concept and narrative of the Anthropocene provides us a chance to develop more prudent, non-hubristic leadership practices that contribute to practically wise decisions, judgements and actions. We believe that a storied wisdom perspective can help us to see the broader process of the problematization of global, regional and local survival that induces interrogating and reworking foundational relationships between and among living and natural beings.

In order to explain more clearly and carefully what we mean, we first develop a critical understanding of practical wisdom, and its links to leadership as well as to narratives are outlined. Therefore, in the following section, we explain in more detail what we mean by 'wisdom' and by 'narrative', weaving them together in relation to the process of 'educating wise leaders'. Then, we provide an overview of all chapters, interpreting them and raising questions for further discussion about the lessons or messages they may have for leadership in the Anthropocene Age. Finally, we invite you, dear readers, to join us in an ongoing conversation about how we can share stories that help create a more sustainable future.

Wisdom and Narrative: Weaving Words and Worlds (Texts and Contexts) Together

What Do We Mean by 'Wisdom'?

The term practical wisdom has been used by philosophers and throughout various cultural traditions. The Western understanding is very much influenced by Aristotle's interpretation of practical wisdom as practical reasoning, knowledge and virtuous habit (Aristotle, 1985, 1998; Eikeland, 2006). Correspondingly, practical wisdom was defined from Aristotle onwards as an intellectual virtue that guides decisions and actions to serve the common good or enhance societal well-being. In this sense, practical wisdom refers to an enacted moral excellence involving individual and collective 'eudaimonia', translated as happiness, thriving, flourishing, and even as utility (Aristotle, 1998: 1144a4–5). This Aristotelian tradition (Eikeland, 2008; Dunne, 1993/1997) has distinguished practical wisdom (phrónêsis) from both the more abstract contemplative and theoretical wisdom (sophia) as well as from the more technical know-how and calculating (tékhnê), connected to activities of making (poiêsis); although theoretical and practical dimensions of wisdom enacted as an art (Küpers, 2013).

Being interested in what is practically wise focuses on making the 'right' use of knowledge and preferential choices or judgements for action. Accordingly, practical wisdom can be understood as an embodied, reflective and morally committed doing (Kemmis & Smith, 2008) that is situationally realized at the right time, for the right reasons and by the right means, rendering right effects and consequences. In order to strike these balances, it is necessary to determine suitable conducts for achieving virtuous aims while finding a proper balanced middle way between undesirable extremes. Moving on this pathway is avoiding states that are 'too hot' (experiencing the agitation of excess) as much as 'too cold' (experiencing inert states of sterility and indifference). This balanced orientation requires an openness to each situation and the ability to perceive as well as to have the appropriate feelings or desires about it, and then to deliberate on what is appropriate in specific circumstances, to value, to respond and to act adequately (Aristotle, 1985; Schwartz & Sharpe, 2006). Importantly, such wisdom is also embodied practically in the sense of incorporating and operating through the integration of various modes in relation to the world, including bodily, affective, sensual and tacit or implicit knowing, and intuition, all of which are highly relevant for organizational life and management (Roca, 2007; Küpers & Statler, 2008; Rooney et al., 2010). All of these modes of wisdom are gained through acquired experience, and can be cultivated through reflection on experience (Statler, 2014).

In recent decades, positive psychologists have built on this ancient tradition and oriented toward wisdom as one of the virtues or excellences associated with human thriving. The psychologists who established part of the theoretical basis for contemporary study of wisdom began by focusing on 'folk conceptions of wisdom'. Synonyms for wisdom like sagacity, sapience, discernment or insight (or antonyms such as folly, foolishness, knavery), for example, demonstrate a link to common sense, often implicitly. The research carried out on these more implicit theories of wisdom (i.e., common sense theories, or folk conceptions), analyzes the terms used to describe both wisdom and those said to be wise, as well as the most typical indicators of wisdom. Results of these studies (e.g., Clayton & Birren, 1980; Holliday & Chandler, 1986; Sternberg, 1985; 1987; Sternberg & Jordan, 2005) have shown that the concepts of wisdom and the wise person are an integral part of everyday human life.

In these philosophical and psychological research traditions, practical wisdom has been consistently associated with leadership (e.g., Yang, 2011; Grint, 2007; Shotter & Tsoukas, 2014). Accordingly, organizational scholars have built on these insights, exploring practical wisdom as an art (Küpers, 2013) that is highly relevant for leadership. Drawing on philosophy, psychology and even theology and spirituality, organizational scholars have researched various dimensions and roles of wisdom. In particular, scholars have explored how wise leader(-ship) involves a capacity for ontological acuity, that is, to discern, integrate and narrate various situated complexities and appropriated responses (McKenna et al., 2009). Illustrating the point by contrast, other recent studies and reports have shown that massive failures by leaders and leadership result from leaders' neglect of wisdom-related qualities (Grossmann & Brienza, 2018; Fortune Editors, 2016). In such cases, leaders appear to hold high levels of intelligence, yet fail in their jobs because they lack wisdom. Speaking of hope in the Anthropocene Age (Küpers, 2019), we can affirm the notion that leaders today, and in the future to come, are called to employ enlightened wise judgements. Those include consideration of the consequences of decisions and actions for the self, others, the organization, stakeholder and society at large. Thus, the exercise of integrity, courage and careful concern for the common good (Bierly & Kolodinsky, 2008) comprises raising questions about what is the 'good', and for whom.

In practice, actions are always constrained to some extent by all kinds of forces, like fate, destiny, luck or contextual conditions and contingent circumstances. These influences imply the need for continuous reappraisal of strategies for approaching the status of virtuosity and goodness of wisdom, respectively the potential for the 'good' in the particular (Gadamer, 1982). We can undertake such an appraisal by reflecting on our own experiences, and also by reflecting on the experiences of others as we encounter them through narratives. Thus, the cultivation of wisdom has always involved telling stories about what someone did, and learning from that person's experience about how to handle similar conditions in one's own lives. Becoming wise, in this sense, always involves narrative.

What Do We Mean by 'Narrative'?

Stories and storytelling have been an integral part of human existence throughout history. A storytelling person or '*homo narrans*' (Fisher, 1987) lives in and through stories; s/he does not know the world other than as a storied realm (Mair, 1988: 127). Throughout life, humans are inextricably entangled in stories, and stories shape our individual identities as well as our social and cultural milieu. Especially as a way of organizing action, stories are creative accomplishments that are bridging oral and written cultures as well as bring together mundane facts and fiction, while incorporating time and place (Sarbin, 1986: 9). Moreover, stories provide media not only to make sense of experiences, but also to challenge, change or preserve deeply rooted meanings, inherent in fictions and myths, across generations (Armstrong, 2006).

While students of the humanities often become familiar with folktales as well as the more refined narrative traditions that have grown from these roots, business students or practitioners are rarely exposed to them – with the notable exceptions of 'case studies'. Nevertheless, organizational and management researchers have, however, extensively explored the significance of stories as fiction for organizational life (see, e.g., Magala & Flory, 2012; Boje, 2010; Gabriel, 2000: Gabriel et al. 2011: Holt & Zundel, 2018).[2]

Stories and narratives open valuable entry gates into a wide assortment of organizational phenomena, including knowledge culture, politics, the dynamics of groups and management, etc. Various streams of research have explored how stories, for example, offer a means of disseminating a vision or message (Gabriel, 2000), sharing knowledge and sense-making (Gabriel & Connell, 2010), constructing gender identity (Gherardi, 1996), encouraging critical reflection on management (Gherardi & Poggio, 2007) or developing authentic leadership (Shamir & Eilam, 2005). Stories also play important roles in strategy development (Küpers et al. 2012) and in the context of transformational change (Brown et al. 2009; Küpers, 2012).

With the rise of digital media, new dialogical forms of co-creational, digital organizational storytelling have emerged that displace narrative monologism and afford a fluid, responsive plasticity of meaning making via protocols of amateurism, affinity and authenticity that generates spaces for critical, minority, grassroots and individual voices (Bell & Leonard, 2016).

Whatever the media, organizational values and beliefs are produced, reproduced and transformed through stories (Smircich, 1983). Not only defining and crossing boundaries, stories constitute filtering frames of reference for interpreting organization actions and form a coherence and order for experienced events. The power of stories lies in their capacity to encompass thinking and feeling about issues as well as to compel and convince others.

At the same time, stories and narrative expression can serve as premises of arguments, persuasive appeals and as an implicit mechanism of cultural control. As organizational stories can generate commitment, they can then be used for vested interests, exerting political power and social control (Wilkins, 1983). Not only organizing anticipated reaction based on an invented tradition, stories also provide models of permissible behaviour and rules, as they are imparting values and affecting problem definitions (Witten, 1993). Witten asserts that "narrative is a singularly potent discursive form through which control can be dramatized, because it compels belief while at the same time it shields truth claims from testing and debate" (ibid: 100). In this way, stories and narratives become tacit means or insidious ways for constructing and reinforcing ideologies or can be used performatively as a discursive resource for influencing events, and its interpretations.

For example, narratives can induce workers to internalize an ideology of 'empowerment' for enhancing performance that is turned to purposes of tightening the iron cage of managerialist control and manipulation (Barker, 1993). Likewise, there exists an ideological deception in storytelling and narrative methodology (Essers, 2012). One of the powers of stories lies in their capacity to encompass and infold feelings and thoughts about issues while compelling others. In this way, storied practices and narratives can also be instrumentalized and appropriated as tools for legitimation to gain and retain dominant power-relationships and structures. Thus, they play a legitimating 'author-ity' and hegemonic role, for example in hospitals (Currie & Brown, 2003), and privileging politically some interest over others (Mumby, 1987).

As stories include rhetorical ploys and shadow themes (Stacey, 2003: 379), they may become mechanisms of mystification. "The Dark Side of Narratives" (Geiger, 2008) makes organizations unreceptive for change. For example, narratives can create self-reinforcing blind spots and sources of organizational or interpretative inertia and path-dependency. These are then preventing an organization from questioning their 'success' principle and limiting its ability to change (Geiger & Antonacopoulou, 2009).

More specifically with regard to leadership, narratives are an embodied way by which humans experience and process the world, while reflecting systematically on their contextual dimensions, including implicit and narrative knowing (Küpers, 2005b). Whereas all stories involve expression and reflection on experience, when leaders in organizations intentionally deploy narratives, there is a danger that the interpretative process can become instrumentalized, leading to closure rather than openness to the future. Animating stories and clusters of narrated tale-worlds and story-realms (Young, 1987) are an expressive form of an original flux, ambiguity and opaqueness of lived experiences of individuals and collectives that need to be kept open. Living narratives both resist finitude, while remaining open to multiple meanings in an ongoing process also related to flows in organizational life-worlds and leadership. Therefore, we need to consider the problem of a generally prescriptive or moralizing 'narrativity', striving for a unity and normative direction of the narrative quest and its lessons. Such normative imposition or 'storyfying' is particularly problematic as it "risks a strange commodification of life and time – of soul" (Strawson, 2004: 450) or can turn into a misused 'story-selling' (Lapp & Carr, 2010).

While reflecting possible uses and abuses of storytelling in organizations (Carr & Ann, 2011), the challenging task for researchers is to try to re-construct voices or tell stories of those that are ostracized, marginalized or exploited. This is important as dominant organizational narratives that celebrate an organization's core values, aspirations and achievements might exclude oppositional stories that challenge, resist, subvert or sidestep the prevailing narratives.

Furthermore, it seems important to inquire why and in which ways stories are retro-regressive or overly progressive; that is, either following a nostalgic path toward supposedly better, good old days, or reaching towards escapist utopian futures. On the one hand, storytelling can oppress by subordinating employees to one grand strategic narrative. On the other hand, ingeniously performed narrative practices can be creatively liberating, serving for contestation and resistance as well as showing organizational members that there are always a multiplicity of stories, storytellers and story-events (Boje, 1995). Finally, "story-tellers ... should not pretend that stories have a magic power of healing for the community or that stories can work wonders for each troublesome situation" (Zipes, 1995: 223). In other words, it will be vital not to over-privilege the role of narratives in human lives in the form of a reductive 'narrative imperialism' (Phelan, 2005).

The addressed dangers and many more problems or risks notwithstanding, stories provide symbolic forms of activity, through which people in organizations express and deal with experiences, ideas or values in their everyday life, and thus they dramatically influence organizational processes and realities as well as developing 'tales of the future' (Goddall, 2010) and of wisdom.

How Can Narratives Contribute to the Education of Wise Leaders? Simulation and Emulation

> I can only answer the question 'What am I to do?' if I can answer the prior question, 'Of what story or stories do I find myself a part?'
>
> (MacIntyre, 1981/1984: 216)

Just as tales and stories have been employed as forms of expressive creating, communal sharing and learning for ages, the relation between narrative and practical wisdom is an ancient one. Historical and cross-cultural studies showed how wisdom was understood as a wholesome knowledge (e.g., Assmann, 1994) that was expressed through song and parable as a sort of pragmatic tool to make sense of, for example, human sufferings and the paradoxical nature of life (Takahashi & Overton, 2005).

Most, if not all, cultures and civilizations possess and process narratives that inform and teach about how to make sense of the world and how to respond to challenges with wise feelings, thoughts, judgements and deeds. These sources of folk wisdom provide a foundation for character or group development, educational formation as well as decision-making about what should be done in ambiguous and uncertain circumstances, or when facing paradoxes or dilemmas. Indeed, the protagonists of such folktales offer exemplary illustrations of virtue and vice and of decision-making and unintended consequences as well as moral implications that follow from each. These stories portray what it means to be a 'good' person and do the 'right' thing across many cultures and eras in human history, and now more and more beyond an anthropocentric orientation.

This book here is part of a 'narrative turn' that takes places also in wisdom research (Ferrari et al., 2013). According to Ferrari et al. (2013), stories of wisdom – as those to live by – can mediate empathizing reasoning and transformational processes. Narrative processes affect personality development across the lifespan via story-making and storytelling. In particular, the development of personal and collective wisdom is bound to wisdom in a narrative mode.[3]

As Bruya and Ardelt (2018a, 2018b) have recently shown, fostering wisdom in the classroom and enacting a wisdom pedagogy can be realized by processing narratives or didactic texts and fostering a community of inquiry. While narratives helped to engage the moral imagination, to cultivate moral emotional sensitivity, and to prompt perspective taking, didactic and speculative philosophical texts provide examples of principles to live by and frameworks for the exploration of interconnected beliefs about the world. As their empirical study showed, storied texts – along with guidance from the instructor[4] – aid to supply perspectives, principles, frameworks and vocabulary, hence; concepts that students need to make sophisticated, nuanced distinctions about their values and beliefs. Integrating stories in education not only helps to challenge beliefs, prompt the articulation of values and encourage self-reflection and self-development, but also sympathetically evaluates the perspectives of others and the grooming of moral emotions.

More broadly, the Carnegie Foundation for Excellence in Teaching has issued a report (Colby et al., 2011) suggesting that business education should in the future seek to integrate professional business education with liberal learning. This 'double helix' approach to business education would, they suggest, help to develop future leaders who are capable of dealing well with complexity and ambiguity, and who take actions and make decisions with an eye toward the common good as the ultimate goal of business practice.

The deep philosophical and psychological questions about the relationship between narrative and the development of wisdom have inspired a range of carefully considered responses especially including Walter Benjamin,[5] Paul Ricoeur[6] and Martha Nussbaum.[7] These writers and others have shown how stories express, communicate and thus support practical wisdom in many ways while allowing people to make sense of wiser practice or do pass moral judgements on actions and decisions of others or of themselves.

Rather than discussing these philosophical interpretations and other significant theoretical projects that argue for the educative value of storytelling here, we focus only on specific approaches pragmatically. We presuppose that narrative wisdom is a capability to show critical insight when solving social problems, guided by the idea of relevance realization – that is, flexible selection of and integration of information so as to enable decisions and actions promoting good life (Vervaeke & Ferraro, 2013).

In this practical spirit, we propose two basic frameworks for understanding why teachers in business and management schools would engage in the exercise of choosing and interpreting narratives, and why their students in a leadership class would spend time reading a textbook that presents these interpretations related to wisdom. The following subsections describe two ways in which narratives can contribute to the development of wisdom for leaders, namely (a) simulation exemplarity, (b) emulation exemplars.

Simulation Exemplarity

By hearing a tale or reading a text or context we might identify with characters, plots and situations, and assimilate these into our stories about ourselves and our organizations. In simulating events experienced by others and reasoning through their own life experiences retrospectively, individuals extract life lessons and insights for future application when making sense of the vicissitudes of their life as lived. In running simulations of hypothetical situations, that is, in casting themselves as a protagonist in a hypothetical narrative, individuals may discern the wisest course of action. By projecting themselves mentally into narrative simulations, people gain access to experiences, not otherwise accessible directly, and can extract personal and general wisdom from them. Resonating with narrative simulations allows them to indirectly learn and gain wisdom by sensing and reflecting on the experiences of others and the complex multi-causal network of contexts and relationships.

In this sense, narratives become part of a specific way of 'wise' sense-making, also accessible through an in-between, including those fictional and real persons who have come before.

> In understanding a story, readers or listeners participate in a meaning-making process whereby they 'read between the lines' of the story, interpreting and analyzing their lived experiences to achieve a deeper meaning in the text, and through this process, extract lessons to live by.
>
> (Ferrari et al., 2013: 147)

Such processes include but extend beyond simple prescriptions, or rule-based accounts of action: "Unlike didactic theoretical explanations, narrative simulations allow us to experience events vicariously by putting ourselves in the story-world—heightening sympathy and empathy and extending our general and social knowledge" (Ferrari et al., 2013: 147). In this respect, the creative or imaginative projection of possible alternative futures for the collective appears as more important than the deductive application of a principle in practice for the individual.

As Ferrari et al. (2013: 147) state: "Hypothetical simulation is simulating situations that the listener or reader could potentially encounter while being linked to cultural master narratives engagement critically". The latter are important as relatively wise persons are aware of and engage critically with master narratives of wisdom. Following a "wisdom of experience approach" (Bluck & Glück, 2004), there can be a learning of generic lessons taking place from wisdom-related events. Accordingly, for example, ways of coping with hardships and obstacles in the life of a protagonist can be seen as both a hallmark and one pathway to one's own possible wisdom practices.

With Staudinger and Glück (2011), we can distinguish between *personal wisdom* (i.e., wisdom as self-related knowledge acquired through direct personal experience) and *general wisdom* (i.e., wisdom as world knowledge that can also be acquired in more indirect ways). Related to processing exemplary simulations, wisdom is learned and cultivatable incrementally over the life course as it occurs through some level of confrontation, direct or indirect, with the fundamental themes and questions of human existence expressed in stories. However, there is the need for some translational work and transfer based on being sensitive to specific situational contexts. "Without sensitivity to cultural–historical, experiential, and situational contexts, it would be difficult to draw wisdom related lessons from exemplars' lives" (Grossmann, 2017a: 246).

Emulation Exemplars

Similar to hypothetical simulations, stories enable people to emulate exemplars as role models for their own lives. These exemplars may include cultural–historical representations or present public figures and especially leaders, who appear to embody significant wisdom-related characteristics through stories. "Wisdom is not merely an abstract concept but a real-life resource used daily to enhance human lives. Exemplars present ways of living that are significant models for everyday people who seek to emulate them in their own lives" (Weststrate et al., 2016: 674).

Stories make people emulate literary, historical, political, religious or philosophical figures as exemplars of what it means to be wise and to tales of their lives. Actually, these are often specially crafted to provide narrative instances of their exemplary ways of perceiving, judging and behaving. For emulation, a projective mode and analogical reasoning (Küpers, 2012) play powerful roles:

> We project or immerse ourselves in the story-world of these wise characters, reasoning through an event from their perspective to gain deeper understanding of their thoughts, feelings, and motivations. This insight can then be generalized, by analogy, to our own lives.
>
> (Ferrari et al., 2013: 148)

From a phenomenological perspective, emulation can be interpreted as a form of embodiment, a bodily response way of resonating. Striving to emulate exemplars, people embody various, distinct wisdom prototypes in their own lives.

Possible emulated exemplars reveal specific practical, philosophical and benevolent prototypes (Weststrate et al., 2016). Weststrate and his colleagues differentiate these prototypes as follows: While practical prototypes are connected to prudential, everyday, strategic, judicious forms in the sense of phrónêsis, philosophical ones are connected more to contemplative, intellectual, scientific forms in the sense of sophia.

By contrast or complementing, benevolent types resonate with moral, compassionate, sacrificial, spiritual and in the sense of agape. Each of these types invite you to emulate specific personal qualities of the wisdom exemplar. For phrónêsis, this entails deep insight; knowledge about life; exceptional judgement; ability to balance multiple interests; foresight; creativity; strategic and skillful communication; that are all relevant for charismatic leadership. Furthermore, all of them relate to particular contexts in which wisdom is exercised. Again, for practical wisdom this implies real-life contexts that involve decision-making, advice giving or problem solving in ambiguous and difficult situations.

The narrative themes of the phronetic type are strategic decision that may turn the tide, or enable a person to find creative ways to overcome an obstacle or refer to a 'secret' that is shared for how to live the 'good life'. Phronetic prototypes are connected to associated characters like advisor, strategist and (political) leader. In their empirical study on nomination of types, Westrate et al. (2016: 673) found surprisingly that the philosophical and benevolent prototypes were rated as wiser than the practical prototypes – although the latter one received many more nominations of the North American sample than did the other prototypes. This may perhaps be explainable by prevailing cultural tendencies toward agency and instrumentality in North America. Additionally, the researchers mention the influence of education, gender and degree of self-assessed wisdom on a person's conception of wisdom at the level of prototype. And again, as for simulation also for emulation of intentions and actions in the narratives of wisdom exemplars' lives, the process depends on cultural–historical, personal–motivational and situational contexts that play a critical role for wisdom, its development and its application in daily life (Grossmann, 2017b).

Developing Storied Wisdom: Please Join Us in Co-Creating a Poly-Logue!

> Do not tell people how to live their lives. Just tell them stories. And they will figure out how those stories apply to them.
>
> (Pausch, 2008)

This book is an attempt to revive and invigorate storytelling about wisdom in relation to leadership and its education in particular. Seeing narrated, practical wisdom as part of a democratic education (Broadhead & Greson, 2018), teaching business and learning leadership can be enhanced by tales of sageness. As we have seen this can be realized in narrated forms of astute orientation to enable and encourage students to exercise practical wisdom in order to make good judgements, decision-making, actions and consequences that contribute towards living a good life for themselves and stakeholders. In that kind of learning, students are not just an inactive audience passively receiving a story from the teller or author(ity). Rather, all are actively and responsively involved in a co-creative process. As a medium for constructing, sharing, interpreting and offering the content and meaning of a story to and with an audience, stories emerge from the interaction and cooperative efforts of teller and audience.

Accordingly, we invite you as readers to co-create the hermeneutically and interpretatively possible meanings of wisdom conveyed in and between the lines of the chapters. This includes being sensitive for the oblique, meanings and allusions for revealing other and transformative ways of being and becoming. Thus, when you enter the storied world of this book, you will hear different voices express and convey ideas, arguments, channeling thoughts, but may also experience affects and feelings or intuitive musings related to wisdom, connected to leadership.

We would like to invite you as co-inquiring inter-locutors to perceive what is happening also *in-between* the positions and statements. In this way, various questions, utterances, insights and interpretations with their nuanced meanings are propelled, sometimes only hinting to associations and possible horizons, which could invite further exploration. Situating the topic of wisdom in such a conversational context and storied texts brings to life and gives flesh to ideas also by examples and illustrations; also related to practical concerns as well as critical reflections.

In a way, the diverse chapters present and weave together a multi-layered poly- or meta-logue. Rather than constructing separate, fixed or closed individual-based definitions of realities or rational-lines of argument, these poly-logical practices open up to a living relationality and possibilities of disclosing co-emerging and spiraling flows. Polyphonic voices, expressed here interwoven in an arguing chorus of different tales of wisdom, such as presentational practices uncover and allow other modes of communication, including felt sense, touching affects, imaginative sounds, visual associations, etc. Accordingly, such dia- and/or polyloguing is opening for a multi-sensuous interplay of tasted, gestured and viewed expressions that are a living narrative, with a colourful diversity of points of standing and moving into and around possibilities of practical wisdom, for organizations and leadership. Not aiming for a single vision or finalizable version, these inter-exchanges are an array of juxta-positioned reasons, concerns about and perspectives on various angles of shades and shapes of wisdom.

In terms of epistemology, this implies that if there is any truth (about wisdom) to be found or, better to say, co-created, it happens through a multitude of simultaneous expressions with their quests and questions, engagements and commitments. This kind of heteroglossia[8] can help to question, test and contest our own and others' ideas, those established and those merging or to be developed. Much like a sounding board the expressions of narrated tales of wisdom here open up for complexity, ambiguity and emotional resonance. Such resonance comes from making the words and its worlds alive, embody what they are about and make them breathe experiences. Hopefully, you as a perceptive and listening reader can relate to those or invoke in them likewise sensory experiences that may lead to a more refined understanding, and invite you to extend the text, or relate and inquire into your own or other life-worldly con-texts.

As an active audience or engaged readers of this concert of voices, we all are becoming involved recipients, and perhaps are provoked to comments or to ask possible questions, state contestations or find other forms to contribute with your own ideas and interpretations. This can lead to a further weaving of con-textures, advancing the ongoing, unfolding fluid discourses to emerge. Therefore, please feel invited to share your responses, reflections or imaginations by writing, drawing or other forms of expressing them and, if you like, forward them to the editors for co-creating a hyper-contextual repository.[9]

After moving thought this introduction as a kind of spiraling and rhizomeatic antenarrative (Boje, 2010) being in the middle and in-between (Boje, 2001: 293) with its dis-symmetrical trajectories, we now invite you to enter the tales. Because "It is a foolish thing to make a long prologue and to be short in the story itself" (II Maccabees, II. 32), let us move into the storied chapters now....

Notes

1 Eco-eschatology and eco-eschatological narratives as end-of-the-world fantasies suspend the present between a geologically deep past and an indefinitely distant future. As Toadvine (2017) elaborated, our obsession with the end of the world found expression in the form of the eco-eschatological narrative frames speculative fiction as well as environmental prediction. It is a phantasm that reflects our desires and anxieties in the present and that leaves its mark, directly or indirectly, on our individual and collective identities, institutions and sense of the world here and now.

2 Holt and Zundel (2018) showed how rejecting the binary truth/non-truth relationship between science and fiction opens up interesting questions and quests

as well as possibilities for research. For them, more implicitly, fiction can play a role in development of scientific accounts. In such 'fictional research', while characteristics of non-truthfulness are not lost, research is itself fictionalized, or draws upon fictional elements. More explicitly, fiction can serve as inspiration; that is, instances where fictionalized accounts are providing ideas and legitimacy for organizational theorizing. Fiction can serve as a source of data or sites of empirical research as well as fiction as research can become a means of attributing science-like qualities to fiction. For them:

> fiction can illuminate phenomena that are hard to capture, measure, or relate to theoretical ideas. They can do so across the full spectrum of human affairs, tying together emotions, hopes, fears, connecting spatio-temporally dispersed affairs, and do so without concern for the limits of specialist silos.

While Levine (2015: 60) argues that "fiction, especially novels, enable us to appreciate our social condition in complex and subtle ways because they, like life, refuse to be easily distilled into simple elements and chains of cause and effect."

3 According to Ferrari et al. (2013: 138) there are two ways in which this is processed: First, the narrative simulations individuals create of (a) hypothetical situations that may come to pass and (b) situations lived by others (e.g., literary or historical exemplars, or others personally known), as well as the reasoning processes through which individuals make meaning of these simulations; second, how individuals actively reflect on their own past life experiences that are relevant to wisdom by crafting stories about these events, a process that has become known as autobiographical reasoning.

4 In one experimental course this involved requiring the students to employ techniques of interpretation to understand the writer's full meaning. This included:

> imaginatively adopting the perspective of the writer, which in turn involves attempting to place oneself in the writer's time and place and to view the ideas through the writer's foreign-language vocabulary, with its unique connotations and associations. For example, students were given available historical background for each text and encouraged to imagine themselves living in that time and responding to the concerns of the writer in that context. Although these texts were primarily didactic, with recommendations on what to believe and how to act, they also contained narratives in the form of brief vignettes.
> (Bruya & Ardelt, 2018b: 113)

Importantly, the guidance of the instructors was embedded in fostering a 'community of inquiry' in which all participants (students and teacher) are mutually supportive and committed to the pursuit of understanding and self-improvement: "In a community of inquiry, students feel comfortable constructing understanding and knowledge as a cooperative venture" (ibid).

5 For Benjamin, the mark of a true storyteller is that they take these morals and 'universal' truths and share this experience with the reader or listener, that "the moral of the story" comes through (Benjamin, 1968: 99). Stories serve not only a 'purpose' but have power over how we view our own experiences

and live (Benjamin, 1968: 87). Originally and still alive in oral traditions, these were shared experiences of the storyteller and those the storyteller listened to, related to wider human experience. However, for Benjamin, as much as wisdom is counsel woven into the fabric of real life, for him "the art of storytelling is reaching its end because the epic side of truth, wisdom, is dying out" (1968: 87):

> The storyteller is a man who has counsel for his readers. But if today 'having counsel' is beginning to have an old-fashioned ring, this is because the communicability of experience is decreasing. In consequence, we have no counsel either for ourselves or for others. After all, counsel is less an answer to a question than a proposal concerning the continuation of a story, which is just unfolding. To seek this counsel one would first have to be able to tell the story. ... Counsel woven into the fabric of real life is wisdom. The art of storytelling is reaching its end because the epic side of truth, wisdom, is dying out. ... For storytelling is always the art of repeating stories, and this art is lost when the stories are no longer retained.
>
> (ibid: 91)

Benjamin believed that (in contrast to individualized novels) storytelling is a unique form of communication that was centrally tied to this idea of artisans and craftsmanship. For him this link to craft is the "web in which the gift of storytelling is cradled" and that its loss is what led to the death of storytelling (ibid: 91). But is storytelling and wisdom really dying or does it find new forms of expression and retelling of 'story-esque' works? Artful stories are still developed and shared to entertain or to enlighten, and continue to capture the popular imagination via novels, movies, stories expressed by songwriters and playwrights using new media and genres; including Wisdom in Movies (Gilmore, 2017).

6 For Ricoeur: (1991) life as quest in search for a narrative. And, in a way, wisdom requires narrative coherence, expression and processing, while stories are a form of organized experience, and one that is organizing experiences. Correspondingly, stories do offer and mediate a form that 'carries' wisdom, which helps for enacting trans-forming practices. Like wisdom, stories link particular events and characters or protagonists (of wise action) causally and meaningfully in a plot, while also suggesting a certain ethical take on the world. Fragmented, nonlinear, incoherent unplotted human experience are tending toward being expressed and processed, thus having an "inchoate narrativity" (Ricoeur, 1984: 74). Such proto-narrative quality of experiencing constitutes a genuine demand for a narrative that can be related to an emplotment of wisdom as the integrating of diverse, discontinuous, unstable events with permanence-in-time. Ricoeur's extensive philosophical study on narrative and ethics (Ricoeur, 1984, 1991, 1992) shows that through telling stories the ethical meaning of practical experience is elucidated and communicated. For him all narrative processes move through a three-folded mimesis from entering with a pre-understanding, then leading to emplotment and to a reconfiguring enactment. First, informed by storytelling and tales, we as human beings have

a pre-understanding of the world of action, which is narrative. Second, then the plot offers a configuring capacity that constructs meaning from events, thus structuring human experience. This is realized through an emplotment as the way in which 'the knower' arranges events, knowing and action that give a sense of wholeness to the story with a beginning and an end. In some way, emplotment is what makes a story intelligible, shareable and actionable. Finally, when we read or listen to a story the same models our experience, thus we also enact the same and we can reconfigure them toward a different future plot of our life. For Ricoeur, emplotment is specifically the ability to take discordant events and heterogeneous episodes of human action and tie them together into a coherent plot, permitting a concordant readability to our lives. On Ricoeur's account, the meaning effect or semantic innovation of narratives arises from its bringing about a "synthesis of the heterogeneous" whereby "goals, causes, and chance are brought together within the temporal unity of a whole and complete action" (Ricoeur 1984: ix). This ordering of events does also imply that one is not free to include in the story all that takes place, but primarily that which is relevant to the story's conclusion. Thus, the point of wisdom-oriented narrativity grows out of surprise, betrayal of expectations, the discordance of life (Ricoeur 1984) processed through integrative emplotment and reconfiguring enactment making them relevant. For Ricoeuer narratives involve both the description and moral evaluation and action, that are all significant for integrating ethics and sapiential dimension also in organizations and institutions (Rhodes et al. 2010; Deslandes, 2012; Habisch & Bachmann, 2016). Moreover, the storied nature of human life and conduct (Sarbin, 1986; Scheibe, & Barrett, 2017) can be connected to wisdom or wisdom-related practices that are poetic. As Sarbin (1986: 8) stated when he argued for treating the narrative as an organizing principle in human action: "human beings think, perceive and imagine, and make moral choices according to narrative structure. … The narrative allows for the inclusion of actors' reasons for their act, as well as the causes of happening." Not only is orientating and thinking narratively characteristic of situation-evaluating practical wisdom, narratives are also 'productive' in a critical and responsive sense, performing a poietic function in that they bring forth realities, concepts and values via a responsive practice (see also Küpers, 2005a). Accordingly, and following Ricoeur's hermeneutical phenomenology, a critical phrónêsis allows viewing narratives of practical wisdom as being responsively *poiêtic* (Wall, 2005). What does it mean? Wisdom is narrative and "*phrónêsis* is poetic in that it implies at its very core the endless re-creation of concrete social relations" (Wall, 2003: 337), by involving the self's dialectical capacity for "creating or innovating ever more responsively inclusive social meaning" (Wall 2003: 334). Such a view is analogous to art and artisanship in that not only is the practically wise in many respects a poet or storyteller, but also that poetic practical wisdom "has an end other than itself" (Wall, 2005: 337) while also generating newly re(con)figured narrative relations. Importantly, these narrative relationships are qualified as advancing toward greater inclusivity and social participation on the basis of otherwise diverse and unrelated 'materials', that is, of narrative otherness (Wall, 2005). Understanding others' perspectives is to understand how they might tell their stories, which itself requires a *phrónêtic* sensibility to the dialogical, temporal and contextualized nature of their lives. Practically, storytelling as a narrative practice has a significant history as a playful method for developing virtuous habits of practical wisdom in leadership (Statler & Roos, 2007), especially in relation to strategy as practice (Küpers et al., 2012). Such a process is not happening apolitical vacuum. Poetically conceived, phrónêsis creates new narratives of life and new inclusivity, which engages with issues of power and conflicts as well as ambiguities, dilemmas and paradoxes as they appear in tragic differences and (moral) incommensurabilities in attempts to accomplish common goods. Living a wise life, also in relation to or as part of organizations, involves immersion in the messy discordances and tragedies of actual current life-worlds and embracing the task of forming together in a radically uncertain future. Based on considering the situated interplay and integration of means and ends in a critical poetic phrónêsis of narrative meaning and social inclusivity, it may be extended toward ecological meanings and systemic inclusivity, generating untold possibilities.

7 As Nussbaum (1990), among many others, has shown, certain wisdom is best expressed and processed in the form of a story. Nussbaum argues that, if we meaningfully engage with and practise an ethical mode of attention to scenarios and characters depicted in stories or fictional story-world, this can enable us to learn moral concerns, truth and about human flourishing; what it means to live a good life. The focus here is on the role of narratives as a '*poiêsis*' of means toward which practical wisdom should be directed. In particular, literature and stories are seen as being a vital instrument or media for becoming a practically wise person and grasping nuances of moral judgement. Narrative forms are requiring and providing a unique and important education in what Nussbaum calls 'moral attention', that is, attention to the concrete particularities of actual persons and situations around us (1990: 162). Narratively informed practical wisdom helps over-come 'moral obtuseness' and 'simplification'. It is through literary narratives that we can sensitize ourselves and cultivate our capacities for 'moral perception', 'moral imagination' and 'moral sensibility' (1990: 154, 164, 183–5; see also Nussbaum, 2001). These phrónêtic capacities are for Nussbaum the very end and completion of moral life as such. Moral wisdom consists precisely in narratively gained attention, care and perception of human particularities. It is the detail and nuance of good narrative artworks that allow for sympathetic engagement with the characters' thoughts, intentions, feelings, behaviour and circumstances. Thus, poetics and narratives – especially as literary means for great public and social catharsis – are media to accomplish *phrónêtic* ends. This includes the need for poetic attention to the tragic and fragile of goodness, related to expressed vulnerabilities, particularities, happening of contingencies, fortunes or luck as well as changeability of the human (moral) situation (Nussbaum, 2001: 5, 138).

With Nussbaum (2001, 2011), there is a need for literature and stories in our life, because:

- novels make apparent and 'salient' features of our lives and situation that would otherwise be overlooked and thus absent from moral reflection;

- novels both instantiate in themselves and reproduce in the attentive and sympathetic reader superior forms of reflective consciousness which bring us closer to grasping the truth than any other procedures or me;
- novels in particular (and fictional forms in general) give expression to 'our sense of life' which must serve as the ultimate reference for all thinking about values and morals.

The link to lived existence here implies also a link to qualities of embodied story-ing that is mediated in tales of wisdom. Stories are effective also in terms of wisdom, because they are affective, that is, there is felt experience of living within a storied cosmos, a tactile, visual and auditory enveloping cosmos sometimes processing and expressing chaos, thus a '*c(ha)osmos*' – a state between chaos and cosmos, disorder and order that is part of being alive. Tales of wisdom are expressing in accordance with the senses, reflectively without severing our sensorial bond. In a way, these tales as modes of cultural languaging are honouring the participatory nature of bodily mediated perception and imagination, including the more-than-human world. Tales, epics and storied expressions even from long ago still strike a chord with people today. Various forms of stories and narratives have been shared in every culture as a means of entertainment, education, cultural preservation and in order to instill moral or wisdom-related values and practices. Stories of wisdom have been, are and will be powerful media for guidance, education, learning and 'healing', that implies also enabling the practise of virtuous conduct and ethical decision-making in our everyday lives.

8 The term heteroglossia refers to the qualities of a language that are *extralinguistic*, but common to all languages. These include qualities such as perspective, evaluation and ideological positioning. In this way most languages are incapable of neutrality, for every word is inextricably bound to the context in which it exists. Heteroglossia is produced by means of the internal differentiation and stratification of different registers in a language.

> The novel can be defined as a diversity of social speech types (sometimes even diversity of languages) and a diversity of individual voices, artistically organized. The internal stratification of any single national language into social dialects, characteristic group behaviour, professional jargons, generic language: languages of generations and age groups, tendentious languages, languages of authorities, of various circles and of passing fashions, languages that serve specific sociopolitical purposes of the day, even of the hour, (each clay has its own slogan, its own vocabulary, its own emphases) – this internal stratification present in any language at any given moment of its historical existence is the indispensable prerequisite of the novel as a genre.
>
> (Bakhtin, 1981: 262–263)

9 Wendelin Küpers can be contacted via: wendelin.kuepers@icn-artem.com, and Matt Statler can be reached at: mstatler@stern.nyu.edu. The idea is to set up a web forum or blogging space on-line, where all comments will be gathered, as a forwarding feedback and continuation of an ongoing inter-involving conversation.

References

Aristotle (1985). *Nicomachean Ethics*. Indianapolis: Hackett.

Aristotle (1998). *Politics*. Indianapolis: Hackett.

Armstrong, K. (2006). *A Short History of Myth*. Edinburgh: Canongate.

Assmann, A. (1994). Wholesome knowledge: Concepts of wisdom in a historical and cross-cultural perspective. In D. L. Featherman, R. M. Learner & M. Perlmutter (Eds.), *Life-Span Development and Behavior* (Vol. 12, pp. 187–224). Hillsdale, NJ: Lawrence Erlbaum.

Bakhtin, M. M. (1981). *The Dialogic Imagination: Four Essays*. (C. Emerson & M. Holquist, Trans.). Austin: University of Texas Press.

Barker, J. R. (1993). Tightening the iron cage: Concertive control in self-managing teams. *Administrative Science Quarterly*, 38: 408–437.

Barker, W. (2001). *The Adages of Erasmus*. Toronto: University of Toronto Press.

Baskin, J. (2015). Paradigm dressed as Epoch: The Ideology of the Anthropocene. Environmental Values, 24, 9–29.

Bell, E. & Leonard, P. (2016). Digital organizational storytelling on YouTube: Constructing plausibility through network protocols of amateurism, affinity and authenticity. *Journal of Management*, 1–13. Inquiry. DOI: 1056492616660765.

Benjamin, W. (1968). The storyteller: Reflections on the works of Nikolai Leskov. In H. Arendt (Ed.), *Walter Benjamin: Illuminations*. London: Jonathan Cape.

Bierly, P. & Kolodinsky, R. (2008). Strategic logic – toward a wisdom-based approach to strategic management. In *Handbook of Organizational and Managerial Wisdom* (pp. 61–88). London: Sage.

Bluck, S. & Glück, J. (2004). Making things better and learning a lesson: Experiencing wisdom across the life span. Journal of Personality, 72, 543–572.

Boje, D. (1995). Stories of the storytelling organisation: A postmodern analysis of Disney as "Tamara-land". *Academy of Management Journal*, 38(4): 997–1035.

Boje, D. M. (2001). *Narrative Methods for Organizational and Communication Research*. London: Sage.

Boje, D. M. (2010). *Storytelling and the Future of Organizations: An Antenarrative Handbook*. London: Routledge.

Broadhead, S. & Greson, M. (2018). *Practical Wisdom and Democratic Education*. Dordrecht: Springer.

Brown, A. D., Gabriel, Y. & Gherardi, S. (2009). Storytelling and change: An unfolding story. *Organization*, 16(3): 323–333.

Bruya, B. & Ardelt, M. (2018a). Fostering wisdom in the classroom, Part 1: A general theory of wisdom pedagogy. *Teaching Philosophy*, 41(3): 239–253.

Bruya, B. & Ardelt, M. (2018b). Wisdom can be taught: A proof-of-concept study for fostering wisdom in the classroom. *Learning and Instruction*, 58: 106–114

Carr, A. & Ann, C. (formerly Lapp) (2011). The use and abuse of storytelling in organizations. *Journal of Management Development*, 30(3): 236–246.

Clayton, V. P. & Birren, J. E. (1980). The development of wisdom across the life-span. A re-examination of an ancient topic. *Life-Span Development and Behavior*, 3, 103–135.

Colby, A., Ehrlich, T., Sullivan, W. & Dolle, J. (2011). *Rethinking Undergraduate Business Education: Liberal Learning for the Profession*. New York: Jossey-Bass.

Currie, G. & Brown, A. D. (2003). A narratological approach to understanding processes of organizing in a UK hospital. *Human Relations*, 56(5): 563–586.

Deslandes, G. (2012). Power, profits, and practical wisdom: Ricoeur's perspectives on the possibility of ethics in institutions. *Business & Professional Ethics Journal*, 31(1): 1–24

Dunne, J. (1993/1997). *Back to the Rough Ground. 'Phrónêsis' and 'Techne' in Modern Philosophy and in Aristotle*. Notre Dame: University of Notre Dame Press.

Eikeland, O. (2006). *Phrónêsis*, Aristotle, and action research. *International Journal of Action Research*, 2(1): 5–53.

Eikeland, O. (2008). *The Ways of Aristotle. Aristotelian Phrónesis, Aristotelian Philosophy of Dialogue, and Action Research*. Bern: Peter Lang.

Essers, J. (2012). Re-writing the organization: The ideological deadlock of narrative methodology. *Journal of Organizational Change Management*, 25(2): 332–351

Ferrari, M., Weststrate, N. & Petro, A. (2013). Stories of wisdom to live by: Developing wisdom in a narrative mode. In M. Ferrari & N. M. Weststrate (Eds.), *The Scientific Study of Personal Wisdom: From Contemplative Traditions to Neuroscience* (pp. 137–164). Dordrecht: Springer.

Fisher, W. R. (1987). *Human Communication as Narration: Toward a Philosophy of Reason, Value, and Action*. Columbia, SC: The University of South Carolina Press.

Fortune Editors. (2016). The World's 19 Most Disappointing Leaders. Available online: http://fortune.com/2016/03/30/most-disappointing-leaders/ (accessed on 12.05.2018).

Gabriel, Y. (2000). *Storytelling in Organizations: Facts, Fictions and Fantasies*. Oxford: Oxford University Press.

Gabriel, Y. & Connell, N. A. (2010). Co-creating stories: Collaborative experiments in storytelling. *Management Learning*, 4(5): 507–523.

Gabriel, Y., Geiger, D. & Letiche, H. (2011). The marriage of story and metaphor. *Culture and Organisation*, 17(5): 367–371.

Gadamer, H.-G. (1982). *Truth and Method*. New York: Continuum Press.

Gehmann, U. (2004). Prometheus unleashed: The quest for knowledge and the promise of salvation through technique. In Y. Gabriel (Ed.), *Myths, Stories, And Organizations* (pp. 165–175). Oxford: Oxford University Press.

Geiger, D. (2008). The dark side of narratives: Challenging the epistemological nature of narrative knowledge. *International Journal of Management Concepts and Philosophy*, 3(1): 66–81.

Geiger, D. & Antonacopoulou, E. (2009). Narratives and organizational dynamics: Narratives as a source of blind spots and organizational inertia. *Journal of Applied Behavioral Science*, 45(3): 411–436.

Gherardi, S. (1996). Gendered organizational cultures: Narratives of women travellers in a male world. *Gender, Work & Organization*, 3(4): 187–201.

Gherardi, S. & Poggio, B. (2007). *Gendertelling in Organizations: Narratives from Male Dominated Environments*. Copenhagen: Liber.

Gilmore, R. (2017). *Searching for Wisdom in Movies*. Basingstoke: Palgrave.

Goddall, H. L. (2010). From tales of the field to tales of the future. *Organizational Research Methods*, 13(2) April: 256–267.

Grint, K. (2007). Learning to lead: Can Aristotle help us find the road to wisdom? *Leadership*, 3: 231–246.

Grossmann, I. (2017a). Wisdom in context. *Perspectives on Psychological Science*, 12(2): 233–257.

Grossmann, I. (2017b). Wisdom and how to cultivate it: Review of emerging evidence for a constructivist model of wise thinking. *European Psychologist* 2017, 22(4): 233–246.

Grossmann, I. & Brienza, J. P. (2018). The strengths of wisdom provide unique contributions to improved leadership, sustainability, inequality, gross national happiness, and civic discourse in the face of contemporary world problems. *Journal of Intelligence*, 6: 22; doi:10.3390/jintelligence6020022.

Habisch, A. & Bachmann, C. (2016). Empowering practical wisdom from religious traditions: A ricoeurian approach. *International Journal of Corporate Social Responsibility*, 1(10): 1–9.

Hamilton, C. (2013). *Earthmasters: Playing God with the Climate*. Crows Nest NSW: Allen & Unwin.

Haraway, D. (2003). *The Companion Species Manifesto: Dogs, People, and Significant Otherness*. Vol. 1. Chicago: Prickly Paradigm Press.

Holliday, S. G. & Chandler, M. J. (1986). *Wisdom: Explorations in Adult Competence*. Basel: Karger.

Holt, R. & Zundel, M. O. (2018). Using fiction in organization and management research. In A. Bryman & D. A. Buchanan (Eds.), *Unconventional Methodology in Organization and Management Research*. Oxford: Oxford University Press.

Kemmis, S. & Smith, T. (2008). Prâxis and prâxis development. In S. Kemmis & T. Smith (Eds.), *Enabling Prâxis: Challenges for Education* (pp. 3–13). Rotterdam: Sense.

Küpers, W. (2005a). Embodied implicit and narrative knowing in organizations. *Journal of Knowledge Management*, 9(6): 113–133.

Küpers, W. (2005b). Phenomenology of embodied implicit and narrative knowing. *Journal of Knowledge Management*, 9(6): 114–133.

Küpers, W. (2012). Embodied transformative metaphors and narratives in organisational life-worlds of change. *Journal of Organizational Change Management*, 26(3): 494–528.

Küpers, W. (2013). The art of practical wisdom – phenomenology of an embodied, wise inter-practice in organisation and leadership. In W. Küpers & D. Pauleen, *A Handbook of Practical Wisdom. Leadership, Organization and Integral Business Practice* (pp. 19–45). Imprint. London: Gower.

Küpers, W. (2019). Integrating hope and wisdom in organisation in the Anthropocene. In D. Ericsson & M. Kostera (Eds.), *Organizing Goodness and Hope* (pp. 72–84). Cheltenham: Edward Elgar.

Küpers, W. & Gunnlaugson, O. (2017). Introduction: Contexts and complexities of wisdom learning in management and business education. In W. Küpers & O. Gunnlaugson (Eds.), *Wisdom Learning: Perspectives on Wising-Up Management & Business Education* (pp. 1–38). London: Routledge.

Küpers, W. & Statler, M. (2008). Practically wise leadership: Towards an integral understanding. *Culture and Organization*, 14(4) December 2008: 379–400.

Küpers, W., Mantere, S. & Statler, M. (2012). Strategy as storytelling: A phenomenological collaboration. *Journal for Management Inquiry*, (21)3: 1–18.

Lapp, C. A. & Carr, A. N. (2010). Storyselling. In A. J. Mills, G. Durepos & E. Wiebe (Eds.), *Encyclopedia of Case Study Research* (Vol. 2, pp. 895–898). Thousand Oaks, CA: Sage.

Levine, C. (2015). *Forms: Whole, Rhythm, Hierarchy, Network.* Princeton: Princeton University Press.

MacIntyre, A. (1981/1984). *After Virtue: A Study in Moral Theory.* 2nd ed. Indianapolis, IN: University of Notre Dame Press.

Magala, S. & Flory, M. (2012). The rhetoric and narratives in management research. *Journal of Organizational Change Management*, 25(2): 201–203.

Mair, M. (1988). Psychology as storytelling. *International Journal of Personal Construct Psychology*, 1(2): 125–137.

McKenna, B., Rooney, D. & Boal, K. (2009). Wisdom principles as a metatheoretical basis for evaluating leadership. *The Leadership Quarterly*, 20(2): 177–190.

Moore, J. W. (2016). *Anthropocene or Capitalocene? Nature, History, and the Crisis of Capitalism.* Oakland, CA: PM Press.

Morton, T. (2016). *Dark Ecology: For a Logic of Future Coexistence.* New York: Columbia University Press.

Mumby, D. K. (1987). The political function of narrative in organizations. *Communication. Monographs*, 54: 113–127.

Nussbaum, M. C. (1990). Love's Knowledge: Essays on Philosophy and Literature. New York: Oxford University Press.

Nussbaum, M. (2001). *The Fragility of Goodness: Luck and Ethics in Greek Tragedy and Philosophy.* 2nd ed. Cambridge, UK/New York: Cambridge University Press.

Nussbaum, M. (2011). *Creating Capabilities: The Human Development Approach.* Cambridge, MA: The Belknap Press of Harvard University Press.

Pausch, R. (2008). *The Last Lecture.* New York: Hachette Books.

Phelan, J. (2005). Who's here? Thoughts on narrative identity and narrative imperialism. *Narrative*, 13: 205–211.

Rhodes, C., Pullen, A. & Clegg, S. (2010). 'If I Should Fall From Grace...': Stories of change and organizational ethics. *Journal of Business Ethics*, 91(4): 535–551.

Ricoeur, P. (1984). *Time and Narrative 1.* K. McLaughlin and D. Pellauer (trans.). 3 vols. Vol. 1. Chicago and London: The University of Chicago Press.

Ricoeur P. (1991). Life in quest of narrative. In D. Wood (Ed.), *On Paul Ricoeur: Narrative and Interpretation* (pp. 20–33). London: Routledge.

Ricoeur P. (1992). *Oneself as Another,* Kathleen Blamey (trans.). Chicago: University of Chicago Press.

Roca, E. (2007). Intuitive practical wisdom in organizational life. *Social Epistemology*, 21(2): 195–207.

Rooney, D., McKenna, B. & Liesch, P. (2010). *Wisdom and Management in the Knowledge Economy.* New York: Routledge.

Sarbin, T. R. (Ed.) (1986). *Narrative Psychology: The Storied Nature of Human Conduct.* Westport, CT: Praeger.

Scheibe, K. & Barrett, F. (2017). *The Storied Nature of Human Life. The Life and Work of Theodore R. Sarbin.* Basingstoke: Palgrave.

Schwartz, B. & Sharpe, K. (2006). Practical wisdom: Aristotle meets positive psychology. *Journal of Happiness Studies*, 7(3): 377–395.

Shamir, B. & Eilam, G. (2005). What's your story? A life stories approach to authentic leadership development. *Leadership Quarterly*, 16(3): 385–417.

Shotter, J. & Tsoukas, H. (2014). In search of phronesis: Leadership and the art of judgment. *Academy of Management Learning and Education*, 13(2): 224–243.

Smircich, L. (1983). Concepts of culture and organizational analysis. *Administrative Science Quarterly*, 28(3): 339–358.

Stacey, R. D. (2003). *Strategic Management and Organisational Dynamics – The Challenge of Complexity*. London: Prentice-Hall.

Statler, M. (2014). Developing practical wisdom in a business school? Critical reflections on pedagogical practice. *Management Learning*, 45(4): 397–417.

Statler, M. & Roos, J. (2007). *Everyday Strategic Preparedness: The Role of Practical Wisdom in Organizations*. Basingstoke: Palgrave MacMillan.

Staudinger, U. M. & Glück, J. (2011). Psychological wisdom research: Commonalities and differences in a growing field. Annual Review of Psychology, 62: 215–241.

Sternberg, R. J. (1985). Implicit theories of intelligence, creativity, and wisdom. *Journal of Personality and Social Psychology*, 49: 607–627.

Sternberg, R. (1987). Implicit theories: An alternative to modeling cognition and its development. In J. Bisanz, C. J. Brainerd & R. Kail (Eds.), *Formal Methods in Developmental Psychology: Progress in Cognitive Development Research* (pp. 155–192). New York: Springer.

Sternberg R. J. & Jordan J. (2005). *A Handbook of Wisdom: Psychological Perspectives*. Cambridge, UK: Cambridge University Press.

Strawson, G. (2004). Against narrativity. *Ratio*, 17: 428–452.

Takahashi, M. & Overton, W. F. (2005). Cultural foundations of wisdom. In R. J. Sternberg & J. Jordan (Eds.), *A Handbook of Wisdom: Psychological Perspectives* (pp. 32–60). New York: Cambridge University Press.

Toadvine, T. (2017). Our monstrous futures: Eco-eschatology and the elements. *Cultural Politics 12 Symposium: Canadian Journal of Continental Philosophy*, 21(1) (Spring 2017): 219–230.

Vervaeke, J. & Ferraro, L. (2013). Relevance, meaning and the cognitive science of wisdom. In M. Ferrari & N. M. Weststrate (Eds.), *The Scientific Study of Personal Wisdom* (pp. 325–341). Dordrecht: Springer Netherlands. doi:10.1007/978-94-007-7987-7_15.

Wall, J. (2003). Phrónêsis, poetics, and moral creativity. *Ethical Theory and Moral Practice*, 6(3): 317–341.

Wall, J. (2005). *Moral Creativity: Paul Ricoeur and the Poetics of Possibility*. New York: Oxford University Press.

Weststrate, N. M., Ferrari, M. & Ardelt, M. (2016). The many faces of wisdom: An investigation of cultural-historical wisdom exemplars reveals practical, philosophical, and benevolent prototypes. Personality & Social Psychology Bulletin, 42: 662–676.

Wilkins, A. (1983). Organisational stories as symbols, which control the organisation. In L. R. Pondy, P. J. Frost, G. Morgan & T. Dandridge (Eds.),

Organisational Symbolism: Monographs in Organisational and Industrial Relations (Vol. 1, pp. 81–92). Greenwich, CT: JAI Press.

Witten, M. (1993). Narrative and the culture of obedience at the workplace. In D. K. Mumby (Ed.), *Narrative and Social Control: Critical Perspectives* (pp. 97–118). London: Sage.

Yang, S.-Y. (2011). Wisdom displayed through leadership: Exploring leadership-related wisdom. *Leadership Quarterly*, 22(4): 616–632.

Young, K. G. (1987). *Taleworlds and Storyrealms: The Phenomenology of Narrative*. Hingham, MA: Kluwer.

Zipes, J. (1995). *Creative Storytelling: Building Community Changing Lives*. New York: Routledge.

Zylinska, J. (2014). *Minimal Ethics for the Anthropocene*. Ann Arbor: Open Humanities Press.

1

THE SANDPIPER AND THE CLAM STRUGGLE

Christopher Michaelson

[This ancient folktale is called 鷸蚌相争 (Yù bàng xiāng zhēng), or The Sandpiper and the Clam Struggle. The following version is my mother's, Margaret Wong's, translation, with some minor embellishment.]

A clam had just emerged at the edge of the shore. It unlocked its shell to dry itself in the sun. At the same time, a sandpiper was flying overhead, observing its prospective prey avariciously.

The sandpiper swooped down as the clam's shell opened, extending its long beak to devour the clam's flesh. The clam suddenly and forcefully closed its shell, tightly clenching the sandpiper's beak. The sandpiper pulled with the strength of its spindly legs to break free, but it could not liberate itself from the clam's grasp. Meanwhile, the clam could not return to the water, as it did not have the muscle to move itself while also dragging the sandpiper.

The sandpiper said, "If you insist on holding on to me, and it does not rain today or tomorrow, you will dry out and die of thirst." This angered the clam, who retorted, "If I do not release you today or tomorrow, you will not be able to eat, and you will die of hunger."

[At this point, one of my children asks, sarcastically: How can they each talk to the other when their mouths are both occupied?]

Neither the sandpiper nor the clam would yield to the other. As they struggled, by chance, a fisherman walked by. When he saw that both animals were unable to move, he snatched them up in one motion and took them home for his dinner.

[The traditional folktale concludes with the proverb, 鷸蚌相争渔人得力 (Yù bàng xiāng zhēng, yúrén dé lì), or "The Sandpiper and the Clam Struggle, and the Fisherman Gets the Benefit."]

THE SANDPIPER AND THE CLAM STRUGGLE

Introduction

This story was related to my children and me by my mother when we were on a beach. She teaches my children Chinese language and culture, although she left her native country when she was only 8 years old. We were together in Florida, where relatives from around the world had gathered for a family reunion. In two boats, we sailed from the marina to a crescent-shaped beach, where so many seashells had collected that we could hear them as though they were chimes that nature had dropped into the surf. The animals occupying the shells attracted sandpipers and other birds, looking for a meal. Further down the beach, fishermen were casting their fishing rods.

Coquinas – tiny invertebrates whose pastel-hued, bivalve homes are barely the size of a fingernail – were revealed at the edge of the shore with each retreating wave. They would race to burrow into the sand again before a sandpiper's pointy beak reached into the shell to eat them. This sequence repeated all day long. As each wave crashed on to the shore, the sandpipers ran away, the coquinas appeared and attempted to disappear, and the sandpipers ran back toward the water, hoping to dine before they were chased away by the next wave. It was such a soothing ritual from my vantage point that it was easy to forget that the participants were battling for survival.

Like many scenes of natural competition, this one offers an allegory for business competition. Each of Porter's five forces (1980) are present. There are predators and prey, but there are also threats from competing predators, the risk of too many competitors for an insufficient quantity of food, the peril of bad weather and other environmental factors influencing the availability of supply, not to mention the intrusion of alien species like me, there to collect empty coquina shells as the sandpipers flee when my steps come uncomfortably close.

Even when they bury themselves beneath the sand, the coquinas leave air holes on the surface that give away their locations. A coquina's only real protections are the other coquinas, that there might be one slower or more enticing than oneself, and the waves, that they might return faster than the sandpipers. Meanwhile, when there are more sandpipers vying for coquinas than there are coquinas visible on the wet sand, they must compete with each other for the spoils while remaining watchful for their enemies.

The struggle between the sandpiper and clam seems a fairer fight, between an irresistible force (the sandpiper) and an immovable object (the clam). Hoping to seize the advantage in this natural competition, the sandpiper has swooped in to attack a nearly immobile target. The clam has no means by which to attack, but it has ample resources to

37

defend itself from a small predator like the sandpiper. They lock themselves together, each unwilling to renounce its position. Neither wants to risk loss by letting go of its grip, which means that sooner or later, both of them will lose. Having chosen together the worst possible outcome, their fate comes earlier than expected in the form of a lucky fisherman.

The Sandpiper and Clam as a Battle for Survival

One way to read this tale is as a Darwinian drama. And, because Darwinian competition has been evoked by ethicists (e.g., Michaelson, 2012) and economists (e.g., Frank, 2011) as a metaphor for business competition, the tale can also be understood as an allegory for Darwinian business competition. From this perspective, business is a zero-sum contest in which, for there to be a winner, there must be a loser. If neither wins, both lose. There is no scenario from this point of view in which both can win.

The tale reminds me of the scene in Theodore Dreiser's *The Financier* (1912/1995), in which the young protagonist who will grow up to become an unscrupulous investment banker develops his worldview of Darwinian competition. Frank Cowperwood, on his walks home from school, passes a fish market every day. One day, he notices a rectangular tank has been put on display, containing a lobster and a squid. The lobster is confined to the bottom of the tank, and the squid occupies the water above.

Like the sandpiper and clam, the lobster and squid are locked in a zero-sum competition. They are one another's only potential source of food, and if neither captures the other, they will both die. When Frank sees that the lobster has seized the first of the squid's tentacles, coming back for more each day thereafter, Frank resolves that he wants to be a lobster, not a squid. He does not stay around to find out what happens to the lobster after its meal is complete, but it portends Frank's future. The lobster is trapped, alone in a cage with no allies. It will likely become somebody else's meal.

How can the sandpiper and clam avoid the fate of becoming the fisherman's meal? For one thing, they would have to collaborate. They would have to free one another from the mutual embrace, and in doing so, the sandpiper would have to sacrifice a meal. The reward for its sacrifice would be the ability to fly away, unencumbered, hungry but free to live another day.

Perhaps, in the course of its escape, the sandpiper might help push the clam back into the water, out of the baking sun and the sight of the fisherman. It does not altogether solve the problem that the sandpiper originally flew here to solve, but it is a happier ending than the alternative.

The Sandpiper and Clam as a Tale of Greed

The sandpiper is the aggressor in this tale, accused of greed by the clam. The clam is unwilling to change its position, not wanting to test whether the sandpiper will pull away or push further in if the clam loosens its grip. Had the sandpiper sought out a smaller mollusk, it would not be locked in this battle. It also would have had a chance for a much smaller bite, but as it is, it risks no meal at all.

The sandpiper's stubborn pursuit of its satisfaction reminds me of a tactic I saw on television as a child, used by hunters in tribal Africa to capture monkeys. The hunters would hollow out a small hole in a tree, large enough for the empty hand of a monkey to reach in for some nuts that the hunters would leave there to attract their victim. The monkey would grab a fistful of nuts, only to discover that a full hand could not exit the hole as easily as an empty one had entered.

Unwilling to let go of its reward, the monkey traps itself with greed and is captured easily by the hunter. When my own children were young, I observed this same monkey behavior when they grabbed in a jar for fistfuls of candy. They were like a cartoon bank robber, who cannot outrun the police because the sack of money is too heavy.

The tale evokes a familiar truism: Do not bite off more than you can chew. This is true in dining and in life in general, but it is particularly salient in business. If material survival is a project akin to a business venture, this story warns us not to try to accomplish our goals in one fell swoop. Success more often requires hard work and persistence, not one single stroke of luck. The bad news for the sandpipers on the beach of coquinas is that they have to work hard all day long to find enough coquinas to satiate their hunger. The good news for them is that they do not face the existential threat posed by the struggle with the clam.

The Sandpiper and Clam as a Prisoner's Dilemma about Trust

Why will the sandpiper and clam not let go of each other and move on to pick another fight? If the sandpiper relents, it will lose its meal, the reason it is here in the first place. If the clam relents, it risks being eaten by its adversary that it hopes will fly away. As alluded to earlier, the clam in particular mistrusts the sandpiper, and with good reason. Without trust, no movement can occur.

As any business negotiator can attest, even competitive business requires trust. Trust must obtain between supplier and customer that products and services will be delivered and that compensation will be returned. Trust must exist between manufacturer and user, that products will perform as intended and will be recalled if defective. Business functions more effectively in jurisdictions in which the rule of law reinforces trust, and corruption reigns and inefficiency mounts where trust is lacking (e.g., Donaldson & Dunfee, 1999). Trust enables financial markets to forge trading relationships among distant strangers (e.g., Redding & Witt, 2007).

The situation in which the sandpiper and clam find themselves is a kind of Prisoner's Dilemma. While that classic of decision theory can take several forms, the essential elements of it are that two prisoners will serve less time and realize the best mutual outcome if they both trust each other, they will serve more time if they both betray each other and realize the worst mutual outcome, but if one betrays the other, the betrayer will be set free, and the betrayed will serve the most possible time. As with the two animals, so with the two prisoners, there is a collectivistic incentive to cooperate and an individualistic incentive to betray each other.

Much is made by sociologists and other culture scholars of the differences between an ostensibly collectivist East and an ostensibly individualist West (e.g., Nisbett, 2003). While it is important not to exaggerate these differences and not to resort to simplistic stereotypes, the general claim that Eastern civilizations sometimes skew more collectivist than Western civilizations has some merit. In China, from which my mother's family emigrated, the family may be considered the basic unit of social analysis from which identity flows. For example, as in many Asian cultures, my family's surnames come before their given names. My uncles have the character of our Chinese last name embossed on the furniture in their homes. My mother knows her siblings in relation to their position in the family: big sister, little big sister, little brother, and so on. By contrast, in the United States, where my father's family settled a few generations ago from Western Europe, the individual is the basic unit of social analysis. The given name comes before the first name, and family keepsakes sometimes have the initials of their individual owners monogrammed on them.

The capitalism inherited from a Western-dominated 20th century tends to emphasize individualism. It has given rise to a "winner-take-all" society (Frank & Cook, 1995) in which first movers and leveraged capital translates into massive spoils for a few (Piketty, 2014). Small performance differences can yield large differences in rewards, sometimes resulting as much from luck as from quality. Former competitors like MySpace and Betamax were rendered defunct by single competitors Facebook and VHS that happened to attract enough early adopters to corner their respective markets (Frank, 2016).

However, the capitalism that will evolve over the 21st century may well lean more collectivist if the cultural values of the largest and fastest-growing emerging markets take hold. The oft-perceived lack of regard in the East for intellectual property, antitrust, and other inventions of Western legal systems are sometimes taken by their detractors to mean disrespect for the rule of law. Viewed through a collectivist lens, though, intelligence is meant to be shared, and collaboration among market participants can sometimes yield more mutual benefits than competition among them (Michaelson, 2010). The tale of the sandpiper and clam might well be teaching us to collaborate with our competitors for our mutual survival.

The Fisherman as a Disruptive Innovator

When neither party to the competition between the sandpiper and clam is able to gain the upper hand, the combatants stay too focused on their immediate adversaries. In the course of their struggle, a third, stronger party, of which they were previously unaware, enters the fray and acquires both of their assets.

The fisherman who seizes the opportunity that the inertia of the sandpiper and clam has gifted to him is like a disruptor who changes the field on which the antiquated competition was played (Christensen, 1997). He is like the technology entrepreneurs who changed the way car services are hailed and hotel accommodations are booked, who took market share from competitors who were locked in competition with each other and did not foresee the emergence of another combatant.

The failure of the sandpiper and clam to look around them at the world around their immediate skirmish reminds me of another fish story, as told by David Foster Wallace in "This is Water" (2009):

> There are these two young fish swimming along and they happen to meet an older fish swimming the other way, who nods at them and says, 'Morning boys. How's the water?' And the two young fish swim on for a bit, and then eventually one of them looks over at the other and goes, 'What the hell is water?'

The moral of Wallace's fish tale is to live consciously, lest we take the live-giving forces around us for granted.

The tale of the sandpiper and clam is like the story of Wallace's fish in that they both persist in their daily struggle without a conscious awareness of the things around them that will have a much greater impact on their well-being than they know. It is unlike Wallace's story in that what the sandpiper and clam are missing, while they are so locked into the narrow frame of their struggle, is the greatest threat to their survival.

The Fertility of a Folktale

There is not a great deal of mystery in the original proverb of the sandpiper and clam. So fixated are they on their adversarial relationship that they fail to heed their common interest in avoiding the fisherman. The concluding proverb – "The Sandpiper and the Clam Struggle, and the Fisherman Gets the Benefit" – aptly sums it up.

Yet so much more meaning can be read into a simple folktale. It has personal resonance for me, of idle moments of recreation as opportunities to interact with and learn from relatives and to consider and reconsider the rewards and risks of nature.

It has professional resonance for any of us. It connects to modern management wisdom about the experience of competition, the role of luck in success, the value of institutions to maintaining order, and the ability for disruption to bring about success and failure. We like to consider ourselves to be the authors of our own success, but this proverb reminds us of the significant potential for our plans to be upset by circumstances beyond our control or anticipation.

Furthermore, it evokes other folk wisdom, tales with morals of their own that intersect with the lessons of this one in complementary and potentially contradictory ways. Is there more to this tale than mutual avoidance of catastrophe? Can the sandpiper and clam achieve a win–win in the end? I am still pondering over this one. In the happiest ending I can realistically imagine, the sandpiper is still hungry and will have to prey on some other unsuspecting clams or coquinas. It seems far-fetched to suppose that they might all become vegetarians.

Folk wisdom makes plentiful use of animal metaphors, reminding us of our animal instincts. Usually, an animal allegory is a maneuver intended to humble us, to remind us that despite our intelligence and capacity to reason that we are as vulnerable to pride, ignorance, rashness, and other vices as any other animal. In recent years, however, scientists have shown that animals have the capacity for moral reciprocity and other apparently virtuous behaviors (e.g., de Waal, 2009). This lesson suggests that even in the state of nature, there is room for cooperation for the common good.

References

Christensen, C.M. (1997). *The innovator's dilemma: When new technologies cause great firms to fail*. Boston, Massachusetts: Harvard Business School Publishing.

de Waal, F. (2009). *The age of empathy: Nature's lesson for a kinder society*. New York: Random House.

Donaldson, T., & Dunfee, T.W. (1999). *Ties that bind: A social contracts approach to business ethics*. Cambridge, Massachusetts: Harvard Business School Press.

Dreiser, T. (1995) (originally published 1912). *The financier*. New York: Penguin Books.

Frank, R.H. (2011). *The Darwin economy: Liberty, competition, and the common good*. Princeton, New Jersey: Princeton University Press.

Frank, R.H. (2016). *Success and luck: Good fortune and the myth of meritocracy*. Princeton, New Jersey: Princeton University Press.

Frank, R.H., & Cook, P.J. (1995). *The winner-take-all society: Why so few at the top get so much more than the rest of us*. New York: Penguin Books.

Michaelson, C. (2010). Revisiting the global business ethics question. *Business Ethics Quarterly* 20(2): 237–251.

Michaelson, C. (2012). Reading leaders' minds: In search of the canon of 21st century global capitalism. *Asian Journal of Business Ethics* 1(1): 47–61.

Nisbett, R. (2003). *The geography of thought: How Asians and Westerners think differently...and why*. New York: Simon & Schuster.

Piketty, T. (2014). *Capital in the twenty-first century* (trans. A. Goldhammer). Cambridge, Massachusetts: The Belknap Press of Harvard University Press.

Porter, M.E. (1980). *Competitive strategy: Techniques for analyzing industries and competitions*. New York: The Free Press.

Redding, R., & Witt, M.A. (2007). *The future of Chinese capitalism: Choices and chances*. New York: Oxford University Press.

Wallace, D.F. (2009). *This is water: Some thoughts, delivered on a significant occasion, about living a compassionate life*. New York: Little, Brown.

2

"DON'T FLY TOO CLOSE TO THE SUN"

Using Myth to Understand the Hazards of Hubristic Leadership

Eugene Sadler-Smith

Introduction

Quis hoc credit, nisi sit pro teste uetustas?

('Who would believe this, if it were not sanctioned by antiquity?')
(Ovid, *Metamorphoses* Book I, Line 400)

The use of stories and myths in leadership development is part of an aesthetic leadership scholarship (Hansen et al., 2007) which uses arts-based methods to catalyse inspiration, reflection and critique, and enable educators and students to "counteract an over-reliance on rational models of decision making" (Schedlitzki et al., 2015: 413). Stories and myths have the power to communicate important messages in emotionally charged and compelling ways. Myths are ways of explaining human beings' relationship to the universe using plotlines in which characters embody easy-to-recognise and easy-to-relate-to human traits, reveal patterns that are archetypal in human affairs, and are as relevant today as they were in the case of Greek myths, two and a half millennia ago (Spence, 1994). The archetypal plotline of hubris-leading-to-nemesis is one way in which leadership educators can bring the hazards of hubris to the attention of their students.

The use of storytelling and management learning and education enables students to engage in different forms of sensemaking based on the knowledge of a story and its plotlines (Boje, 2008). Retrospective sensemaking enables students to ask what the situation was and what caused it to arise, whereas prospective sensemaking enables students to ask how might the similar situations in the future unfold as a result of their knowledge of the story? The use of myth in relation to hubristic leadership may help students of leadership to surface and critique assumptions and beliefs about leadership; generate alternative meanings and interpretations of events and experiences in their own organisations; engage more actively with ethical, social and political issues in organisations; and help individuals and groups to come to terms with or militate against the destructive consequences of hubristic leadership (Gray, 2007; Mead, 2011; Sadler-Smith, 2019; Schedlitzki et al., 2015).

Doing so enables students to ask the following questions: what are the characteristics, causes and consequences of hubristic leadership (retrospective sensemaking) and how can the consequences of destructive leadership be contained or constrained in the future (prospective sensemaking)? These different forms of sensemaking can be applied to the study of hubristic leadership in the classroom by appealing to the hubris-followed-by-nemesis archetypal pattern (see Ronfeldt, 1994). Using this approach it is assumed that hubristic leadership is a type of destructive leadership and is associated with negative unintended consequences or 'nasty surprises' (Padilla et al., 2007; Sadler-Smith, 2019). Hubristic leadership is destructive because it implicates volitional, systematic and repeated leader behaviours that ultimately violate the legitimate interests of organisations and their members through a misuse of power or position in ways which invite destructive outcomes, but not necessarily with any intent to harm (Einarsen et al., 2007; Krasikova, et al., 2013). Hubristic leadership has consequences that are not accidental, but this is not because there is some provable causal link between over-confidence and contempt and destructive outcomes, rather there are effects that hubrists invite by acting in the way that they do and as a result commit themselves to accepting (Midgley, 2004).

Myth

Myths are a special type of emotionally charged narrative, they concern human experiences which are neither true or plausible, are not mere 'passing enjoyment' but express something that is important, serious, even sacred, which has immediate cultural relevance (Graf, 2006). Myths compel us, often through a tragic aesthetic, to take note and therefore have an emotive, explanatory and educative potential in personal and professional domains. Myths are an effective yet non-coercive way to inform and regulate moral behaviour. They serve an aetiological function in that they explain and help readers to make sense of natural and social phenomena in events rooted in an imagined distant past. As aetiologies, myths fulfil a prescriptive need in the immediate present, but lend themselves to constant adaptation in changing circumstances while their object remains the same (Graf, 2006).

Even though myths have retained their unassailable niche in the modern and post-modern world, it appears that, with a small number of exceptions, myth is an under-used resource in the management learning and education classroom (Austin et al., 2009; Hatch et al., 2005; Joullié, 2016; Schedlitzki et al., 2015). For management and leadership educators myths provide a fundamental form of narrative knowledge which is embedded in a cultural memory and transmitted from one generation to the next through allegory, metaphor and archetype; moreover, their universality makes them as applicable to modern-day life as to the cultural milieu in which they were first assembled (Gherardi, 2004; Hatch et al., 2005; Schedlitzki et al., 2015). Myth offers management and leadership educators an almost inexhaustible resource for reconfiguring the present according to the past and its enduring archetypes. The re-telling of the past by authors (including educators and their students) supports them in making sense of events in their current or recent experiences that are shaped by the complexities (cognitive, conative, affective and ethical) that are implicit in the myth's plotline (Boje, 1991, 2008; Schedlitzki et al., 2015). The archetypal nature of the characters and plotlines of Greek mythology render them highly transferable to current situations since they embody fundamental aspects of the human experience (Hatch et al., 2005).

Myths, fables, folk and fairy tales inform and educate about how to make sense vicariously of our experiences of the world and how to respond to challenges with practically wise thoughts, words and deeds. One of the reasons for using stories and myths in leadership classes is that it can evoke aesthetic and emotional responses which go beyond rational modes of thinking, deciding and problem solving and situate managerial experience in potentially disruptive management and leadership spaces which are messy, uncertain and ambiguous (Gabriel, 2000).

Different types of myths may embody different types of plotlines such as comic, tragic, epic and romantic (Gabriel, 2000) or combinations of these, for example the 'Echo-Narcissus' myth is both romantic and tragic (self-love and unrequited love, and the tragic deaths of both protagonists). Likewise, the theme of the tragic hero can be used to alert students to the possibility that all leaders are potentially tragic (for example, Achilles is the supreme Greek hero but, being human, he is flawed) and sensitise them to how a pattern of rise and fall might be anticipated and avoided.

Storytelling and mythology are linked strongly to emotion and memory, and emotion can have a strong impact on students' learning experiences (Schedlitzki et al., 2015). The classroom presents a relatively safe space in which strong emotions can be evoked and made sense of. One way in which emotional responses can be evoked is through the mechanisms of experiential processing (Epstein, 2010). The experiential system is an intuitive information processing system—sometimes referred to as 'System 1'—which is more 'primitive' and is associated with direct experience and emotion and which "encodes experience in the form of concrete exemplars and narratives" (Epstein, 1994: 713). The rational system on the other hand is a 'cold' analytical information processing system, sometimes referred to as 'System 2'.

Narratives appeal to and connect directly with the experiential system because they are concretive, specific, personally convincing, imagistic and interpersonal (Bruner, 1986). Their characters, settings, intentions, emotions and actions give them a veracity to real-life that abstract representations can neither achieve or possess. This is one reason why the use of anecdotes increases the persuasiveness of messages and why poetry and other forms of serious literature are valued beyond their entertainment function because they are a "vicarious source of significant experience" (Epstein, 1994: 711); as such they afford readers and listeners with indirect encounters with "lived situations" (Küpers and Statler, 2008: 379).

Appealing to experiential processing redresses the current imbalance in management learning and education's pedagogy. The latter is biased towards rational thinking (Burke and Sadler-Smith, 2006). Experiential processing enables educators and their students to strike a balance between the phenomenological and cognitive approaches and helps to de-biase current discourses (Küpers and Statler, 2008). The conjoining of myth and experiential processing has significant practical and pedagogical implications for management learning and education because appealing to experiential processing via potent narratives is an effective means to communicate knowledge of hazards and risk perception, and motivate positive behavioural change (Dillard and Hisler, 2015; Tyler and Guth, 1999; Tyler and Reynolds, 1998).

Greek Myth and Ovid

Myth and emotionally charged narrative come together in the poetry of Ovid (43BC–17AD), especially in his re-telling of Greek myths in the *Metamorphoses*. Ovid was a Roman poet who lived during the reign of Augustus. He was a contemporary of the older Virgil and Horace, with whom he is often ranked as one of the three canonical poets of Latin literature. Ovid's *Metamorphoses* is the principal source from which European culture drew its knowledge of the myths produced by numerous unknown, learned Hellenistic poets of the past. Predating Ovid, Homer is the absolute master text, whilst in the Renaissance and beyond both Dante and Milton drew inter-textually on Ovid in the *Divina Commedia* and *Paradise Lost*. *Metamorphoses* contains over 250 traditional tales, or *fabula*, concerning human experiences which are neither true or plausible, often with a tragic element, but which have an immediate interpersonal, social or cultural relevance (Galinksy, 1975; Graf, 2006; Quint, 2004).

The myths Ovid retold are chosen and gain authority according to their aesthetic values and, as noted earlier, serve an aetiological function in that they explain and, by explaining, organise current social phenomena in terms of events in the distant past; they also legitimate social facts and in doing so they fulfil a cognitive need in the immediate present (Graf, 2006). The myths often concern natural phenomena (animals, plants, rock formations, constellations, etc.) and the metamorphoses of humans into stags, flowers, trees, stars, etc. (Wise, 1977). Ironically, the Dædalus-Icarus episode is one of the few that does not contain a metamorphosis as such even though some have claimed, implausibly, that the metamorphosis is from human to bird—literally speaking it is not since Dædalus and Icarus remain human, albeit humans with the god-like power of flight which ultimately led to Icarus' downfall (Hoefmans, 1994).

Ovid's skill as a poet is that he uses myth to "effortlessly elucidate" complex social, emotional and moral situations (Graf, 2006: 119) and throughout the narrative he is keen to point out the power of divine influence on human life—"it was the gods who did all this" (op cit.: 120)—and the punishment meted out, often by forfeiture of the protagonist's life (in Icarus' case by drowning), is as a result of some form of divine influence if not direct intervention (Pavlock, 1998: 154).

The *Metamorphoses* is permeated with knowledge and wisdom, moreover didacticism is a fundamental component of Ovid's narrative strategy, used in order to be able to describe and prescribe in a human world of uncertainty (the human world is firmly in the grip of the divinities or their agents) (Graf, 2006). Indeed, one of the motivations of the *Metamorphoses* is to explore the nexus between the aesthetics of poetry and the abstractness of knowledge, but also to offer "practical recommendations" (Graf, 2006: 62). As will be seen in the following pages, the advice Dædalus offered to, but which went unheeded by, Icarus accorded with the Greek maxim of moderation or 'nothing in excess' as inscribed at Delphi (Chappell, 2006: 146) (cf. the Aristotelian 'doctrine of the mean').

In Book 8 of the *Metamorphoses* Ovid relates the fable of the father (Dædalus, a master) and his son (Icarus) who had been detained against their wishes by King Minos on the island of Crete. So as to be able to escape from captivity, Dædalus used his craftsmanship to fashion two pairs of wings made from feathers and wax. The wings gave Dædalus and his son the god-like power of flight which they duly used to flee the island. Before their escape, Dædalus entreated Icarus to exercise restraint, however, things did not go exactly as Dædalus had hoped for or as Icarus had planned. Icarus—as the result of an unintended consequence of his exuberant over-confidence allied to his contempt for his father's advice—plunged to his self-inflicted doom in the Icárian Sea, "And then he caught sight of the wings in the water. Dædalus cursed the skill of his hands and buried his dear son's corpse in a grave" (Lines 233–235). Dædalus is left at the end of Book 8 lamenting the tragic death of his son and cursing his inventions: "He laid the body to rest, in a tomb, and the island was named Icária after his buried child" (Lines 233–235).[1]

Hubris and Hubristic Leadership

In ancient Greece the capital sin of hubris was fundamentally a lack of balance and represented the antithesis of two qualities greatly prized by the ancient Greeks, *aidos* (Αἰδώς, humble reverence for law, human and divine) and *sophrosyne* (σωφροσύνη, self-restraint and a sense for proper limits) (Sheard et al., 2012; Wassermann, 1953). Hubris is bad because it is a disturbance of equilibrium which can lead to unintended negative consequences, for example in business this could involve taking to excess the factors which drove success in the first place but which then become sources of decline, for example growth-driven, entrepreneurial builders become impulsive, greedy imperialists expanding their businesses helter-skelter into areas they know little about (see 'The Icarus Paradox', Miller, 1990). Balancing tensions and steering a course between excess and deficiency and maintaining a well-calibrated equilibrium is vital in navigating the paradox of hubris and instrumental in avoiding the potentially destructive consequences of hubristic leadership.

Hubris has been referred to as an 'intoxication of power' (see Garrard and Robinson [2016] for an interdisciplinary account on the intoxication of power theme). Hubristic leaders systematically and repeatedly take strategic decision choices that are over-confident and over-ambitious, they show contempt and arrogance towards the advice and criticism of others, and as a result run the risk of over-reaching themselves and inviting unintended negative consequences. Two key attributes of hubristic leadership are leaders' exaggerated and excessive confidence in their own abilities and judgements and the contempt in which they hold the cautionary advice and criticism of others. Examples of hubristic leadership in business and management include: Long-Term Capital Management (Stein, 2003), BP Deepwater Horizon (Mason, 2004), NASA (Ladd, 2012), Royal Bank of Scotland (Brennan and Conroy, 2013), Halifax Bank of Scotland (Perman, 2013), etc. For reviews see: Picone et al., 2014; Sadler-Smith (2016); Sadler-Smith et al., 2017.

The main features of hubris have been captured comprehensively in the concept of 'hubris syndrome' (Owen and Davidson, 2009). Hubris syndrome is a set of fourteen behaviours that appear together and are associated with holding significant positional power under conditions of largely unfettered discretion following a period of considerable prior successes. The consequences of these behaviours manifest as hubristic incompetence. As an intoxication of power, Owen and Davidson (2009) described hubris syndrome as a disorder of position as much as of the person. In essence, the hallmarks of hubris are over-confidence and over-ambition emanating from inflated self-beliefs in one's capabilities and exaggerated expectations of a likelihood of successful outcomes. Over-confidence and over-ambition is accompanied by contempt for advice and criticism of others.

Whilst some of the diagnostic behaviours for hubris syndrome overlap with narcissism, hubris is distinct from narcissism in a number of ways (Asad and Sadler-Smith, 2020). Narcissism is a personality trait characterised by self-absorption, grandiosity and a sense of entitlement. Narcissists believe that they are uniquely special and deserving of praise and admiration and can turn arrogant and hostile if their grandiose yet shallow and fragile self-concept is threatened. Hubris on the other hand is not a personality trait, it is a transitory state which develops in the wake of prior successes and the acquisition of significant power, and abates once power is lost. Comparing the Dædalus–Icarus and Echo–Narcissus episodes from Ovid is a useful teaching strategy for comparing and contrasting hubrism and narcissism.

The paradox of hubris is that leadership attributes such as confidence can be both a strength and a weakness. Confidence can be highly beneficial in achieving results and motivating others but this is true only up to a point after which confidence in its extreme forms can manifest as recklessness and contempt. Hubristic leaders fail to calibrate accurately the balance between a deficiency and an excess of a given leadership capability (such as confidence, ambition, etc.). These mis-calibrations emanate from inflated self-beliefs which tip the balance over into excess (Sadler-Smith, 2019).

Hubristic leaders have inflated self-beliefs in their abilities (inflated ability expectations) and inflated self-beliefs that their strategic choices will lead to successful outcomes (inflated outcome expectations). Hiller and Hambrick (2005) identified four components of inflated self-evaluation (which they labelled hyper core self-evaluation) which predispose a leader to over-confident and over-optimistic strategic choices: self-esteem (for example 'I am worthy'), self-efficacy (for example 'I succeed at tasks'), locus of control (for example 'Life's events are within my control') and emotional stability, (for example 'I am free from anxiety/I am not anxious'). Inflated self-esteem, self-efficacy and locus of control and low anxiety are likely to be associated with less comprehensive (i.e. more intuitive) decision processes, faster (i.e. more instinctive) strategic decision making and greater centralisation of decision making (i.e. more controlling) to the CEO. In believing that they are exceptionally worthy, capable, in control and anxiety-free, individuals with inflated positive self-evaluations are likely to be over-confident and therefore act on the basis that their judgements are correct.

"DON'T FLY TOO CLOSE TO THE SUN"

Other sources of inflated self-belief include: (1) better-than-average effect whereby individuals in general tend to consider themselves above average on positive characteristics, for example, most people will rate their driving skills as above average; (2) attributions of causality whereby individuals tend to attribute successful outcomes to their own actions (a self-serving attribution) whereas failure is put down to others or bad luck; (3) base-rate neglect whereby executives' inflated estimations of their abilities emanate from comparisons to population average (for example, the 'average manager'), rather than 'average CEO'. This factor underlines the importance of CEOs 'keeping their feet on the ground' and making more accurate, i.e. less upwardly-biased, self-evaluations.

The Dædalus and Icarus Episode

The Dædalus–Icarus episode is contained in Ovid's *Metamorphoses*, at Book VIII, Lines 183–235.[2] It has particular contemporary relevance because hubristic leadership is recognised increasingly as a hazard for business organisations and political institutions, as well as for civil society in general (Owen, 2012; Picone et al., 2014). Events on the world stage in 2018 (the time of writing) highlight the hazards of hubristic leadership in the United States and beyond, not only for businesses but perhaps even more importantly for civil society and the stability of the global order. The Dædalus–Icarus episode is recounted in full:

> Meanwhile Daedalus, hating Crete, and his long exile, and filled with a desire to stand on his native soil, was imprisoned by the waves. 'He may thwart our escape by land or sea' he said 'but the sky is surely open to us: we will go that way: Minos rules everything but he does not rule the heavens'. So saying he applied his thought to new invention and altered the natural order of things. He laid down lines of feathers, beginning with the smallest, following the shorter with longer ones, so that you might think they had grown like that, on a slant. In that way, long ago, the rustic pan-pipes were graduated, with lengthening reeds. Then he fastened them together with thread at the middle, and bees'-wax at the base, and, when he had arranged them, he flexed each one into a gentle curve, so that they imitated real bird's wings. His son, Icarus, stood next to him, and, not realising that he was handling things that would endanger him, caught laughingly at the down that blew in the passing breeze, and softened the yellow bees'-wax with his thumb, and, in his play, hindered his father's marvellous work.
>
> When he had put the last touches to what he had begun, the artificer balanced his own body between the two wings and

51

hovered in the moving air. He instructed the boy as well, saying 'Let me warn you, Icarus, to take the middle way, in case the moisture weighs down your wings, if you fly too low, or if you go too high, the sun scorches them. Travel between the extremes. And I order you not to aim towards Bootes, the Herdsman, or Helice, the Great Bear, or towards the drawn sword of Orion: take the course I show you!' At the same time as he laid down the rules of flight, he fitted the newly created wings on the boy's shoulders. While he worked and issued his warnings the ageing man's cheeks were wet with tears: the father's hands trembled.

He gave a never to be repeated kiss to his son, and lifting upwards on his wings, flew ahead, anxious for his companion, like a bird, leading her fledglings out of a nest above, into the empty air. He urged the boy to follow, and showed him the dangerous art of flying, moving his own wings, and then looking back at his son. Some angler catching fish with a quivering rod, or a shepherd leaning on his crook, or a ploughman resting on the handles of his plough, saw them, perhaps, and stood there amazed, believing them to be gods able to travel the sky.

And now Samos, sacred to Juno, lay ahead to the left (Delos and Paros were behind them), Lebinthos, and Calymne, rich in honey, to the right, when the boy began to delight in his daring flight, and abandoning his guide, drawn by desire for the heavens, soared higher. His nearness to the devouring sun softened the fragrant wax that held the wings: and the wax melted: he flailed with bare arms, but losing his oar-like wings, could not ride the air. Even as his mouth was crying his father's name, it vanished into the dark blue sea, the Icarian Sea, called after him. The unhappy father, now no longer a father, shouted 'Icarus, Icarus where are you? Which way should I be looking, to see you?' 'Icarus' he called again. Then he caught sight of the feathers on the waves, and cursed his inventions. He laid the body to rest, in a tomb, and the island was named Icaria after his buried child.

Icarus, in common with leaders in business and politics who become intoxicated with their power and success, became intoxicated with his power of flight. The principal, but not the only, moral lesson of this emotionally charged story is 'don't fly too close to the sun'. In this and other myths Ovid explored morally ambiguous situations (James, 2009) and offered a commentary on the negative consequences of excess. Ovid communicates and reinforces the enduring folk wisdom that over-confidence and arrogance (two of the hallmarks of hubris) are vices which must be avoided. He communicates the moral lesson via the dramatic death of Icarus who, as the embodiment of excess and aspiration (Quint,

2004: 847), ends-up being the hapless victim of his own hubristic excess. The *Metamorphoses* contains many other such moments of "high emotional intensity" (Brunner, 1966: 356) and affords management and leadership educators an extensive and largely untapped repository of relevant myths (e.g. Phaethon and Phoebus, Echo and Narcissus, etc.).

Interpretation

Icarus dared to fly too close to the sun using wings fashioned expertly from feathers and wax (the height of technological sophistication at that mythological time) and in so doing over-reached himself and against Dædalus' express advice. Icarus' demise was an unintended negative consequence of his hubristic over-confidence and exuberance. In this episode of the *Metamorphoses* Ovid, via tragedy, submits a moral critique of Icarus; the myth admonishes his hubristic over-confidence and espouses moral guidance via the explicit message of the story: 'don't fly too close to the sun'. The emotional reaction derived from the tragic aesthetic which Ovid mobilises is a feeling which also makes possible moral action, namely identification and sympathy with, and a compassion for, the welfare of human beings (Feagin, 1983) but also exasperation at their foolishness. Icarus, amongst all of Ovid's myths, is always germane because "wisdom … is the antidote to human overconfidence and the managerial *hubris*" that often follows the inability to recognise and accept our limitations (Chia, 2013: xv, emphasis added).

One of the principles of hubris in Classical mythology is that of a 'cosmic order'. The corollary of this is that hubris on the part of mortals invites punishment for transgressions of that order: mortals are born mortals, and with a few exceptions, so it must always remain. Indeed, the code is so strict that even minor deities are not allowed to compete with major deities (Hansen, 2004). Mortals are expected most certainly to understand their position in the pecking-order of the Universe. Any who have the temerity to transgress this rule by acting as though they were equal or superior to the deities (for example, by daring to fly) will naturally, and inevitably, incur divine wrath. The Dædalus–Icarus episode is a cautionary narrative which is told with the purpose in the mind of the narrator of dissuading the hearer from over-ambitious and over-confident behaviours that invite, and therefore risk bringing about, negative unintended consequences (Hansen, 2004).

A further relevant, but sometimes overlooked, aspect of the Icarus myth is that Dædalus exhorted his son not only to avoid flying too high but also to avoid flying too low ("if you fly too low the water will clog your wings", in other words to "keep to the middle way" (*Metamorphoses*, Book 8, Line 203). This theme is also to be found in the Phaethon myth where Phoebus (the Sun God) urges his son (Phaethon) to follow the middle way: "Venture to climb too high and you'll burn the ceiling of heaven, the earth if you sink too low; for safety remain in the middle" (*Metamorphoses*, Book 2, Lines 136–139). Hubris researchers see parallels in this with CEOs who need to 'fly at the right height' and strike the right balance between confidence and over-confidence, ambition and over-ambition and authentic pride and hubristic pride (Petit and Bollaert, 2012: 268). This creates tension with the view that 'for big results you have to take big risks'; there danger of 'falling hard' is ever-present given that risky behaviours are associated with extreme results (both positive and negative; see Chaterjee and Hambrick, 2007).

Sensemaking and Re-Storying the Myth

Seen through the lens of the Dædalus–Icarus episode, hubristic leadership can be made sense of retrospectively and prospectively. In making sense of Icarus' hubris retrospectively students could be tasked with asking what were the characteristics, causes and consequences of Icarus' irrational exuberance and contempt for Dædalus' wise advice? In making sense of hubris prospectively students could be tasked with asking what might Icarus and/or Dædalus have done to avoid hubristic excess or contain its calamitous consequences? With regard to sensemaking and hubris more generally, Robinson (2016), drawing on Karl Weick's work, remarked that in a world that is volatile, uncertain, complex and ambiguous, bold action is adaptive because its opposite, overly cautious deliberation is potentially futile in a changing world where perceptions can never be accurate because by the time something has been grasped it has become something else. In Robinson's analysis this may help to explain why it is that leaders with the courage (or perhaps the temerity) to be bold risk takers "and who once were regarded as heroes are seen in retrospect to have suffered from hubris—but only in the wake of events that laid them low" (p. 14).

Re-storying a myth is a useful pedagogical device for familiarising students with the plotline and pattern which is implicit in the myth and for the purposes of retrospective and prospective sensemaking (Schedlitzki et al., 2015). Myths are not open-ended plotlines. They have well-defined characters and a well-circumscribed train of events, and as such their core elements are open to multiple interpretations but they are not necessarily open to improvisation of the plot as such since it represents an archetypal pattern. The Greek myths Ovid re-told are not open-ended, their plotline is given; however, they are open to re-storying in terms of contemporary technologies, social structures, relationships and systems. For example, the Dædalus–Icarus myth could be re-storied in terms of modern-day hubristic leaders such as Richard Fuld at Lehman Brothers or Fred Goodwin at Royal Bank of Scotland, or hubristic organisations such as Long-Term Capital Management (Lowenstein, 2000) or BP in the Deepwater Horizon blowout (Mason, 2004).

The myths' characters and plotline provide a scaffolding whereby organisational events in the students' experience can be framed in terms of a meaningful pattern (hubris-to-nemesis) in order that they may determine similarities and differences between their experiences and the hubris-to-nemesis archetype. This may assist students in determining the characteristics, causes and consequences of relevant events that they may have experienced (for example, where they were involved in a process of hubristic leadership either as leader or follower or bystander), or on the other hand it may open up a deeper analysis and critique of the experience which could reveal in fact that their organisational story was not hubris as entailed in in Dædalus–Icarus myth but was a related, but substantively different phenomenon. By re-storying organisational events that, on the face of it, appeared hubristic may actually reveal that the destructive consequences did not emanate from hubrist leadership, rather they were a consequence of some other form of destructive leadership such as narcissistic leadership, and this distinction could be conceptually important given that hubrism is sometimes conflated with narcissism (Asad and Sadler-Smith, 2020; Sadler-Smith, 2019). In this case, analysis and reinterpretation could initiate a new and different process of storying and re-storying around the Echo and Narcissus episode from *Metamorphoses*, Book II. In this way the use of myth becomes more fluid, emergent and open ended, and forges broader connections between relevant leadership constructs.

Mitigating Hubristic Leadership through Practical Wisdom

Practical wisdom is a means by which the vice of hubris might be countered, and the hazard of hubristic leadership mitigated; it also provides a foundation for moral character development as a force for good in times of crisis and uncertainty. This chapter has sought to understand how myth can provide educators and leaders with a resource for making sense of and mitigating hubristic leadership on the basis that: (1) the aesthetics of myths (as told for example by Ovid) have a powerful and compelling effect on the reader or listener by appealing directly to the experiential system (System 1) which entails an intuitive, emotive and embodied way of knowing; (2) hubris arises when leadership strengths such as ambition, confidence, pride and self-esteem become over-developed and give rise to negative, albeit unintended, consequences (nasty surprises), as such they represent an excess of leadership strengths (a 'strengths-into-weaknesses' paradox, see Sadler-Smith, 2019); (3) in straying from the middle course, hubris as a form of excess may be considered a leadership vice; (4) by appealing to experientiality via myth has the potential to leverage practical wisdom (*phronēsis*) which can militate against the deleterious consequences of the confidence, arrogance, pride and contempt that are the hallmarks of hubristic leadership.

Myths do have a given plotline but they are open to multiple interpretations, for example as well as castigating Icarus for his over-ambition and over-confidence, as noted earlier, Ovid also incorporates explicitly into the narrative the concept of the "middle way" (Pavlock, 1998: 152): Dædalus is presented as a "model [moral prototype] of moderation" exhorting Icarus to "stay away from all excessiveness" (Hoefmans, 1994: 145). He specifically lectures Icarus on flying a middle course offering strictures about not flying too low or too high; he explains to Icarus that the wings will be damaged by the sun's heat if they fly too high and by the dampness of the sea if they fly too low. The Dædalus–Icarus myth can be interpreted as counsel against the excesses of over-confidence, over-ambition and exuberance which ultimately lead to recklessness, hubris and nemesis. In this regard hubris exists in a duality with its contrastive, nemesis: "hubris calls for nemesis, and in one form or another it's going to get it, not as a punishment from outside but as the completion of a pattern already started" (Midgley, 2004: 148).

Turning to Aristotle and moral education more explicitly, virtue ethics exhorts moderation rather than deficiency or excess. CEO hubris is an excess of the leadership strengths of, amongst other things, confidence, ambition and self-esteem. Furnham (2004) illustrates this point with regard to the related idea of narcissism (defined as malignant self-love, overbearing self-confidence, inexplicably high self-esteem). The problem for the high-flyer is that "you probably need a great deal of self-esteem to get the job, but you need to lose some of it while on the job" (Furnham, 2004: 143). Too much, as well as too little, self-esteem can be both a cause and a consequence of management failure. Even when people with low self-esteem get into positions of power, low self-esteem prevents risk-taking, bold decision making, etc., however "those with seemingly limitless self-esteem and concomitant hubris are the real problem" (Furnham, 2004: 143). Aristotle's doctrine of the mean locates virtue "between two vices one of excess and one of deficiency"; and virtuous action is "intermediate between the actions expressive of those vices" (Young, 2006: 192). In this interpretation, excesses of confidence, ambition and self-esteem are leadership vices, therefore hubris is a vice. Leaders whose trajectories parallel that of Icarus and who are unable to moderate excess may show a lack of practical wisdom.

Practical wisdom is defined by Aristotle as a 'truthful disposition' to get things right in action (Chappell, 2006). Icarus failed to get things right in action. Practical wisdom is a virtue (*Nicomachean Ethics*, 6.5.1140b-24) instantiated in a capacity for a "prudential judgement by which equivocal circumstances are negotiated and acted upon for the common good" perfected through practice and habituation (Chia, 2013: xv). Icarus was too young and too inexperienced to have perfected a disposition which according to Aristotle becomes "familiar with experience, but a young man has no experience" (cited in Epstein, 1994: 712). This was in spite of the wise Dædalus' exhortations as to the perils of a deficiency or excess of altitude. *Phronēsis* is as *phronimos* does (Chia, 2013), and Dædalus steered wisely the middle flight path and lived to tell the tale.

Practical wisdom also creates a "bridge between the emotive [which has cognitive 'weight'] and the rational" (Roca, 2008: 612). Experiential processing activates the emotive, whereas rational processing articulates knowing; neither is sufficient of itself nor are they separable. The interaction of the experiential with the rational system is a "source of intuitive wisdom and creativity" (Epstein, 1994: 715). Phronetic (that is 'practically wise') leaders, through experientiality and rationality, are able to intuitively grasp important features of ambiguous situations in making choices "driven by the pursuit of the common good" (Shotter and Tsoukas, 2014: 224). Practical wisdom (phronēsis) is one means by which actors can reconcile the competing demands of the common good and commercial success (Zhu et al., 2016).

As noted earlier, myth not only allows space for the examination of complex social matters such as morality and ethics (Graf, 2006), it also allows for multiple interpretations (Furnham, 2004). The theme of moral criticism (Pavlock, 1998) in the reading presented here is directed at boldness and temerity (both in Icarus' flight and, in a different reading, Dædalus' making) and is equated with flawed judgement. Myths can provide moral education but in doing so management educators should be mindful of the dangers of manipulation and control and be aware of the ethical implications of poetic license and the interpretation that is adopted (Gabriel, 2004; Schedlitzki et al., 2015).

Implications and Conclusions

The protagonists in myths offer exemplary illustrations of the consequences of virtue and vice and, in the case of Icarus, of the unintended consequences of over-confident and over-ambitious judgements and behaviour. Greek myth as re-told by Ovid provides a gateway not only to a broader discussion of the relationships between narrative, aesthetics and wisdom, but also to lessons that might be learned from modern narratives of hubristic excess.

Hubrists of recent times who have brought about negative, not to say calamitous, consequences for themselves, their organisations, institutions and society did not, it would be logical and reasonable to assume, set out deliberately to be destructive. In the same way that Icarus did not set out to drown himself, Richard Fuld did not set out to contribute to the bankruptcy of his beloved Lehman Brothers, nonetheless severe and harmful unintended consequences (a nasty surprise) accrued from the interactions between his hubristic leadership, the behaviour of followers and the propitiousness of the 2007 context for a destructive outcome. The modern-day hubrists mentioned earlier displayed a lack of practical wisdom borne out of excessive confidence, ambition and self-esteem, and when allied to a contempt for the advice and criticism of others it became a toxic mix. Accordingly, ancient myths and stories of modern hubrists engagingly told in management and leadership education and development via emotionally charged narratives could be used to catalyse both experientiality (intuition, System 1) *and* rationality (analysis, System 2) configured as a duality, not a dichotomy, and retrospective *and* prospective sensemaking, thereby sensitising managers and leaders to the perils of hubris and drawing attention to the moral character strengths required of a leader (Crossan et al., 2013) and, ultimately, to the wisdom of humility which is the antithesis of hubristic excess.

Notes

1 The complete Daedalus-Icarus episode from the *Metamorphoses* is reproduced in: http://ovid.lib.virginia.edu/trans/ Metamorph8.htm Accessed 23 03 2018.
2 http://ovid.lib.virginia.edu/trans/Metamorph8.htm Accessed 23 03 2018.

References

Asad, S., & Sadler-Smith, E. (2020). Differntiating leader hubris and narcissism on the basis of power. Leadership (in press).
Austin, R. D., Nolan, R. L., & O'Donnell, S. (2009). The technology manager's journey: An extended narrative approach to educating technical leaders. *Academy of Management Learning & Education, 8*(3), 337–355.
Boje, D. M. (1991). The storytelling organisation: A study of story performance in an office-supply firm. *Administrative Science Quarterly, 36*(1): 106–126.
Boje, D. M. (2008). *Storytelling Organizations*. London: SAGE.
Brennan, N. M., & Conroy, J. P. (2013). Executive hubris: The case of a bank CEO. *Accounting, Auditing & Accountability Journal, 26*(2), 172–195.
Bruner, J. S. (1986). *Actual Minds, Possible Worlds*. Cambridge MA: Harvard University Press.
Brunner, T. F. (1966). The function of the simile in Ovid's 'Metamorphoses'. *The Classical Journal, 61*(8), 354–363.
Burke, L. A., & Sadler-Smith, E. (2006). Instructor intuition in the educational setting. Academy of Management Learning & Education, 5(2), 169–181.
Chappell, T. (2006). The variety of life and the unity of practical wisdom. In T. Chappell (Ed.) *Values and Virtues: Aristotelianism in Contemporary Ethics*. 136–157. Oxford: Oxford University Press.

Chatterjee, A., & Hambrick, D. C. (2007). It's all about me: Narcissistic chief executive officers and their effects on company strategy and performance. Administrative Science Quarterly, 52(3), 351–386.

Chia, R. (2013). Foreword. In W. Küpers and D. J. Pauleen (Eds). *A Handbook of Practical Wisdom: Leadership, Organization and Integral Business Practice.* xv–xvi. Abingdon: Routledge.

Crossan, M., Mazutis, D., Seijts, G., & Gandz, J. (2013). Developing leadership character in business programs. *Academy of Management Learning & Education, 12*(2), 285–305.

Dillard, A. J., & Hisler, G. (2015). Enhancing the effects of a narrative message through experiential information processing: An experimental study. *Psychology & Health, 30*(7), 803–820.

Einarsen, S., Aasland, M. S., & Skogstad, A. (2007). Destructive leadership behaviour: A definition and conceptual model. *The Leadership Quarterly, 18*(3), 207–216.

Epstein, S. (1994). Integration of the cognitive and the psychodynamic unconscious. *American Psychologist, 49*(8), 709–724.

Epstein, S. (2010). Demystifying intuition: What it is, what it does, and how it does it. *Psychological Inquiry, 21,* 295–312.

Feagin, S. L. (1983). The pleasures of tragedy. *American Philosophical Quarterly, 20*(1), 95–104.

Furnham, A. (2004). *Management and Myths.* UK: Palgrave Macmillan.

Gabriel, Y. (2000). *Storytelling in Organisations: Facts, Fictions, and Fantasies.* Oxford: Oxford University Press.

Gabriel, Y. (Ed.) (2004). *Myths, Stories and Organisations: Premodern Narratives for Our Times.* Oxford: Oxford University Press.

Galinsky, K. (1975). *Ovid's Metamorphoses: An introduction to the basic aspects.* Los Angeles: University of California Press.

Garrard, P., & Robinson, G. (Eds) (2016). *The Intoxication of Power: Interdisciplinary Insights.* Basingstoke: Palgrave Macmillan.

Gherardi, S. (2004). Knowing as desire: Dante's Ulysses at the end of the known world. In Y. Gabriel (Ed.) *Myths, Stories and Organisations: Premodern Narratives for Our Times.* 32–48. Oxford: Oxford University Press.

Graf, F. (2006). Myth in Ovid. In P. Hardie (Ed.) *Cambridge Companion to Ovid.* 108–121. Cambridge: Cambridge University Press.

Gray, D. (2007). Facilitating management learning: Developing critical reflection through reflective tools. *Management Learning, 38*(5), 495–517.

Hansen, W. F. (2004). *Handbook of Classical Mythology.* Oxford: Oxford University Press.

Hansen, H., Ropo, A., & Sauer, E. (2007). Aesthetic leadership. *The Leadership Quarterly, 18*(6), 544–560.

Hatch, M. J., Kostera, M., & Kozminski, A. J. (2005). *The Three Faces of Leadership: Manager, Artist, Priest.* Oxford: Blackwell Publishing.

Hiller, N. J., & Hambrick, D. C. (2005). Conceptualizing executive hubris: The role of (hyper) core self-evaluations in strategic decision-making. *Strategic Management Journal, 26*(4), 297–319.

Hoefmans, M. (1994). Myth into reality: The Metamorphosis of Daedalus and Icarus (Ovid, Metamorphoses, VIII, 183–235). *L'antiquité Classique, 63*, 137–160.

James, H. (2009). Ovid in Renaissance English literature. In P. E. Knox (Ed.) *A Companion to Ovid*. 423–441. Chichester: John Wiley & Sons.

Joullié, J. E. (2016). The philosophical foundations of management thought. *Academy of Management Learning & Education, 15*(1), 157–179.

Krasikova, D. V., Green, S. G., & LeBreton, J. M. (2013). Destructive leadership: A theoretical review, integration, and future research agenda. *Journal of Management, 39*(5), 1308–1338.

Küpers, W., & Statler, M. (2008). Practically wise leadership: Toward an integral understanding. *Culture and Organization, 14*(4), 379–400.

Ladd, A. E. (2012). Pandora's well: Hubris, deregulation, fossil fuels, and the BP oil disaster in the Gulf. *American Behavioral Scientist, 56*, 104–127.

Lowenstein, R. (2000). *When Genius Failed: The Rise and Fall of Long-Term Capital Management*. New York: Random House.

Mason, R. O. (2004). Lessons in organizational ethics from the Columbia disaster: Can a culture be lethal? *Organizational Dynamics, 33*(2), 128–142.

Mead, G. (2011). *Coming Home to Story: Storytelling beyond Happily Ever After*. Bristol: Vala Publishing Cooperative.

Midgley, M. (2004). *The Myths We Live By*. Abingdon: Routledge.

Miller, D. (1990). *The Icarus Paradox: How Excellent Organizations Can Bring About Their Own Downfall*. New York, NY: Harper Business.

Owen, D. (2012). *The Hubris Syndrome: Bush, Blair and the Intoxication of Power*. 2nd Edition. York: Methuen.

Owen, D., & Davidson, J. (2009). Hubris syndrome: An acquired personality disorder? A study of US Presidents and UK Prime Ministers over the last 100 years. *Brain, 132*(5), 1396–1406.

Padilla, A., Hogan, R., & Kaiser, R. B. (2007). The toxic triangle: Destructive leaders, susceptible followers, and conducive environments. *The Leadership Quarterly, 18*, 176–194.

Pavlock, B. (1998). Daedalus in the labyrinth of Ovid's 'Metamorphoses'. *The Classical World, 92*(2), 141–157.

Perman, R. (2013). *Hubris: How HBOS Wrecked the Best Bank in Britain*. Edinburgh: Birlinn.

Petit, V., & Bollaert, H. (2012). Flying too close to the sun? Hubris among CEOs and how to prevent it. *Journal of Business Ethics, 108*(3), 265–283.

Picone, P. M., Dagnino, G. B., & Mina, A. (2014). The origin of failure: A multidisciplinary appraisal of the hubris hypothesis and proposed research agenda. *The Academy of Management Perspectives, 28*(4), 447–468.

Quint, D. (2004). Fear of falling: Icarus, Phaethon, and Lucretius in 'Paradise Lost'. *Renaissance Quarterly, 57*(3), 847–881.

Robinson, G. (2016). Making sense of hubris. In P. Garrard & G. Robinson (Eds) *The Intoxication of Power: Interdisciplinary Insights*. 1–16. Basingstoke: Palgrave.

Roca, E. (2008). Introducing practical wisdom in business schools. *Journal of Business Ethics, 82*(3), 607–620.

Ronfeldt, D. (1994). Beware the *Hubris–Nemesis Complex: A Concept for Leadership Analysis*. Santa Monica, CA: RAND.

Sadler-Smith, E. (2019). *Hubristic Leadership*. London: SAGE.

Sadler-Smith, E. (2016). Hubris in business and management research: A 30-year review of studies. In P. Garrard & G. Robinson (Eds) *The Intoxication of Power: Interdisciplinary Insights*. 39–74. Basingstoke: Palgrave Macmillan.

Sadler-Smith, E., Akstinaite, V., Robinson, G., & Wray, T. (2017). Hubristic leadership: A review. *Leadership* (forthcoming). http://dx.doi.org/10.1177/1742715016680666

Schedlitzki, D., Jarvis, C., & MacInnes, J. (2015). Leadership development: A place for storytelling and Greek mythology? *Management Learning, 46*(4), 412–426.

Sheard, A. G., Kakabadse, N. K., & Kakabadse, A. P. (2012). Leadership hubris: Achilles' heel of success. In *Global Elites*. 308–331. UK: Palgrave Macmillan.

Shotter, J., & Tsoukas, H. (2014). In search of phronēsis: Leadership and the art of judgment. *Academy of Management Learning & Education, 13*(2), 224–243.

Spence, L. (1994). *Introduction to Mythology*. London: Senate.

Stein, M. (2003). Unbounded irrationality: Risk and organizational narcissism at long term capital management. *Human Relations, 56*(5), 523–540.

Tyler, J. M., & Guth, L. J. (1999). Using media to create experiential learning in multicultural and diversity issues. *Journal of Multicultural Counselling and Development, 27*(3), 153.

Tyler, J. M., & Reynolds, T. (1998). Using feature films to teach group counselling. *Journal for Specialists in Group Work, 23*(1), 7–21.

Wassermann, F. M. (1953). The speeches of King Archidamus in Thucydides. *The Classical Journal, 48*(6), 193–200.

Wise, V. M. (1977). Flight myths in Ovid's 'Metamorphoses': An interpretation of Phaethon and Daedalus. *Ramus, 6*(1), 44–59.

Young, C. M. (2006). Aristotle's justice. In R. Kraut (Ed.) *The Blackwell Guide to Aristotle's Nicomachean Ethics*. 179–197. Oxford: Blackwell Publishing.

Zhu, Y., Rooney, D., & Phillips, N. (2016). Practice-based wisdom theory for integrating institutional logics: A new model for social entrepreneurship learning and education. *Academy of Management Learning & Education, 15*(3), 607–625.

3

CHOOSING OUR CROSS WITH WISDOM

A Folktale for Living and Leading

Elena P. Antonacopoulou and Regina Bento

The Folktale: Picking a Cross

There once was a man who was always complaining about his life:

"This is so unfair, why is life so hard for me? I can't carry my cross any longer, it's too heavy … Other people have it so much easier!"

One night he had a dream. An angel took him to a room, where all sorts of crosses were on display.

"Go ahead," said the angel. "Choose the cross that's right for you. These are the crosses of all the people you know. Just pick any of them, and you can trade it for yours."

"That's easy," answered the man. "Just get me the lightest one."

"But remember," warned the angel. "The cross you pick should help your soul grow stronger."

The man went carefully around the room, examining each cross. "This one is really light, I can easily carry it. But maybe it is not challenging enough, I know I can handle more." And, moving to the next one: "Oh, my! This one is too heavy, there's no way I could carry it."

And so he continued examining the crosses, trying some on, and discarding one after another. Finally, he spotted one that seemed just right.

"That's it! That's the cross for me…"

"Why don't you try it?" invited the angel.

The man walked around a bit with the cross he had chosen, just to make sure how it felt.

"Yes, this one is just right. It is heavy enough to help me grow, but not so heavy that I can't bear it in the long run. That's it, that's the one I want. But whose is it?"

The angel answered: "Well, turn it around and look at the name on the back."

Why This Folktale?

This folktale has far-reaching implications for the personal and professional lives of leaders, no matter where we are in our journeys of learning leadership. From beginners to seasoned leaders, we all carry our burdens, and we can help or hinder others' ability to carry their own. Here we take a secular perspective, rooted in the philosophical traditions of stoicism, to explore the importance of choosing our "cross" with wisdom: suffering is an inescapable part of life, but our ability to deal with it depends on the wisdom of our choices. Those choices can sometimes influence the very *causes* of our suffering – for example, when the suffering relates to something that is conceivably under our control. And perhaps more importantly, those choices can also influence the *effects* that suffering has on us, even when we cannot do anything about the suffering itself.

This folktale's use of a cross to symbolize our burdens in life can be traced back to the weight of the cross that Jesus had to bear on the way to Golgotha for his crucifixion. And yet, we note that the moral of the folktale goes beyond Christianity, and finds resonance in other religious and spiritual traditions (for example, in the Jewish tale about carrying one's load). The enduring power of this tale might be puzzling since on the one hand, it does not provide easy answers to the question of human suffering. On the other hand, it carries universal moral meanings: "don't complain, it could be worse;" "don't worry: we're not given more to suffer than we can bear;" "your life is the way it was meant to be: your cross has your name on it."

In its multiple variations across diverse cultural traditions, a shared meaning for this folktale is preserved: the core wisdom it holds about *choice*. We may complain and rebel against the heavy burdens we carry in life, we may think that those burdens are unfair or unbearable, and we may crumble under their weight or struggle to bear them with equanimity and faith (as in the Book of Job). But, no matter how heavy our burden, we become better able to carry it when we trust (or realize) that we are carrying the "right" burden, and that our burden has been chosen with wisdom: i.e., with a loving understanding of what we can actually (and sustainably) bear, and with a teleological (if not theological) understanding that bearing this burden serves some higher purpose.

When we approach suffering with wisdom, we gradually find ourselves able to extract learning and growth from the experience, and to move a little further in our human search for meaning (Frankl, 2015). Here we will not attempt to answer the question that has been asked through the millennia: why suffering? Rather, we will start with the notion that suffering exists, and that it can serve a purpose. The dilemmas that are presented to us can create moments when we experience learning the most, whether in extraordinary circumstances, or in the struggles of everyday life, or in the quotidian practice of leadership, or in developmental activities such as Outward Bound. These moments of struggle can help us develop the capacity to "feel safe being vulnerable" (Antonacopoulou, 2014). Such safety in vulnerability can transform suffering into a rite of passage, from which we can learn to distill the wisdom to choose. Choosing wisely is integral to discovering our humanity, and involves learning both how to act and how to experience such suffering, even when its nature and intensity cannot be altered. Therefore, our ability to make those choices with wisdom is not fixed and static. It is emergent and unfolding as part of our journey of becoming. Akin to Ulysses' struggle to reach "Ithaca," this makes the journey so much more critical than the destination.

Our personal and professional struggles can help us develop and grow through daily reflexive critique and practicing, so that we not only refine what we do to better ends, but also refine ourselves in the process, thus carving our character and conscience (as much as our competence) in what we do (Antonacopoulou, 2010). When our burdens threaten to bring us down, we may find the strength to choose to carry on regardless, cultivating our own practical judgment – *phronesis* – and picking ourselves up, determined to use this vulnerable state to achieve as much learning as possible. In this respect, picking up our cross is an invitation to choose to lead life with purpose, drawing meaning and cultivating our humanity from the pedagogy – education/*paideia* – that learning to live life is itself an invitation for (Antonacopoulou, 2016). As we will argue, this is where lies the possibility of wisdom which we will explicate also in relation to leadership.

The "Moral" of the Story

Our intent in this chapter is neither to propose a defense of suffering, or to make the argument that suffering is good for its own sake. Rather, our goal is to use our opening folktale to explore the idea that we do not need to see suffering as something to be feared and avoided, but as an integral aspect of our growth and appreciation of what it takes to learn leadership.

In other words, we can develop our ability to approach suffering with wisdom, and this can allow us to use our own suffering as one of the paths that life offers us to grow in strength, resilience and equanimity. Such growth may hold the key to appreciating leadership (or lack thereof) in ourselves and in others as we experience the learning necessary to make choices.

Perhaps one of the most fundamental of choices is to not live in fear. We can, instead, approach daily life with the implicit trust that, if something "bad" happens, we will be able to handle it – or, at least, that we can develop, gradually, such ability. Similarly, when things do not go to plan, or what we seek does not materialize in the ways we imagined or would prefer, that is not a mark of failure we can retreat from. Instead, it is an invitation to return and revise our intentions and plans as well as the way we imagine, so that we can grow from that process the trust in the process of learning. It is this trust in surrendering to the invitation to learn that propels us to grow by enabling us to continue to "show up" for life, putting things in perspective, curving our character and conscience using the inevitable burdens as ways to develop our "core" strength, rather than being paralyzed by the possibility that we might inexorably crumble under their weight. Different from physical strength, the core strength we propose here refers to the way we can stand our ground, firm and strong, for our convictions, reflecting the core virtues that form the person we are. This is a source of power and strength that is central to growing our humanity and – unlike physical growth and muscle strength – it is acquired through reflexivity and critique, not merely by following a fitness regime, even if our "core" strength enhances our fitness for living and by implication well-being.

Moreover, when we approach our cross(es) with wisdom, suffering can become more than a path for individual growth. It can also turn out to be a path for collective growth. Such collective growth extends our humanity towards serving the common good, because our collective *phronesis* – practical judgment – is then directed towards a higher purpose. We suggest that one such higher purpose is in learning how to love. Suffering is humbling, and is not an individual experience. Our pain teaches us our limits, and makes us more sensitive to the pains and limits of others. It also makes us more appreciative of the strength and grace of others. Through suffering, we can become both more willing to help others, and more able to seek or accept their help. When we are able to choose our cross with wisdom, and to help others with theirs, we improve our lives through learning, and we restore a sense of meaningfulness as to why the struggle is worth the experience of suffering. These would be the moments we collectively grow.

In our human search for meaning, we so often spend much of our life searching for happiness and feeling like the man in the folktale, complaining about our cross and wondering how much better life would be if we had "that," instead of "this." We concentrate so much of our effort into looking for a "better" cross – one lighter than the one we have – as if "possessing" that "other" cross might somehow magically create happiness, release the big secret of how that cherished "other" state of being may hold the key to all that we long for. But what if, as the man in the story ultimately succeeds in doing, we could learn to go beyond momentary pain when choosing our cross? We would then realize that a "lighter" cross is not necessarily better – that maybe happiness is not the ultimate goal, and that suffering is not to be avoided at all costs. We would then take on what we can actually handle, even if that implies a struggle. We transform at that point the struggle itself into the weight we lift to increase our core strength. We enhance our fitness for life, by becoming more solid in our capacity to weather storms that life throws at us. We celebrate what it means to feel alive. We feel pain in the struggle because our perseverance in our core strength is what enables us to carry on regardless.

Choosing our cross with wisdom involves the realization that Western society's obsession about being happy leads us to a "checklist" limbo, where we are constantly revising and adding up to the list of conditions that need to be fulfilled and preserved in order for us to feel "happy." If we are constantly assessing the gap between that ideal scenario and our current situation, we cannot truly appreciate what we already have; we will live in fear of not attaining the items in the checklist, and – perhaps worse – in fear of the possibility of losing what we do have. Trying to attain and protect all the items in an ever-growing checklist of happiness leads to a life beset by considerations about "what if," and "if only."

In affluent Western societies, this happiness checklist is constantly reinforced by advertising messages, both blatant and subtle. Our desires and regrets are further inflated in the "sharing" environment of our digital communities in Instagram, Facebook and Twitter, where we are constantly confronted with how others are "scoring" on the checklist for happiness; it is easy to be tempted into envy or shame, if we forget that what we are seeing is a carefully curated version of their life. Once we become unable to limit what we "want," we also lose the ability to differentiate it from what we "need." We then live at the mercy of a never-ending spiral of appetite and hunger.

In contrast, as we learn to choose our cross with wisdom, we find that we are also learning to face our fear of suffering. We come to learn that the fear of suffering involves a fear of losing control – and further, a fear of losing even the illusion of control. Once we relinquish the checklist of happiness, we become open to the possibility of choosing our cross with wisdom.

Implicit in such wisdom is the idea that we cannot control everything that happens to us, but we can still strive to control how we react to it. Accepting this idea is a freeing and empowering experience, since, as the stoics (Inwood, 2007; Long, 2002) would remind us, it helps us deal with suffering in two significant and interrelated ways. First, it helps us realize that no matter how bad a situation is, it could be even worse. And second, if we cannot think of anything worse, it can help us find some degree of peace at the bottom of the deepest well. If we cannot say that "it could be worse," we can still find consolation in realizing that this also means that "it can't get any worse," since the situation is already as bad as it can get at this moment when we are experiencing it. Either way, this implies that losing control over events does not necessarily mean that we lose control over our experience of those events.

This idea helps us work with our fear of the suffering that is already being experienced, as well as the fear of the suffering that might still lie ahead. We find that happiness and suffering are intertwined in an exquisite braid, as inseparable as the double helix in the DNA that forms the building blocks of our personal and professional lives.

This idea can be an exhilarating experience. It goes beyond helping us deal with suffering – it opens us to the possibility of *joy*. We see joy as different from happiness: not a transitory and conditional emotion, but as a force field of energy rooted in a deep and enduring appreciation for life with all that it entails, including both suffering and happiness. The fear of suffering can keep us from experiencing joy, in the same way that the fear of nightmares can keep us from sleeping, and therefore can deprive us from dreaming, imagining and aspiring to create what may seem impossible. Learning to choose our cross(es) with wisdom means that we are better equipped to carry our burdens, and also that we are more open to be "surprised by joy" (Lewis, 2017). That joy is the injection of energy that propels us to move forward, to carry on regardless, and to *transform breakdowns into breakthroughs*.

Relevance in Our Own Personal Experience

We, the co-authors of this chapter (Elena and Regina), have been friends and collaborators for almost twenty years. In a recent email, Elena shared a particularly difficult struggle, and Regina responded by quoting this tale from the folklore of her native country, often retold by her father as she was growing up. Elena reacted immediately: "We have the same story in my country! My Mother was always telling it." This surprised us both, because we come from different cultural traditions (Greece and Brazil, respectively).

We were even more delighted to find out that this tale has played a significant role in how we have looked at so many challenges through the years, both in our personal and professional lives. This folktale has resonated throughout our lives, rekindling in difficult moments our appreciation of struggle as integral to personal growth; and we have both been inspired to pass it on to our children, and to use it in our leadership courses and seminars. It was stunning for us to realize how this story endures and resonates across cultures, generations and contexts. This inspired us to share in this chapter the folktale's broader messages about the significance of choosing our cross with wisdom.

When Elena was growing up in Cyprus, her parents urged her to "learn to cherish your cross." This meant learning to see her cross not just as a symbol of Crucifixion and death, but one of expansion and abundance: not despairing from the struggle, but finding joy in the realization that, little by little, we can learn to carry even what might otherwise have seemed an unbearable weight. In such a radical twist of interpretation of the cross as something to be cherished, joy comes from learning that suffering and happiness are inextricably intertwined.

The joy that springs from this living cross of wisdom is an outcome of learning, not an end in itself – just as the suffering involved in choosing and carrying that cross is a pathway to learning, not something to be sought for its own sake. When Regina was growing up in Brazil, she was reminded of this in a vivid way. Struggling with adolescence, one night Regina found a note that her father had left on her pillow. The one-line note said, very simply: "don't worry about happiness." Regina then went to her father to ask him to explain what he meant. He answered: "happiness is a by-product, not a goal to be pursued. The more you seek it, the less likely you will be to find it." He went on:

> if you pursue happiness as a goal, you might end up with a checklist of things you need to have in order to be happy, and this will make you focus on pursuing those things, and live in fear of losing them. If that happens, you will lose track of what really matters in life, all that gives it meaning.

He concluded with a phrase that would haunt, and console, Regina throughout her life: "we should not seek to have something we could not lose with a smile."

Now, decades later, we (Elena and Regina) realized the enduring relevance that the "choosing your cross" folktale had for our personal experiences. We also realized that, given the difference in our backgrounds and current contexts, such commonality in relevance was also an indication that we needed to explore the reasons for the universality of the folktale. Why does this story have such power to transcend time and space, reverberating across cultures and generations? This question prompted us to examine this folktale more closely, going beyond the tensions and extensions we were experiencing in our own lives to distill its core wisdom about *choice* in the broader context of leaders and leadership.

Relevance for Leadership Practice

The lifelong journey of learning and practicing leadership requires wisdom in the choice of the burdens we carry – and the choices of how we carry them – in our personal and professional lives. How can we "pick" our cross with wisdom, in a way that enables us to then "pick up" and carry it through life, opening ourselves to joy, and greeting both happiness and suffering with equanimity? The answer(s) may be shaped as we form our philosophy of life, which evolves over the course of a lifetime as we learn the power of choosing, the significance of our *phronesis* in making such choices and the endurance we grow as we learn to navigate life's lesson in the *paideia* it provides to grow our core strength.

When striving to choose our cross with wisdom, we as leaders can put ourselves in the place of the dreamer in the folktale, taking into consideration both the elements in the story: we are not only "picking" our cross (i.e., choosing a cross in terms of its characteristics, the weight of the burdens to be borne), but we are also "picking *up*" our cross (i.e., choosing a cross in terms of our own potentialities and constraints – our willingness and ability to carry those burdens).

Moreover, the assessments we make are not only in terms of what "is" but also in terms of what "can" be. In other words, in making those assessments (about the burdens and about ourselves) leaders might find wisdom in the Serenity Prayer:

> Lord, grant me the serenity to accept the things I cannot change,
> the courage to change the things I can,
> and the wisdom to know the difference.
>
> (Morris, 2014: 2)

It is a testimony to the power of the Serenity Prayer that it has been a source of inspiration in so many different situations, not only in religious contexts but also in addiction recovery programs and in multiple secular situations where it has helped people from all walks of life to choose and carry their particular burdens. It is also a testimony to the universality of the Serenity Prayer that it has been attributed to so many different secular thinkers and spiritual leaders: Cicero, Reinhold Niebuhr, St. Thomas Aquinas, St. Augustine, St. Francis of Assisi and others.

The classical formulation of the Serenity Prayer suggests that wisdom is necessary to analyze a dichotomy: what can and cannot be changed. This analysis can be approached as a trichotomy (Irvine, 2009): what we have full control over (can change), have some control (might be able to change, at least partially) or have no control over (cannot change). Here we extend the idea even further, and use the Serenity Prayer to assess what we "can" and "cannot" change as a continuum that helps us choose our cross with wisdom.

Let us imagine a metaphor: *a living cross of wisdom*. The horizontal beam represents the burdens of life (the weight to be borne), and the vertical beam represents the bearer of those burdens (our capacity to bear their weight). Here we propose that in choosing our cross with wisdom we assess each of those beams (guided by the Serenity Prayer), so that their edges become stretching points, pulling each beam outward, horizontally and vertically, and expressing the elasticity of our potential to connect them to form our core symbolized in the cross itself. The core becomes the meeting point where these dimensions coming together energize our responses to reflect our *phronesis* in serving the common good with openness, readiness and resilience but also elasticity. Such elasticity reflects the strength of our choice to transform tensions into extensions, breakdowns into breakthroughs.

One approach we have found helpful in applying this metaphor to the practice of leadership is for leaders to approach their "cross" as a way of forming practical judgments: this involves assessing both the burden (the weight to be borne), and the bearer (our capacity to bear that weight), in the context of man's broader search for meaning (Frankl, 2015).

Assessing the Burden. One way to strengthen our choices is to assess our burden (the weight to be borne), by questioning which elements of the horizontal beam of the cross we can or cannot readjust. For example, we may pursue such readjustment by examining the temporal nature of our burdens, in order to discern whether their weight stems from the past, the present or the future.

Carrying around the weight of *past* events and experiences, as if they were still happening right now, leads to suffering the pangs of regret and prolonging grievances. Choosing our cross with wisdom involves letting go of burdens that come from our past, lightening the horizontal beam by learning forgiveness and compassion for ourselves and for others. Worline and Dutton (2017) remind us that "awakening compassion" in our workplaces is a "quiet power" capable of elevating both people and organizations.

Even if we cannot change what has already happened in the past, there may still be something we can strive to do about it in the present and in the future. First, we can strive to reframe the past in ways that do not involve clinging or regret, that do not dwell on the alternative universe of "what if?" and "if only," and that do not involve blame, either in terms of guilt or recrimination. Second, we can strive to identify patterns in the past that might enable us, from now on, to change what we still can change. Instead of incurring the same mistakes over and over again, once we identify a recurring pattern we might learn that it is possible to stop repeatedly adding their weight to the burdens in the horizontal beam of our cross. There can be great wisdom in studying the patterns revealed by our recurring problems so that we can learn to avoid repeating or further growing them from this point on.

This learning from the past is powerfully expressed in Portia Nelson's poem, "Autobiography in Five Short Chapters:" when we first walk down one street and fall into a deep hole in the sidewalk, we feel helpless, figure that it is not our fault and discover that it is very difficult to find a way out; the second time we walk down the same street, but ignore the hole, we fall into it again, refuse to believe that it happened once more or that it might be our fault and keep finding it difficult to climb out; the third time, we see the hole and still fall in it, out of habit, but then we recognize that it is our fault and manage to get out more easily; the fourth time we take that street, we have now learned to see the hole and therefore are able to walk around it; the fifth time, we choose to "walk down another street" (Nelson, 2012).

The weight of our *present* burdens can often be substantially alleviated when we learn from the past what we can change right now, whether by walking around the "hole in the sidewalk," or by taking a different "street" entirely. Present burdens, be they related or unrelated to past events, can also be lightened when we realize that, even when we have very little control over what is happening to us, it may still be possible to change how we react to them. In other words, we may be able to lighten the experienced weight, if not the weight itself, as discussed in the next section about expanding our capacity to bear life's burdens.

The horizontal beam of our cross can be further lightened if we learn to refrain from adding to it the weight of our *future* burdens. There may be room for individual agency, i.e., things we can do right now, and in the future, to change the nature and weight of those future burdens. But even in situations where such agency to change future burdens is quite limited, and where there are aspects of our future that are more path-dependent and difficult to change, we can still control something very important, which we might be able to change right now: we can learn not to carry those burdens in advance, worrying about them before they even happen. In other words: let us keep changing what we can, but not fret about the future.

Assessing the horizontal beam of the cross by applying the wisdom of the Serenity Prayer to discern what we can change, or not change, in each of its three temporal elements may help us carry the burdens by being present in the moment we are invited to act – lightening them as we can, without the extra weight of looking to the past with regrets or grievances, and the extra weight of looking to the future with fear or anxiety.

Assessing Our Capacity to Carry Burdens

The wisdom of the Serenity Prayer can also be applied to discerning what can or cannot be changed in the vertical beam of the cross. Whereas in the previous section we focused on how to work with the weight of our burdens, here we explore how to increase our capacity, our strength to bear them. A good place to start building this capacity is the realization that doing so is in our best interest. Since suffering cannot be eliminated, we might as well learn how to live with it, and how to derive benefit from it.

Stoic philosophers such as Zeno of Citium (in Cyprus), Seneca, Epictetus and the Emperor Marcus Aurelius offer helpful guidance on how to deal with suffering (Sellars, 2016a, 2016b; Sorabji, 2000; Stephens, 2007), and stoicism remains a modern, practical philosophy (Irvine, 2009; Sellars, 2016a). According to stoicism, there are aspects of our reality that cannot be changed, but even for those there still remains the possibility of learning and changing the way we respond to them. As discussed in the previous section, it is more fruitful to strive for control over ourselves than over external circumstances. The stoics see great value in striving to learn this type of self-mastery:

> Don't demand that things happen as you wish, but with that they happen as they do happen, and you will go on well.
>
> (Epictetus, 135: 8).

> If then everything else is common to all that I have mentioned, there remains that which is peculiar to the good man, to be pleased and content with what happens, and with the thread which is spun for him.
>
> (Marcus Aurelius, 167: Book 3).

We can change our experience of our burdens, if not the burdens themselves, if we strive to follow the stoic advice to put things in perspective by contrasting our current suffering with the worst that could possibly happen. And, if that comparison leads us to conclude that the current scenario is indeed the worst we can imagine, we can still strive to find consolation in the thought that this means we cannot fall any further, as we argued earlier: "Be like the promontory against which the waves continually break, but it stands firm and tames the fury of the water around it" (Marcus Aurelius, 167: Book 4).

This sort of self-control may come more easily to some than to others, depending on factors such as personality (e.g., internal vs. external locus of control), upbringing, culture, and so on. But still, our capacity to carry our burdens can be increased through practice, when we, as leaders, learn to embed elasticity in our reactions to external events. This practice can be pursued in a variety of ways (Antonacopoulou & Bento, 2010, 2016; Irvine, 2009):

- small acts of self-denial or sacrifice to serve as inoculations against reversals of fortune;

- resistance against short-term temptations, in order to use those victories to build self-confidence in our ability to stand hardship, choose goals wisely and delay gratification;
- subordination of desires to values, so that we may welcome pleasure, worldly success and rewards when they come, but still recognize that they are not worth pursuing for their own sake, nor clinging to at all costs.

These and other daily practices move us along the continuum of the Serenity Prayer, transforming things we could not change into things we can. They help us change both our strength and our patience, as we learn to develop our capacity to endure the weight of our burden, and bear the wait for the time this learning might take.

Choosing the Cross Within a Broader Search for Meaning

Learning to be "worthy of our suffering" is part of our broader search for meaning (Frankl, 2015). Quoting Nietzsche, Frankl reminds us of the radical importance of this search for meaning: "He who has a *'why'* to live for can bear almost any *'how'*" (Frankl, 2015: 96). A crucial benefit from suffering, therefore, is that it carries its own cure. It leads us to ask "why," and thus, prepares us to deal with "how."

Even when the loom of fate weaves the most terrible experiences, and seems to take away from us absolutely everything, there is still something we must strive to retain: *our freedom to choose how to react to this suffering*. Reflecting about his life in a Nazi concentration camp, Victor Frankl reminds us: "(...) everything can be taken from a man but one thing: the last of the human freedoms – to choose one's attitude in any given set of circumstances, to choose one's own way" (Frankl, 2015: 62).

Confronted with unimaginable horrors, Frankl was constantly reminded of a quote from Dostoevski: "There is only one thing that I dread: not to be worthy of my sufferings" (Frankl, 2015: 62). Those words came particularly alive for Frankl when he witnessed the behavior of those who, in their martyrdom, preserved their "last inner freedom" in how they approached suffering and death, denying the Nazis' ultimate control: "It can be said that they were worthy of their sufferings; the way they bore their suffering was a genuine inner achievement. It is this spiritual freedom – which cannot be taken away – that makes life meaningful and purposeful" (Frankl, 2015: 62).

Choosing our own cross with wisdom allows a deep sense of appreciation of our human condition. We are no longer conquered victims, stuck without hope in impossible circumstances. Instead, we become learners: no matter how reluctant at first, we eventually find ourselves on the way to being transformed into athletes in training, who can find joy in the struggle of daily practice, as the pain of exertion starts yielding the pleasure of lifting heavier and heavier weights, and running longer and longer distances reaching levels of fitness not thought humanly possible.

Once we acknowledge the possibility and reality of suffering without becoming victimized, or paralyzed by it, we start learning how to embrace vulnerability without fear. Buoyed by the notion that what matters is not whether we fall, but the fact that we strive to get up again, we find courage in the exhortation of the mindfulness mantra to "begin again." This allows us to prepare for the worst, hope for the best and know that we can be ready for whatever comes, because we have been practicing to face challenges without fear or anxiety, and practicing to enjoy the good that may come our way without coveting or clinging to it. What has real value – our essence – our core – cannot be taken away.

Suffering is one among many paths in life's search for meaning: "(...) let me make it perfectly clear that in no way is suffering necessary to find meaning. I only insist that meaning is possible even in spite of suffering" (Frankl, 2015: 106).

Life offers us multiple paths to learn core lessons: suffering is one of those paths, and it can help us learn about ourselves, and about others – a path both for inward and outward growth, learning and love. This, we would suggest, is where leadership also stands a better chance to emerge. Hence, whilst the preceding paragraphs explain the choosing of our cross with wisdom, they also offer a new framing of what leadership may be and how such leading may be demonstrated.

We would suggest that leadership involves the process of choosing our cross with wisdom, as reflected in our individual and collective *phronesis* to "pick" the cross(es) as a pathway for learning. Leadership also involves the process of "picking up" not only our cross(es) when we might temporarily bend in their weight, finding the "Courage, Commitment, Confidence and Curiosity" (Antonacopoulou & Bento, 2018) to stand up strong; it is also about picking up each other, showing each other compassion, love and support. Leadership, in this sense, implies a special challenge in the process of picking (up)/choosing our cross(es) with wisdom, because it reflects our learning to cultivate our core strength to stand with and for each other to preserve our human right to be free.

Leadership, conceptualized in these terms, not only changes the conversation in the leadership field with all its rich variations and interpretations focusing on the person – as Hero, Olympian or just Human (Antonacopoulou, 2008, Petriglieri & Petriglieri, 2015; Liu & Baker, 2016) – or the collective practices that define shared and distributed leading (Küpers & Weibler, 2008; Cunliffe & Eriksen, 2011; Raelin, 2016) and the learning that is done both individually and organizationally (Grint, 2007; Antonacopoulou & Bento, 2003; 2010). We also seek

74

through this new conceptualization of leadership to cast new light to one of the most fundamental purposes of leadership – to energize us in living life well, with joy, with contentment, with meaning and with purpose, because we are learning to endure the challenge of learning to *lead our lives from within*, using our core strength, the essence of who we are.

Implications for the Personal and Professional Development of Leaders

This folktale holds an important lesson for leadership development: it signals the need to continuously learn how to face the personal and professional challenges of "leadership from within." When we go deep within ourselves to learn how to pick (up) our cross with wisdom this also opens us for an expanded understanding of leadership. In this expanded view, leadership is not just for the privileged few who occupy roles with formal authority, ostensible power or wide-range influence, existing in a "league of their own: a mythical world of possibility that everyone can envision, very few can be a part of, and only a handful can deliver" (Antonacopoulou, 2008: 30). Rather, we step away from this mythologized image of the "leader-as-hero" and into the much broader and more real world of "leaders-as-learners" (Antonacopoulou & Bento, 2018). In this broader world, leadership is a collective responsibility, a "cross to bear" that has our names on it – and a cross that belongs even to those of us who might not think of ourselves as "leaders" in the traditional, heroic view of the term. As Parker Palmer notes:

> Leadership is a concept that we often resist. It seems immodest, even self-aggrandizing, to think of ourselves as leaders. But if it is true that we are made for community, then leadership is everyone's vocation, and it can be an evasion to insist that it is not. When we live in the close-knit ecosystem called community, everyone follows and everyone leads.
>
> (Palmer, 2000: 74)

When we go into the metaphorical room in the folktale, the work of assessing the weight of the crosses and the bearer's capacity to carry them is not just an individual quest. Rather, this "walk around the room" is part of a search for meaning that enables us to learn about the burdens of other bearers in our community, and to develop the empathy and compassion to alleviate those burdens and improve the coping capacity of our fellow bearers. This is what we recognize as "learning leadership" (Antonacopoulou & Bento, 2003; 2010), because as leaders we learn to embrace the challenge and burden of leadership; and in doing so, we learn to strengthen our capacity to feel safe being vulnerable as we commit to *learning from the experience of leading and leading from the experience of learning.*

This is not an easy path to leadership. It requires us to confront and examine our deepest fears and desires, instead of simply projecting them into the external world. When we pick (up) the cross of leadership that bears our name, the responsibility that comes with it may, at times, feel too overwhelming. But, as we have seen in the previous sections, suffering is not something to be automatically and unreflectively avoided. Palmer (2000) invites us to learn how to face leadership challenges and crucibles from the motto of Outward Bound programs: "If you can't get out of it, get into it." He explains further that:

> We capitalists have a long and crippling legacy of believing in the power of external realities much more deeply than we believe in the power of the inner life. How many times have you heard or said, 'Those are inspiring notions, but the hard reality is…'? How many times have you worked in systems based on the belief that the only changes that matter are the ones you can measure or count? How many times have you watched people kill off creativity by treating traditional policies and practices as absolute constraints on what we can do? (…) But the great insight of our spiritual traditions is that we – especially those of us who enjoy political freedom and relative affluence – are not victims of that society: we are its co-creators. We live in and through a complex interaction of spirit and matter, of the powers inside of us and the stuff 'out there' in the world. (…) Our complicity in world-making is a source of awesome and sometimes painful responsibility – and a source of profound hope for change. It is the ground of our common call to leadership, the truth that makes leaders of us all.
>
> (Palmer, 2000: 77)

Suffering is one of the paths in the "leader-as-learner" (Antonacopoulou & Bento, 2018) search for meaning, and to find our way out we must learn to go in (deep inside) and through. Palmer tells us about a bestiary of five "monsters" he works with when he leads "retreats where leaders of many sorts – CEO's, clergy, parents, teachers, citizens, and seekers – take an inward journey toward common ground" (Palmer, 2000: 85–86). In the journey of learning leadership from within we deal with each of those five monsters, and receive corresponding *gifts of learning.*

According to Palmer, the first monster that must be faced when learning to lead from within is "insecurity about identity and worth." This insecurity often leads us to use extroversion as a coping mechanism

CHOOSING OUR CROSS WITH WISDOM

against self-doubt, to become dependent on external activity as a distraction or as evidence of self-worth (which sometimes leads to depression, or even death, when those activities are taken away), and to deprive others of their identities in order to enhance our own. As we learn how to deal with this first monster, our painful inner journey gives us the first gift of learning:

> (...) the knowledge that identity does not depend on the role we play or the power it gives us over others. (...) When a leader is grounded in that knowledge, what happens in the family, the office, the classroom, the hospital can be life-giving for all concerned.
>
> (Palmer, 2000: 87)

The second monster is the belief that the world is a battleground, to be conquered through fiercely competitive "tactics and strategies, allies and enemies, wins and losses, do or die" (Palmer, 2000: 87). This can become a self-fulfilling prophecy, transforming workplaces and organizations into ruthless combat zones where leaders trample over followers and fight for the spoils of war. When we learn to deal with this second monster, seeking instead for "consensual, cooperative, communal" ways of doing business and living in society, our inner journey yields yet another gift of learning:

> The structure of reality is not the structure of a battle. (...) Yes, there is death, but it is part of the cycle of life, and when we learn to move gracefully with that cycle, a great harmony comes into our lives. The spiritual truth that harmony is more fundamental than warfare in the nature of reality itself could transform this leadership shadow – and transform our institutions as well.
>
> (Palmer, 2000: 88)

The third monster is the belief that we must have ultimate control and responsibility over everything. It impels leaders to micro-manage and relate to others in abusive and manipulative ways, succumbing to "burn-out, depression and despair" when reality shatters that illusion of control. But if we learn how to refuse to be deceived by this third monster, we earn the third gift of learning:

> The gift we receive on the inner journey is the knowledge that ours is not the only act in town. Not only are there other acts out there, but some of them are even better than ours, at least occasionally! *We learn that we need not carry the whole load but*

can share it with others, liberating us and empowering them. We learn that sometimes we are free to lay the load down altogether. The great community asks us to do only what we are able and trust the rest to other hands.

(Palmer, 2000: 89). (Emphasis is ours)

The fourth monster is fear, particularly the fear of chaos in life and organizations. Closely related to the need for control, it can seduce leaders into protecting the status quo at all costs, in an ethos that imprisons others (and themselves) within the bounds of rigid rules, procedures and precedent, and stifles "dissent, innovation, challenge and change." When we learn the courage to confront this fourth monster, we reap the fourth gift of learning:

> ... chaos is the precondition to creativity: as every creation myth has it, life itself emerged from the void. Even what has been created needs to be returned to chaos from time to time so that it can be regenerated in more vital form. When a leader fears chaos so deeply as to try to eliminate it, the shadow of death will fall across everything that leader approaches – for the ultimate answer to all of life's messiness is death.

(Palmer, 2000: 89–90)

The fifth monster is the leader's fear of death and failure, breeding an insecurity to let anything die or fail "on his or her watch." This fear can tempt leaders into paradoxical traps: sometimes "killing" projects prematurely, before they have a real chance to yield results; sometimes keeping other projects artificially alive, long after they should have been terminated; and sometimes resuscitating other projects without any revitalization of their ability to succeed. All these traps inhibit the leader's capacity for transforming such projects into sources of new learning. However, when we learn to face this fifth monster, we open ourselves to the possibility of receiving the fifth gift of learning: "(...) death finally comes to everything – and yet death does not have the final word. By allowing something to die when its time is due, we create the conditions under which new life can emerge" (Palmer, 2000: 91)

Those five monsters add weight to the cross of leadership – increasing the burdens of leaders and those around them, and draining their individual and collective capacity to carry those burdens. But when we are willing to learn from within, and to find out what we can and cannot control about the suffering caused by those monsters, we will have a better chance to pick (up) that cross of leadership with wisdom and to benefit from the ensuing gifts of learning. We will have learned to lead life from within – with and from our core.

Implications for the Development of More Responsible and Sustainable Leadership Practices

Traditional leadership education and development efforts tend to focus on the heroic model of leadership and on "competencies" that are externally oriented. This folktale suggests, instead, the need to focus on leaders-as-learners, who are never completely formed and do not have all the answers, but who are not afraid to keep asking deeper and more challenging questions in their quest for meaning, and for learning to lead from within.

The further one ventures into the exploration of this kind of leadership, the more one needs to learn about the sense-making, connection-building, choice-making, vision-inspiring, reality-creating roles of leaders. This is a journey not just of the mind, but of the spirit, something that cannot really be "taught" in the traditional sense of this word – but fortunately it is something that can be learned.

This learning can be facilitated by expanding leadership education and development beyond traditional management topics, to include philosophy, history, literature and art, and by encouraging "practices of deep reflection:" storytelling, historical inquiry, reflective reading and writing, dialogue, action research (Wisely & Lynn, 1994). Palmer (2000) encourages us to help each other explore our inner lives as we learn leadership from within, and offers three recommendations.

First, Palmer urges us to "lift up the value of inner work" in leadership education and development: "Inner work is as real as outer work and involves skills one can develop" (Palmer, 2000: 91). He suggests, for example, the use of journaling, reflective reading and meditation, and cautions that our inner work cannot be sacrificed without cost to our outer work as well.

Second, he asks us to spread the word that inner work, though deeply personal, does not need to remain a private endeavor. Indeed, it is often helpful to pursue it in community, where we can support each other's efforts. This support must, however, remain non-invasive. As is the practice in Quaker communities, it must restrain from offering advice or quick fixes, focusing instead on listening attentively, and posing questions to help us discern our own answers.

Third, Palmer encourages us to remind each other of the role of fear in our lives: a fear that can drive us to either try to "fix" or abandon one another; and even a fear of being afraid, since this might imply the realization that we are not perfect. In contrast, all the wisdom traditions, no matter how diverse, share a common exhortation: "Be not afraid."

> 'Be not afraid' does not mean that we cannot **have** fear. Everyone has fear, and people who embrace the call to leadership often

find fear abounding. Instead, the words say we do not need to **be** the fear we have. We do not have to lead from a place of fear, thereby engendering a world in which fear is multiplied.

(Palmer, 2000: 93–94)

Palmer's three recommendations become even more urgent when we consider Worline and Dutton's (2017) observation that suffering and compassion deserve renewed attention in leadership education and development:

Suffering is a heavy word. Most of the time, we try to avoid it. 'Suffering' is also a word you might not connect to work life. Suffering doesn't typically show up on lists of businesses' most significant concerns or make the cut of the many issues that can occupy a manager's agenda. But it should. A new science of compassion, based in extensive research, helps us to see that suffering, and the compassion that helps address suffering directly, is one of the most important ideas for business today.

(Worline & Dutton, 2017: 1)

Worline and Dutton see suffering as pervasive in the workplace, whether flowing in from our lives outside (illness, losses, divorce, finances, addictions, etc.) or arising within the organization itself (workload, performance pressures, downsizing, interpersonal conflicts, mismanaged change efforts, etc.). If we do not want our workplaces to become "amplifiers of human suffering" (Worline & Dutton, 2017: 11), current and prospective leaders must practice compassion, a process that involves building personal and collective capacities for attention (noticing suffering), interpretation (framing problems and failures as opportunities for learning), empathic concern (being present and appreciating different perspectives), and action (changing what can be changed) to alleviate suffering.

As we go around the room in our folktale, picking (up) our crosses with wisdom, we gradually learn, individually and collectively, who we are, how we can behold suffering with compassion towards ourselves and others, and how we can retain the ultimate freedom of choosing how we react to circumstances we cannot control. Adler and Delbecq remind us that "leadership is not a place where suffering is avoided or courage is unnecessary" (2017: 11). But, while leadership "from within" requires courage, this does not mean that we need to be perfect, nor heroic, to be leaders. We can just be leaders-as-learners, wounded healers who know that neither success or failure lasts forever, that suffering is one of the paths to wisdom, and that what matters is finding our "core." It is through this core we also discover the *courage, commitment, confidence and curiosity* to continue, because we also discover *compassion* in our love for life and freedom (Antonacopoulou & Bento, 2018).

Letting go of the regrets and grievances of the past, and the fear and anxiety of the future, we can get ready, each moment, to "begin again."

References

Adler, N.J. & Delbecq, A. L. (2017). Twenty-First Century Leadership: A Return to Beauty. *Journal of Management Inquiry*, Pre-published online. Available at: https://doi.org/10.1177/1056492617710758

Antonacopoulou, E.P. (2008). Practising engaged leadership: Living the myth & embodying the legend of the Olympic athlete. In M. Kostera (ed.) *Organizational Olympians*. London: Palgrave, pp. 30–39.

Antonacopoulou, E.P. (2010). Making the business school more 'critical': Reflexive critique based on phronesis as a foundation for impact. *British Journal of Management*, 21: 6–25.

Antonacopoulou, E.P. (2014). The experience of learning in space and time. *Prometheus*, 32(1): 83–91.

Antonacopoulou, E.P. (2016). Rediscovering paideia and the meaning of a scholarly career: Rejoinder to "identifying research topic development in business and management education research using legitimation code theory". Journal of Management Education, 40(6): 711–721.

Antonacopoulou, E.P. & Bento, R. (2003). Methods of 'learning leadership': Taught and experiential. In J. Storey (ed.) *Current Issues in Leadership and Management Development*. Oxford: Blackwell, pp. 71–92.

Antonacopoulou, E.P. & Bento, R. (2010). Learning leadership in practice. In J. Storey (ed.) *Leadership in Organizations: Current Issues and Key Trends*, 2nd Edition. London: Routledge, pp. 81–102.

Antonacopoulou, E.P. & Bento, R. (2016). Learning leadership: A call to beauty. In J. Storey (Ed.) *Leadership in Organizations: Current Issues and Key Trends*, 3rd Edition. London: Routledge, pp. 99–112.

Antonacopoulou, E.P. & Bento, R. (2018). From Laurels to learning: Leadership with virtue. *Journal of Management Development*, 37(8): 624–633.

Cunliffe, A.L. & Eriksen, M. (2011). Relational leadership. *Human Relations*, 64(11): 1425–1449.

Epictetus. 135. *The Enchiridion*. Available online at http://classics.mit.edu/Epictetus/epicench.html

Frankl, V. (2015). *Man's Search for Meaning*. (Gift Edition). Boston: Beacon Press.

Grint, K. (2007). Learning to lead: Can Aristotle help us find the road to wisdom? *Leadership*, 3(2): 231–246.

Inwood, B. (2007). *Seneca: Selected Philosophical Letters Translated with Introduction and Commentary*. Oxford: Oxford University Press.

Irvine, William B. (2009). *A Guide to the Good Life: The Ancient Art of Stoic Joy*. New York: Oxford University Press.

Küpers, W.M. & Weibler, J. (2008). Inter-leadership: Why and how to think leader- and followership integrally. *Leadership*, 4(4): 443–447.

Lewis, C.S. (2017). *Surprised by Joy: The Shape of My Early Life*. (Epub Edition). San Francisco: HarperOne.

Liu, H. & Baker, C. (2016). White knights: Leadership as the heroicisation of whiteness. *Leadership*, 12(4): 420–448.

Long, A.A. (2002). *Epictetus: A Stoic and Socratic Guide to Life*. Oxford: Oxford University Press.

Marcus Aurelius. 167. *The Meditation*. Available online at http://classics.mit.edu/Antoninus/meditations.html

Morris, J. (2014). *The Way of Serenity: Finding Peace and Happiness in the Serenity Prayer*. New York: Harper Collins.

Nelson, P. (2012). Autobiography in five short chapters. In *There's a Hole in my Sidewalk*. New York: Atria Books, pp. xi–xii. Accessed online at sites.uci.edu/mindful/files/2013/10/Autobiography-in-Five-Short-Chapters.pdf

Palmer, P. (2000). *Let Your Life Speak: Listening for the Voice of Vocation*. San Francisco: Jossey-Bass.

Petriglieri, G., & Petriglieri, J.L. (2015). Can business schools humanize leadership? Academy of Management Learning & Education, 14(4): 625–647.

Raelin, J.A. (2016). It's not about the leaders: It's about the practice of leadership. *Organizational Dynamics*, 45(2): 124–131.

Sellars, J. (2016a). *The Routledge Handbook of the Stoic Tradition*. New York: Routledge.

Sellars, J. (2016b). *Stoicism* (Ancient Philosophies). New York: Routledge.

Sorabji, R. (2000). *Emotion and Peace of Mind: From Stoic Agitation to Christian Temptation*. Oxford: Oxford University Press.

Stephens, W.O. (2007). *Stoic Ethics: Epictetus and Happiness as Freedom*. London: Continuum.

Wisely, D.S. & Lynn, E.M. (1994). Spirited connections: Learning to tap the spiritual resources in our lives and work. In J.A. Conger (Ed.) *Spirit at Work: Discovering the Spirituality in Leadership*. San Francisco: Jossey-Bass.

Worline, M. & Dutton, J. (2017). *Awakening Compassion at Work: The Quiet Power that Elevates People and Organizations*. Oakland, CA: Berrett-Koehler.

4

KING POPIEL, THE KILLER MICE AND THE STORY OF THE POST-LIE LEADERSHIP

Michał Izak and Monika Kostera

The Legend of King Popiel

A very long time ago, at the heart of the land that is now known as Poland, in the ancient city of Gopło, there stood a beautiful tall tower, the pride of the Slavic people inhabiting the area and the symbol of their unity and brotherhood. The Slavs have always believed in these principles – alas, the actual practice of them was not up to the ideal. But the tower was there to remind them, and every time they looked up at it, they knew that it was important for them to strive for them.

The Slavs were then ruled by a king presiding over a council of elders, all coming from the same noble family. The custom was to meet regularly, debate important matters of state and make the most important decisions together. It worked fine for a long time. And so it also was at the times when the young ambitious Popiel became king. He and his German wife Gerda were a glamorous and magnificent couple, infatuated with power, believing themselves to be superior to the rest of the royal family. They looked good and spoke well, they were bright and persuasive, and knew how to make a great impression on others.

Now, it is said that the king had been warned, as a little boy, that mice would bring him misfortune. Therefore, he was very careful about hygiene and grooming thus there were, in fact, no mice in his castle, something of an unusual achievement in those days.

Whilst the queen's foreign ancestry was frowned upon by the more suspicious people, the royal couple grew increasingly prosperous. Yet, they were not satisfied with what they had. They incessantly wanted more and more. Even more, they felt that they deserved better than what was supposed to be the fate of provincial rulers. Increasingly, they were getting impatient with the way things were being done and considered them too slow, old fashioned and, simply, ineffective.

When the date of the next council approached, Gerda addressed her husband and stated:

IZAK AND KOSTERA

"We have been putting up with these old fools for too long. Just look how things are done in other countries. This is a backwards way of ruling a kingdom. Is it, in fact, a kingdom at all, or a party of old men?"

"You are right, my wife", Popiel readily agreed, "these councils are a bore and a burden to the kingdom, and they are an insult to the acumen of the king. We should look for a way of ending the sad spectacle and convert our backwater land into a prosperous, modern kingdom."

"Yes, my husband. We should indeed. Look at these old men, all they think of is diminishing you, your power, one day they will end up disposing of you, I am telling you."

"But pray, how can we rid the country of their sad influence? The people seem to be regrettably attached to this form of government. We cannot just pronounce ourselves monarchs, as the bumpkins are not able to understand the matters of reason and rule."

"Yes, my husband, and that is why we are not telling them about our plans in that vulgar open fashion. We will say that we are coming together for even greater unity and brotherhood. Let us invite these old fools for supper after the next council to our castle. The people will be happy about such a gesture of perfect unity."

"Yes! They will! We shall talk to the people about the virtues of accord, family, brotherhood and involvement! We shall propagate the values of even greater togetherness and harmony! And then?"

"And then we shall kill them," Gerda said.

"Yes, my dear, we shall do that! And to the people we will say that they now are so close to our hearts that they have decided to stay with us and live together with us, until death do us part."

"Until death do us part, indeed!"

And that is what they did actually. Their people were told how important unity and brotherhood were to them and how seriously and literally they were taking them. They invited the councillors for supper. The elders were happy to accept the invitation, believing that their rather troublesome young sibling and his wife were at last ready to engage in building good and close relationships with all the members of the council. After the meeting they all joined the king in his castle to eat and drink together. When they were all quite inebriated with the good mead that was flowing at the table, the hosts produced another jug, this time carrying poison diluted with the mead. While they themselves abstained from the round, all of the elders drank their last toast to brotherhood and unity and fell instantly dead. The royal couple ordered the guards to carry the dead bodies under the cover of night out of the castle and drop them into the nearby Gopło lake, each weighed down with a heavy stone. The next day they announced to the people that the brotherhood and unity had reached a higher level and now all of the council members were living together under one roof. The elders would now focus on work and so they would not leave the castle until some important matters of state were settled. In rapid procession there followed a number of oppressive rulings, which were all explained and justified to the people by invoking the authority of brotherhood and unity. And each time the royal couple claimed that this was a decision of the council, one which would make the kingdom even more excellent and successful in the future.

The land was soon sagging under the tyranny and the people were suffering from increasing pressures and demands from the king, but what could the people do? They believed that the council must be right, that there indeed must be a superior reason to what was happening, something that the elders saw and understood, as they were all working so hard that they were not even able to go out for a walk in the wood. So the peasants and the craftsmen kept on working harder and harder, and the royal couple got richer and richer.

While the unity seemed to prosper and wealth unites all people (or at least those who believed in them), the occasional mice squeaks commenced to be heard in the corridors and chambers of the once impeccably clean and pest-free castle. To Popiel's horror any and all attempts to eradicate the plague were in vain. Then, one particularly dark, moonless night, a multitude of mice emerged from the lake and invaded the royal castle. The mice were born out of the lies of the king and queen, one mouse for each lie, and they fed on the bodies of the dead elders until they grew big and fat. The horde stormed the royal chambers, and the king and the queen woke up in utmost alarm and fled, in their nightgowns, to the upmost floor of the tall tower. But the mice were well fed, so they were good climbers and they followed them up to their topmost hideout. They were now getting ferociously hungry from all the running and climbing. When they found Popiel and Gerda, yelling insults at each other and blaming each other for their plight, they jumped at them and simply ate them for supper. Only the bones remained. When the servants discovered the sad remains, the guards confessed what they had done with the dead bodies of the elders. There was much unrest and alarm among the people, but also much anger which at last surfaced and found a way out.

It all ended in celebration, when people realized what was being done to them behind the façade of pretty declarations, which were in fact all deceit and outright lies. The castle lay deserted as all the servants fled and everything was left to the mice, who devoured everything they found edible and then left too, fleeing into the fields and beyond. The people gathered and decided that they must elect another king. After much deliberation they designated Piast the Wheelright who, together with his wise wife Rzepicha, was running a small workshop, and was known as a careful and devoted craftsman and very much respected by the neighbours. He accepted the nomination with a pure and humble heart and, being a good guild member himself, knew about the real value and meaning of unity and brotherhood. Therefore, he always listened to the council, even when he, as any king, sometimes had ambitions and ideas of his own, tempting him to go off in his own way. He had a son, Ziemowit, who, as it happens, at the day of his father's election, was celebrating his passage from boyhood into manhood. He was blind from birth, but the presence of all the people of the land made his eyes miraculously open and he gained sight on that very day. From that day on, he was watching everything studiously, observing and learning diligently about different people, the soil, the ghosts and the animals. He learned intensively and saw that, taken together, it was all a unity – the Land as such. That is how the tribe acquired its name – Polanie, people of *pola*, which means the land. When his father died after many years of good reign, he took over as the first dynastic king of the Polanie, second in the peaceful and magnificent line of the Piasts, who since ruled the country between the rivers Vistula and Odra for centuries, nurturing the Land and the principles of brotherhood and unity.

Introduction

We have chosen the legend of old king Popiel and the killer mice, because it shows the consequences of disconnecting leadership from the people and the land, and it also points to a way out of the seemingly desperate situation this kind of leadership produces. If there ever was a historical Popiel, his were the times of transition from a society of tribes to a more organized societal form. It must have been a difficult and turbulent time, when old customs were losing their hold on people, yet no new ones were fully formed to replace them. There must have been much trouble and turbulence.

Today, we too live in a time of uncertainty and turbulence. Zygmunt Bauman (2012) adopts the metaphor of the interregnum, coined by Antonio Gramsci, to describe this time as "a time-span of yet unknown length, stretching between a social setting which has run its course and another, as yet under-defined and most certainly under-determined, which we expect or suspect to replace it" (Zygmunt Bauman, in Bauman, Bauman, Kociatkiewicz and Kostera, 2016, p. 17).

Old social institutions are crumbling, become eroded, questioned and purposefully destroyed, and no ready replacements are yet in sight (Streeck, 2016). Considering that social institutions partake in construction of social reality, thus affecting the possibility for collective action (Berger and Luckmann, 1966/1991), such times do not offer much in terms of hope and consolations for the social actors. People are bound to experience loss, fear and anxiety when looking towards the future, as well as trying to make sense of the present: "The old is dying and the new cannot be born. In this interregnum a great variety of morbid symptoms can appear" (Gramsci, 1971, p. 276).

The future will not materialize as if by a good spell, there are too many real and sobering dangers present, posing as a threat to the future of humanity and the whole planet. We must actively look for a viable and sustainable future for human society and it is a task of utmost urgency, as Zygmunt Bauman cautioned us in his book *Retrotopia* which, unfortunately, turned out be his last:

> The present task of lifting human integration to the level of all humanity is likely to prove unprecedentedly arduous, onerous and troublesome to see through and complete. We need to brace ourselves for a long period marked by more questions than answers and more problems than solutions, as well as for acting in the shadow of finely balanced chances of success and defeat [...] More than at any other time, we – human inhabitants of the Earth – are in the either/or situation: we face joining either hands, or common graves.
>
> (Bauman, 2017, p. 167)

Capitalism has always been full of contradictions and conflicts, but now the erosion has reached beyond the limits formerly regulated by a set of socio-economic institutions. We now have an interregnum rather than just another crisis: we are facing an urgent and imminent danger to the planet's ecosystem (Klein, 2014); moreover, the irreversible disintegration of democratic and economic institutions, and the crisis is neither transformative nor adaptive (Streeck, 2016).

The current economic system transgresses the Earth's environmental limits, creating and augmenting man-made climate change, destruction of the bio-sphere and pollution of water (see e.g. Klein, 2014 and Monbiot, 2017 for an extensive discussion of the consequences). Management is no longer about production, but about extraction (Fleming, 2017), ruthless depletion of natural (Klein, 2014) and human commons and resources (Fleming, 2017). Democracy is being destroyed, on the one hand, by the complete disconnection from the living world, as political power is as good as owned by destructive industries (Monbiot, 2017). On the other hand, it is being nullified by the increasing disconnection from others, society, the people supposedly being "led" or represented by leaders, who, instead, base their power by projecting ever more empty, mendacious and narcissistic claims and images of themselves (Alvesson, 2013).

Even though the situation appears exceptionally bleak and, as Gramsci (1971) predicted, many morbid symptoms do indeed appear, there is an ever more noticeable chorus of voices making itself present in the public sphere, proposing ways out of it. In particular, they suggest doing so by engaging imagination (e.g. Graeber, 2015) to reconnect with place and the living planet (e.g. Monbiot, 2017; Klein, 2017) and with our own sociality in a radically altered context (e.g. Wright, 2010; Harvey, 2014; Bauman et al., 2016). And last but not least – the "negative capability" to critically approach claims made by leaders (Alvesson and Spicer, 2016) to detect lies and, ultimately, to reclaim the truth by parrhesia and organizational resistance (Weiskopf and Tobias-Miersch, 2016)

In this text, we use the legend of king Popiel to answer this call: use imagination in order to point to natural and social roots and consequences of leadership and invite to join us in a creative journey to find ways of reclaiming the missing roots, or what we regard as the truth (and practice) of leadership.

Moral of the Story

In short, the moral of the story is pretty straightforward – without a connection to people and the land, power becomes disconnected from the social and natural context, losing legitimization and, ultimately, becomes usurpation in need of a justification to persevere. Such justifications can be constructed out of supposedly superhuman qualities of the leader or by manipulation and empty promises made to the followers. They can also be created by the invocation of ideas out of context, such as assumptions and traditions not sufficiently linked to the present and grand values, employed normatively rather than as actual objects of faith and dedication. Finally, they can be woven from other, similarly fragmented aspects of the cultural process of organizing, such as those conceptualized by Mary Jo Hatch (1993). The way that the whole makes sense in cultural terms and how a leader can approach it to fulfil her or his role is directly linked with the coherence of this process. Mary Jo Hatch, Monika Kostera and Andrzej Koźmiński (2005) explain that leaders both represent what is and encourage the embracing of possible futures by their symbolic role in the cultural dynamics of organizing. They represent order – in spite of the very process of leadership emergence being messy (as discussed below) – and they inspire by engaging an organization's creative potential and the change it brings. Vision and inspiration not only fuel the imagination required to change, but also reassure people as members of an organization, helping them to face their fears. By taking part in the process of organizing in their proper, that is, responsible function (emplaced role), that is as taking symbolic responsibility for the whole, leaders play three important roles: that of *managers*, ensuring order, *artists*, inspiring change and *priests*, keeping alive the most cherished beliefs and values (ibid.). A disconnection from that system of cultural ordering (as happened with Popiel's and Gerda's self-centred leadership) causes a radical separation between power and meaning. In order words, leaders get locked into their own bubbles of meaning, distanced from the experience of the followers as well as stakeholder thus from living sources of legitimization. Leadership becomes self-absorbed, even narcissistic, claiming superhuman entitlement, but effectuating actual control by coercion and deception (Kets de Vries, 2006). Starting out as charismatics, narcissistic leaders lose connection to the outside world, concentrating exclusively on their own bubble and making an increasingly idealized image of themselves and tweak an equally false image of the world to fit their image of self and their own agenda (as per Popiel and Gerda's case). Often, in pursuit of ever more "ambitious" and abstract goals, increasingly distanced from the embedded context from which they derived, maimed by the incessant drive to always aim for the "upper right" (indicating progress), they easily lose their bearings. Furthermore, the detached disconnect between themselves and realities in which other people live intensifies over time. Narcissistic leaders (such as Popiel and Gerda) close themselves to all signals that ruin their sense of entitlement and their heroic efforts. In the end, untruth becomes the only possible approach (ibid.).

Personal Resonances

For one of us, this legend evokes a generalized experience[1] of perils of the "ivory tower syndrome" suffered by management and managers insulated from the wider context of their leadership practice. When understanding of what the organization is about, why it exists and which values it is driven by is either lost or indeed never established by a leader (and the memories of both and either are rather unpleasant to the author), it ceases to be clear what the purpose of leadership is and it risks becoming autotelic. All too often does this conclusion seem to resonate with us in the neoliberally imbued organizational contexts facilitating tolerance for short-termist leadership agendas. These agendas then drive obsession with and towards constant change and which, trading rationality for rationalization, paradoxically draw upon long-term visions and manifestos. In this vein, the legend equally evokes the fear of "not having a vision" and thus being stigmatized as lacking leadership skills. The managerial "postalgia" being a condition of projecting a "Golden Future" was recognized a while ago (Ybema, 2004); it nevertheless seems even more relevant now. In particular, this seems to be the case as its symptoms are worsened, alongside the generally accelerated pace of organizational and societal change. Again, across sectors, countries and industries, the managerial imperative of "looking forward and beyond" strikes a chord with the experiences of one of the authors, thus rendering the re-reading of Popiel's legend both timely and interesting.

Another resonance concerns the second half of the story. Since 2012, one of us has been conducting an ethnographic study of alternative economic organizations, operating on the margins of the capitalist system (Kostera, 2014; 2018). They are self-supporting enterprises and collectives, operating towards other aims than profit. The "profit" they make is regarded as a means towards that end, which typically includes environmental and democratic ideas and ideals. People in all the studied organizations often see the role of work as a higher human need and many were more or less explicitly created in order to be a workplace devoid of alienation. They often express, both in formal interviews and in their everyday conversations, a conviction that they are an alternative for the future, a germ for a new possible economy. As one of the organizers put it succinctly, "capitalism is a giant compost heap" (Łukasz, Good Coop) and these organizations are sprouts of new life in its (less toxic) margins. One of the more radical interlocutors (Paweł, Radical House) likened his organization as a kind of a rat, street smart and nimble, grabbing what it needs to survive from the ruins of the system and making room for itself on its own terms. "Green" ideas, images, goals and connections appear in much of the interview material, and are prominent in everyday conversations, actions and symbolism. Some of the organizers emphasize the importance of direct, constant contact with nature and people living in the countryside, for business reasons (organizations engaging in the cultivation trade and of natural agricultural produce) and because it is good for human beings to be have contact with living nature. For many, if not all, it is also very important to keep and develop close ties with local people and communities (stakeholders) and, more generally, with the place where they operate. Organizers from one organization, a vegan bar, emphasize that the bar is there not just to sell food, but to offer a place where people can hang around without having to pay huge amounts of money. People can sit and talk as long as they like, over just one coffee, if they prefer. Paweł from the Radical House introduced the ethnographer to an even more revolutionary local café, where guests can sit, read or chat entirely for free. The sense of rootedness and physical space and place is prominent in all the studied organizations, and in some it is quite central in conversations and daily operations. In the words of Iphigenia of the Good Coop: "People come around just to have a chat, sometimes. It's a pleasure."

The idea and practice of democracy is also of pivotal importance. The organizers firmly believe in it, and for many it appears as a central issue, even more important than place and product. One of the organizers of Vegan Heaven, a bar in central Warsaw, explained to the researcher that it was far more important to him to sincerely practice democracy than to cook food. True, he loved it, but he could easily do something else, such as building houses, for example. For many democracy was something of a declaration of love, bringing not just the warm feelings of being a family, but also the quarrels and conflicts inherent to sisterhood and brotherhood, or in the words of an organizer, Ania from Rosa Hostel, "like in a good old marriage, we spend most of the time quarrelling with each other". Most of the organizers would consider this hard but good: living relationships are not a harmonious stasis but vibrant conflict, tension and difference.

Leadership is never individual centred in one person, in these organizations. It is shared, from duos to full collective leadership, and/or rotational. As one organizer put it: "I just feel like I don't want to do anything alone, ever again" (Marianna, Space of Games).

Relevance for Leadership Practice

Popiel's legend – as indeed any good story – may be read in a variety of ways and we would merely like to offer three among many alternative interpretations. We also suggest how those readings may help to discuss leadership beyond the rigid notion of "a model" – as outlined in the final section of this chapter.

Certainly, on the most immediate level, dramatic, though well-deserved death of the rulers of Gopło and subsequent twists introducing the new man in charge, can be read as a cautionary tale. No matter how powerful you are, betting on short termism, collusion and forceful solutions, ignoring discord and indignation which it feeds (quite literally so in Popiel's case) will get you nowhere. Ruling from the high tower of self-serving interest, manipulating others towards one's own selfish gain, distancing oneself from the wider social good, all that may be seen as a ready-made recipe for "bad" leadership. Not necessarily entirely ineffective in a short term, it is without any prospects for offering sustainable solutions in a longer run. In this respect, Popiel–Gerda's leadership practice resonates closely with, e.g., discussions on psychopathy in an organizational context (Boddy, 2010; 2011) and other aspects of a dark triad of personality (Paulhus and Williams, 2002). Corporate psychopaths are callous, remorseless and lacking empathy, whilst highly extrovert, influential and often perceived as charming and attractive by those they take advantage of (Boddy, 2006). Similar to our protagonists, psychopaths are "organizational destroyers", highly disruptive to organizational legitimacy and potentially threatening the very existence of organizations, which they lead (Boddy, 2011, p. 3).

The said reading, however, largely ignores the ambivalence and thus the positive model, which from a different perspective may seem espoused in the legend. After all, most of the dominant features of the narrative are matched against incomparably more productive, visionary leadership by Piast the Wheelright, his son Ziemowit and the subsequent

Piast dynasty. "Visionary" is of course a keyword here: not only half-legendary Ziemowit (though his historicity is nowadays relatively rarely questioned, cf. Jasiński, 2007), but also his grand-grandson, Mieszko I – undoubtedly historical figure, 10th century ruler, regarded as a creator of the Polish state – were (after Gallus Anonymous) blind until early adolescence. In both cases, regaining vision (and thus sweeping away their parents' shame, as a child's disability was socially stigmatized at the time) was associated with the rite of passage towards manhood, or metaphorically shedding away of a child's naïve perception of the world. The historical context facilitates such reading, as for both, Ziemowit and Mieszko, the "new gaze" is associated with a new perspective on matters of state and politics of their time – much needed after a period of socially traumatizing rule of Popiel and politically unstable conditions of Mieszko's emergence to power, respectively. In both cases, traditionally at least, the times that follow are comparatively more prosperous.

Similarly, the mice feast at Gopło marks the crucial transition from enclosed, paranoid, exclusive leadership towards the one based on openness and, at least to some extent, readiness towards dialogue and interaction with its people and (some degree) of social participation. In this vein, the social gathering appears productive both for Mieszko and Ziemowit, and Piast the Wheelwright seems to emerge as a leader, through some form of a social consensus – or semblance thereof. Characterizing the latter leadership style as empowering would not do justice to medieval social and political context, yet certainly the previous traits (openness, participation, dialogicity) may invoke conditions necessary for empowerment to occur. Conventionally, the all-embracing vision, courage to implement it and wisdom to do so in a socially empowering manner belong to a professed model of a "good" leader.

And yet, this very model is always contingent and in need of further problematizing – in fact the closer reading of Popiel's legend may encourage such scrutiny. For once, the singularity of leadership needs unpacking in this case: the "anti-model" of leadership evoked earlier in itself seems to consist of two somewhat distinct agencies. The strong, yet conspicuously morally aberrant "voice" of Gerda and somehow less agentic – though in no way morally superior – formal enunciation of Popiel "normalizing" the former. We do not think those distinct presences are necessarily ethically diversifiable (as both can be perhaps seen as equally repulsive), but they do differ in terms of function as well as source of power in both cases, defying expectations. In this respect, the Popiel–Gerda leader–follower relationship may be seen as reversed, due to a formal power element (Popiel) acting as a post-rationalizing agent, normalizing the agency exercised by the tacit element (Gerda). This bi-modal ventriloquism of leadership makes it more difficult to identify the source of power in the name of which actions are undertaken, the

KING POPIEL AND THE KILLER MICE

agencies undertaking them and the underpinning rationale(s), thus rendering the leadership a much more elusive process then it is often purported to be. As this approach opens up the possibility for perceiving leadership in pluralist and processual terms, the questions previously (perhaps) regarded as straightforward assume a new, uncanny shape, and are thus in need of re-visiting:

For example "If and why was Popiel a bad leader?" may be turned (as follows) into "Which aspects of leadership process were decisive in bringing about the change (for the worse)? What were they founded upon and influenced by? Which/whose agencies were involved?"

Those traits are pivotal for discussing the implications of the emergence of an honest, truthful and "sustainable leadership" – as an ongoing (processual) endeavour – which we address in the last section of this chapter.

Questions for Reflection and Discussion

Instead of normative conclusions in this part of our story, we propose a list of points or questions for reflection and discussion, in particular, for students:

1. Consider the role of charisma in leadership. How do you think that leaders like Popiel and Gerda become popular and even worshipped? Think of two similar stories from real history, older and more recent. Are there different kinds of charisma? Different uses?
2. Compare the legend of King Arthur (for this see also Chapter 9 'The Story of Merlin as a Tale of Wisdom') with the story of kings Popiel and Piast. Make a list of similarities and differences. Now consider the role of the Holy Grail in the Arthurian tales. Make a thought experiment – what would happen if Popiel sent his followers to find the Grail? What would happen if Piast did the same thing?
3. Write a fictive tale titled: CEO Popiel of Software Gopło. Re-imagine the legend as a contemporary management case study.
4. Do you think Popiel and Gerda could have been educated to be more honest and truthful leaders, more sensitive to nature and to their people? Make an argument for and against such a possibility. Propose a teaching programme that would, in your opinion, have been useful for Popiel and Gerda in order to make them re-think their position, or at least consider the existence of other alternatives.
5. In your opinion, which aspects and stages of leadership process determined the outcomes (both good and bad) in the case of Popiel and Piast/Ziemowit? Now, list the reasons for which you believe those were the crucial ones.
6. Preferably once you have done (5), assume an alternative scenario, in which Piast and Popiel – as leaders – would trade places (that is, a

93

person with Piast's mentality is now married to Gerda, and a person with Popiel's mindframe is running the small workshop in the vicinity of the castle). How differently would the story evolve in your opinion? What might stay the same?

7. Revisit your list from (5). Consider the factors not related to physical presences of Popiel, Piast and Ziemowit. Which role does the social and cultural context play in the story?

8. Now, assume it is possible that they (Piast, Popiel, Ziemowit) were not exercising their own agency, but rather acted as agents of an external superior power (e.g. God or Nature/the Land). Taking this assumption into account rewrite the legend from the perspective of a commoner living in the 9th century in the Gopło area.

Implications for the Development of More Responsible and Sustainable Leadership Practices

If nowadays organizations indeed exist in the post-truth era (Davis, 2017), the nuanced understanding of the processes underpinning leadership unfolding in them may be more in place then attempts to inform them with any "truly best" practices and models. In the following, final section, we shall build on the notions of *heterogeneous* leadership recognized earlier, to discuss the possibility of sustainable post-lie leadership.

Lying in a leadership context may be identified as a conscious manipulation of somebody else's worldview through intentional misrepresentation of facts on which it is based – thus as an attempt to gain control and gain advantage by remaining "in charge" of the message conveyed. In that respect, post-lie leadership is as much about the alignment of facts with some actually perceived reality, as it is about reshaping the function of the leader as well as relationship between the leader and those who are led. In the post-lie context, recognition of diversity *within* leadership (the multiplicity of voices, rationales and motivations) goes hand in hand with appreciation of heterogeneity in those subjected to it. To embrace post-lie leadership, it is hardly enough to truthfully match ones' statements with underlying facts. Admittedly, this is a good start, as psychopathic manipulators and permanent liars tend to disregard the worlds of others almost by default – which we see as a stumbling precluding sustainability. Therefore, it is not the factual correctness that makes a post-lie leadership model tenable, as the former is equally (if not easier) attainable in highly formalized and mechanical processes, in the absence of the human factor. The post-lie model – the one embracing, but stepping beyond truthful representation – is sustained by the leader's openness regarding its own agendas and motivations. Furthermore, this is also coupled with recognition and appreciation of similar diversity of impulses and dispositions in its followers. Post-lie leadership is therefore about dialogue, establishing understanding and, subsequently, creating a common platform from which to act together.

While theoretical resonances in social theory are in this respect multiple (cf. Habermas, 1984; Bakhtin, 1981), and calls for dialogic and socially embedded leadership are certainly not new, in this chapter we do not aspire to build a new theory on the basis of existing ideas. We would merely like to show that resources for contemplating the alternatives to the current excesses of unethical and downright deceitful leadership modes featuring on the highest echelons of social strata (Keyes, 2004) are available more readily then we often care to admit – often residing in all-too-familiar tales and legends passed between generations. As these tales were repeated over the years and centuries of being conveyed by the diverse people in a variety of social circumstances, chances are that their durability is owed not to uniformity of meanings imposed, but rather to relevance to those peoples and nations at different times.

Therefore, rather than perceiving their protagonists or behaviours which they describe as ideal models – carriers of a set of undisputable attributes imposed on readers and students oppressively – they should be allowed to resonate with a much wider scope of our sensibilities and meanings which we dare making.

In this vein, rather than talking about the model emerging from Popiel's legend, we may identify in it a variety of predispositions, agencies and rationales contrasted against the common themes significant from the leadership perspective. These could, for instance, be the leader's role (e.g. ensuring order vs inspiring change), communication (dialogic vs monologic), style (autocratic vs participatory), and others. Like any good story, the predispositions such as those are only as viable as they are relevant to lived experience of those they pertain to and only as informative and transformative as they are suited to increase our understanding of the world around us. This is where organizational story encounters the myth, and where the opportunity for leadership to learn the lesson from folklore lies.

Note

1 Those experiences were gathered both in the academia and private sector (consulting) in Poland and in the United Kingdom from 2004 onwards.

References

Alvesson, M. (2013). *The triumph of emptiness: consumption, higher education, and work organization.* Oxford: Oxford University Press.

Alvesson, M. and Spicer, A. (2016). *The stupidity paradox: The power and pitfalls of functional stupidity at work*. London: Profile Books.

Bakhtin, M. (1981). *The dialogical imagination*. Austin, TX: University of Texas Press.

Bauman, Z. (2012). Times of interregnum. *Ethics & Global Politics*. 5(1): 49–56.

Bauman, Z. (2017). *Retrotopia*. London: Polity.

Bauman, Z., Bauman, I., Kociatkiewicz, J. and Kostera, M. (2016). *Management in a modern liquid world*. London: Polity.

Berger, P. and Luckmann, T. (1966/1991). *The social construction of reality: A treatise in the sociology of knowledge*. London: Penguin.

Boddy, C.R. (2006). The dark side of management decisions: Organisational psychopaths. *Management Decision*. 44(10): 1461–1475.

Boddy, C.R.P. (2010). Corporate psychopaths and organizational type. *Journal of Public Affairs*. 10(4): 300–312.

Boddy, C.R. (2011). *Corporate psychopaths: Organisational destroyers*. New York: Palgrave Macmillan.

Davis, E. (2017). *Post-truth: Why we have reached peak bullshit and what we can do about it*. London: Little, Brown Book Group.

Fleming, P. (2017). *The death of homo economicus: Work, debt and the myth of endless accumulation*. London: Pluto.

Graeber, D. (2015). *The utopia of rules: On technology, stupidity, and the secret joys of bureaucracy*. Brooklyn: Melville House.

Gramsci, A. (1971). *Selections from the prison notebooks*, ed. and trans. Quintin Hoare and Geoffrey Nowell-Smith. London: Lawrence & Wishart.

Habermas, J. (1984). *Theory of communicative action*. Boston: Beacon Press.

Harvey, D. (2014). Seventeen contradictions and the end of capitalism. London: Profile.

Hatch, M.J. (1993). The dynamic of organizational culture. *Academy of Management Review*. 18(4): 657–693.

Hatch, M.J., Kostera, M. and Koźmiński, A. (2005). *Three faces of leadership: Manager, artist, priest*. London: Blackwell.

Jasiński, K. (2007). *Rodowód Piastów śląskich*. Cracow: Avalon.

Kets de Vries, M. (2006). *The leader on the couch: A clinical approach to changing people and organizations*. New York: John Wiley.

Keyes, R. (2004). *The post-truth era: Dishonesty and deception in contemporary life*. London: St. Martin's Press.

Klein, N. (2014). *This changes everything: Capitalism vs. the climate*. New York: Simon and Schuster.

Klein, N. (2017). *No is not enough: Defeating the new shock politics*. Allen Lane.

Kostera, M. (2014). *Occupy Management! Inspirations and ideas for self-management and self-organization*. London: Routledge.

Kostera, M. (2018). Adventurers and lovers: Organizational heroines and heroes for a new time. *Journal of Genius and Eminence*. Forthcoming.

Monbiot, G. (2017). *Out of the wreckage: A new politics for an age of crisis*. London: Verso.

Paulhus, D.L. and Williams, K.M. (2002). The dark triad of personality: Narcissism, Machiavellianism, and psychopathy. *Journal of Research in Personality*. 36(6): 556–563.

Streeck, W. (2016). *How will capitalism end? Essays on a failing system*. London: Verso.

Weiskopf, R. and Tobias-Miersch, Y. (2016). Whistleblowing, parrhesia and the contestation of truth in the workplace. *Organization Studies*. doi 10.1177/0170840616655497

Wright, E.O. (2010). Envisioning real utopias. London: Verso.

Ybema, S. (2004). Managerial postalgia: Projecting a golden future. *Journal of Managerial Psychology*. 19(8): 825–841.

5

THE WISDOM OF OTHERS
Cultural Acclimatization and Engaged Leadership

Tim Gilman-Ševčík

Foreword for Readers Unfamiliar with *Gulliver's Travels*

This masterpiece of satire by 18th-century Anglo-Irish author Jonathan Swift is widely known, in its bastardized manifestation, as a children's story. It certainly has many of the necessary elements to appeal to the youngest readers and viewers of the mediocre films and other popular media interpretations of the work. Certainly the most famous and popular aspect is the land of the Lilliputians, where natives 1/10th our size bind the gigantic Lemuel Gulliver when they find him shipwrecked on their shores.

This land contrasts with its foil, where the native Brobdingnagians tower 10 times over the terrified narrator. Through the course of the book, Gulliver also visits Laputa, a flying island city modeled on London, which oppresses those beneath it. Those below represent Swift's beloved, native home of Ireland, and the ruling Laputians enforce their sovereignty by casting their shadow over them, stopping the rain and sun, and threatening to crush them. They also send down absurd innovations, promoted by the false home of higher learning, the Academy of Projectors, which dictates absurd innovations that destroy functional native cultures and traditions. Finally, Gulliver finds his paradise in the land of the Houyhnhnms, which you can easily pronounce by making the sound of a horse's whinny. Try it now. He falls completely under the sway of the sentient horses who use repulsive primitive humans they call Yahoos, as their beasts of burden.

After returning to his native England, he is incapable of accepting humanity's failings in the face of the peace-loving, enlightened quadrupeds, who banished him from their midst. Isolated and alienated, he lives out his days disgusted by the reality of the land he called home before his extended exile. The passage that follows is drawn from the very end of the book where the narrator, like many who return home after being abroad, is incapable of finding any redeeming feature in his own culture.

Photo 5.1 Boots in New York
Image courtesy of Pascal Perich: pperich.com

He summarizes his travels and learning and defends his decision to protect these exotic lands from the contaminating presence of his fellow Europeans.

Gulliver's Travels *Into Several Remote Nations of the World, Chapter XII*

It is easy for us who travel into remote countries, which are seldom visited by Englishmen or other Europeans, to form descriptions of wonderful animals both at sea and land. Whereas a traveller's chief aim should be to make men wiser and better, and to improve their minds by the bad, as well as good, example of what they deliver concerning foreign places.

I could heartily wish a law was enacted, that every traveller, before he were permitted to publish his voyages, should be obliged to make oath before the Lord High Chancellor, that all he intended to print was absolutely true to the best of his knowledge; for then the world would no longer be deceived, as it usually is, while some writers, to make their works pass the better upon the public, impose the grossest falsities on the unwary reader. I have perused several books of travels with great delight in my younger days; but having since gone over most parts of the globe, and been able to contradict many fabulous accounts from my own observation, it has given me a great disgust against this part of reading, and some indignation to see the credulity of mankind so impudently abused. Therefore, since my acquaintance were pleased to think my poor endeavours might not be

GILMAN-ŠEVČÍK

unacceptable to my country, I imposed on myself, as a maxim never to be swerved from, that I would strictly adhere to truth; neither indeed can I be ever under the least temptation to vary from it, while I retain in my mind the lectures and example of my noble master and the other illustrious Houyhnhnms of whom I had so long the honour to be an humble hearer.

- *Nec si miserum Fortuna Sinonem Finxit, vanum etiam, mendacemque improba finget.*

"Though Fortune had made Sinon wretched, she has not made him untrue and a liar"[1]

I know very well, how little reputation is to be got by writings which require neither genius nor learning, nor indeed any other talent, except a good memory, or an exact journal. I know likewise, that writers of travels, like dictionary-makers, are sunk into oblivion by the weight and bulk of those who come last, and therefore lie uppermost. And it is highly probable, that such travellers, who shall hereafter visit the countries described in this work of mine, may, by detecting my errors (if there be any), and adding many new discoveries of their own, justle me out of vogue, and stand in my place, making the world forget that ever I was an author is indeed would be too great a mortification, if I wrote for fame: but as my sole intention was the public good, I cannot be altogether disappointed. For who can read of the virtues I have mentioned in the glorious Houyhnhnms, without being ashamed of his own vices, when he considers himself as the reasoning, governing animal of his country? I shall say nothing of those remote nations where Yahoos preside; among which the least corrupted are the Brobdingnagians; whose wise maxims in morality and government it would be our happiness to observe. But I forbear descanting further, and rather leave the judicious reader to his own remarks and application.I am not a little pleased that this work of mine can possibly meet with no censurers: for what objections can be made against a writer, who relates only plain facts, that happened in such distant countries, where we have not the least interest, with respect either to trade or negotiations? I have carefully avoided every fault with which common writers of travels are often too justly charged. Besides, I meddle not the least with any party, but write without passion, prejudice, or ill-will against any man, or number of men, whatsoever. I write for the noblest end, to inform and instruct mankind; over whom I may, without breach of modesty, pretend to some superiority, from the advantages I received by conversing

THE WISDOM OF OTHERS

so long among the most accomplished Houyhnhnms. I write without any view to profit or praise. I never suffer a word to pass that may look like reflection, or possibly give the least offence, even to those who are most ready to take it. So that I hope I may with justice pronounce myself an author perfectly blameless; against whom the tribes of Answerers, Considerers, Observers, Reflectors, Detectors, Remarkers, will never be able to find matter for exercising their talents.I confess, it was whispered to me, 'that I was bound in duty, as a subject of England, to have given in a memorial to a secretary of state at my first coming over; because, what-ever lands are discovered by a subject belong to the crown.' But I doubt whether our conquests in the countries I treat of would be as easy as those of Ferdinando Cortez over the naked Americans. The Lilliputians, I think, are hardly worth the charge of a fleet and army to reduce them; and I question whether it might be prudent or safe to attempt the Brobdingnagians; or whether an English army would be much at their ease with the Flying Island over their heads. The Houyhnhnms indeed appear not to be so well prepared for war, a science to which they are perfect strangers, and especially against missive weapons. However, supposing myself to be a minister of state, I could never give my advice for invading them. Their prudence, unanimity, unacquaintedness with fear, and their love of their country, would amply supply all defects in the military art. Imagine twenty thousand of them breaking into the midst of an European army, confounding the ranks, overturning the carriages, battering the warriors' faces into mummy by terrible yerks from their hinder hoofs; for they would well deserve the character given to Augustus, Recalcitrat undique tutus. [*Your ignorant opponent kicks back*] But, instead of proposals for conquering that magnanimous nation, I rather wish they were in a capacity, or disposition, to send a sufficient number of their inhabitants for civilizing Europe, by teaching us the first principles of honour, justice, truth, temperance, public spirit, fortitude, chastity, friendship, benevolence, and fidelity. The names of all which virtues are still retained among us in most languages, and are to be met with in modern, as well as ancient authors; which I am able to assert from my own small reading.But I had another reason, which made me less forward to enlarge his majesty's dominions by my discoveries. To say the truth, I had conceived a few scruples with relation to the distributive justice of princes upon those occasions. For instance, a crew of pirates are driven by a storm they know not whither; at length a boy discovers land from the topmast; they go on shore to rob and plunder, they see a harmless people, are entertained with kindness; they give the country a new name; they take formal possession of it for their king; they set up a rotten plank, or a stone, for a memorial; they murder two or three dozen of the natives, bring away a couple more, by force, for a sample; return home, and get their pardon. Here commences a new dominion acquired with a title by divine right. Ships are sent with the first opportunity; the natives driven out or destroyed; their princes tortured to discover their gold; a free license given to all acts of inhumanity and lust, the earth reeking with the blood of its inhabitants: and this execrable crew of butchers, employed in so pious an expedition, is a modern colony, sent to convert and civilize an idolatrous and barbarous people!But this description, I confess, does by no means affect the British nation, who may be an example to the whole world for their wisdom, care, and justice in planting colonies; their liberal endowments for the advancement of religion and learning; their choice of devout and able pastors to propagate Christianity; their caution in stocking their provinces with people of sober lives and conversations from this the mother kingdom; their strict regard to the distribution of justice, in supplying the civil administration through all their colonies with officers of the greatest abilities, utter strangers to corruption; and, to crown all, by sending the most vigilant and virtuous governors, who have no other views than the happiness of the people over whom they preside, and the honour of the king their master.But as those countries which I have described do not appear to have any desire of being conquered and enslaved, murdered or driven out by colonies, nor abound either in gold, silver, sugar, or tobacco, I did humbly conceive, they were by no means proper objects of our zeal, our valour, or our interest. However, if those whom it more concerns think to be of another opinion, I am ready to depose, when I shall be lawfully called, that no European did ever visit those countries before me. I mean, if the inhabitants ought to be believed, unless a dispute may arise concerning the two Yahoos, said to have been seen many years ago upon a mountain in Houyhnhnmland. But, as to the formality of taking possession in my sovereign's name, it never came once into my thoughts; and if it had, yet, as my airs then stood, I should perhaps, in point of prudence and self-preservation, have put it to a better opportunity.Having thus answered the only objection that can ever be raised against me as a traveller, I here take a final leave of all my courteous readers, and return to enjoy my own speculations in my little garden at Redriff; to apply those excellent lessons of virtue which I learned among the Houyhnhnms;

THE WISDOM OF OTHERS

to instruct the Yahoos of my own family, as far as I shall find them docible animals; to behold my figure often in a glass, and thus, if possible, habituate myself by time to tolerate the sight of a human creature; to lament the brutality to Houyhnhnms in my own country, but always treat their persons with respect, for the sake of my noble master, his family, his friends, and the whole Houyhnhnm race, whom these of ours have the honour to resemble in all their lineaments, however their intellectuals came to degenerate.I began last week to permit my wife to sit at dinner with me, at the farthest end of a long table; and to answer (but with the utmost brevity) the few questions I asked her. Yet, the smell of a Yahoo continuing very offensive, I always keep my nose well stopped with rue, lavender, or tobacco leaves. And, although it be hard for a man late in life to remove old habits, I am not altogether out of hopes, in some time, to suffer a neighbour Yahoo in my company, without the apprehensions I am yet under of his teeth or his claws.My reconcilement to the Yahoo kind in general might not be so difficult, if they would be content with those vices and follies only which nature has entitled them to. I am not in the least provoked at the sight of a lawyer, a pickpocket, a colonel, a fool, a lord, a gamester, a politician, a whoremonger, a physician, an evidence, a suborner, an attorney, a traitor, or the like; this is all according to the due course of things: but when I behold a lump of deformity and diseases, both in body and mind, smitten with pride, it immediately breaks all the measures of my patience; neither shall I be ever able to comprehend how such an animal, and such a vice, could tally together. The wise and virtuous Houyhnhnms, who abound in all excellences that can adorn a rational creature, have no name for this vice in their language, which has no terms to express any thing that is evil, except those whereby they describe the detestable qualities of their Yahoos, among which they were not able to distinguish this of pride, for want of thoroughly understanding human nature, as it shows itself in other countries where that animal presides. But I, who had more experience, could plainly observe some rudiments of it among the wild Yahoos. But the Houyhnhnms, who live under the government of reason, are no more proud of the good qualities they possess, than I should be for not wanting a leg or an arm; which no man in his wits would boast of, although he must be miserable without them. I dwell the longer upon this subject from the desire I have to make the society of an English Yahoo by any means not insupportable; and therefore I here entreat those who have any tincture of this absurd vice, that they will not presume to come in my sight.

103

When the Falsehoods Fly, Try Slowing Down

Swift starts this passage with a traditional feint or ploy from historical fiction – to insist upon the veracity of this obviously false text. "I imposed on myself, as a maxim never to be swerved from, that I would strictly adhere to truth." He is credited as one of the greatest satirists in the English language, and uses his deadpan style to assail the powers shaping the society he lives within, especially the Catholic and Protestant churches, as well as English rule in his native Ireland. However, to distinguish what is true and what is false in his layered and contradictory writing provides a playful yet complex exercise that can be seen as a lesson relevant for today. How can we ascertain the intent of the author? Our narrator swears that he is credible, but he has already taken a false name, so we know we are reading fiction. Are we attentive enough to the source of news and information we're receiving these days? Can we parse what is being stated, implied, intended, or argued? Swift's narrator, Captain Gulliver, so obviously works his utmost to deceive us, which is for amusement, yet also for insight. He veers from reality into fantasy without changing tone, introducing places and situations that are fantastic and entertaining, and still assert their truthfulness. While we are reading a dense yet humorous work that has managed to remain in print for 300 years, so we can feel our failure to grasp many of his political and social references, nuanced descriptions, and critical barbs, but can we catch the truth among the lies presented as truths of our own times? Driven by the rhetoric of President Trump, much has been made recently about the power of false statements, so-called "fake news", unverified, but passionately presented information that is now so rapidly and widely disseminated online as traditional media outlets struggle to survive. We can see the new breed of young media giants like Facebook and Twitter stumble as it becomes clear that nefarious users have quickly learned to leverage social channels to distribute disinformation more effectively than real information. An MIT study published in *Science Magazine* in Spring 2018 shows how unsubstantiated rumors circulate far faster and further than news that is actually true, specifically on Twitter, but without a doubt the same would be true on all the platforms competing for eyeballs. Swift is famously quoted as saying, "Falsehood flies, and truth comes limping after it, so that when men come to be undeceived, it is too late; the jest is over, and the tale hath had its effect," but he couldn't show the data to support it. It's ironic that this truth has managed to limp along for centuries only to be substantiated with measurable metrics in our time. The wisdom of his insight is still beaten by the speed of the misleading message, we have to slow down to let the truth catch up before we jump to believe what's in front of us.

THE WISDOM OF OTHERS

If we are sharing wisdom for leadership, then we must advise listening on multiple levels. Whether we are "leading" as instructors, managers, researchers, even peers, or just critically aware citizens, there's a need to continually evaluate the information we're receiving. This may pertain to information and knowledge we learn in conversation, in seemingly objective business documents, in the news, or any form that asserts its own veracity through various reassuring signifiers, like logos and letterhead, brand affiliations or the various imprimaturs of authenticity that help us to lower our guard in terms of suspending disbelief. A critical eye, refusing sardonic skepticism, if possible, remains a productive tool for a student, teacher, researcher, entrepreneur, manager or anyone exploring unfamiliar fields. Every beseeching voice has a purpose, a goal that the speaker or writer is seeking to achieve, and grasping the "message behind the message" or "between the lines" represents a higher level of listening, reading or perceiving and watching.

My personal affiliation with this classic work of fiction was deeply rooted in a desire to overcome the disappointment of its nuanced and sophisticated cultural critique, which has faded in the face of its juvenile fantasy contents. Like many wise and revealing stories or "myths", it can be read for pure entertainment, and quickly hollowed of any lasting substance or transformative intention. Accordingly, I endeavored to create a dense re-presentation of the most compromised part of the narrative, that of the miniature Lilliputians. The miniature has an almost universally appealing romantic attraction, as Steven Millhauser explored in his essay, *The Fascination of the Miniature*. But Swift hardly presented the Lilliputians as the lovable little people they've become in our collective conscious. In the original, Gulliver narrowly escapes with his life after overhearing the jealous and conniving miniscule courtiers debating whether to put out his eyes with needles or just poison him, which they are loathe to do because disposing of his massive, rotting body would be such a monumental undertaking.

Gulliver's Travels inspired the name of my last project, a for-profit museum startup in Times Square, which I named Gulliver's Gate, as an homage to the original, and a shift to the present availability of technology to create immersive experiences for audiences. Visitors from around the world were welcome to pass through the "Gate", and experience a distorting mirror of the world outside in highly mechanized miniature models, which they could interact with and even become a part of by being scanned, 3D printed and added permanently as part of the display. Contending with the reference to this complex satirical critique of society while creating a popular cultural destination kept me asking stimulating questions about how we were balancing commercial and creative goals and priorities in a fast-paced development process. My challenge was to give the reference to the original text a new life as a socially critical, yet still popular, commercial

105

entertainment vehicle in my role as Artistic Director of Gulliver's Gate. I helped develop and launch this miniature world the size of a football field in Times Square in New York in 2017. Repurposing Swift's title as an experience visitors could enter and participate in gave me an excuse to read the book several times and to get my colleagues of this project to do the same. My colleagues did try to remain true to the original text, albeit with different interpretations and varying levels of enthusiasm because they could not tolerate any critical commentary that would risk decreasing sales or diminishing the fundamentally commercial viability of the venture.

In terms of practical wisdom, the book offers a moral about the work of the visitor being to essentially translate the various divergent cultures s/he experiences and reconcile them with her/his own knowledge and values. S/he fails to find a place for her/himself in any of these wildly foreign lands, and also loses his connection to his own home. Ultimately s/he becomes alienated from her/himself and all others around her/him once s/he's back home because of her/his actual and perceived differences. Learning to navigate the conflicting aspects of politics, relationships and priorities that we experience within different settings takes more than familiarity with the local language, it requires acceptance and even reinvention to navigate. The danger is that we can fall into the prejudices and limitations of a closed society, and the challenge is to be able to open ourselves and the others that make up the cultures we encounter in our travels.

As a cultural work, *Gulliver's Travels* has inspired more higher quality reinterpretations, such as George Orwell's classic *Animal Farm* or H.G. Wells' *Island of Dr. Moreau*, than re-creations in moving image, such as the campy 1970's film with Richard Harris or the forgettable Jack Black. The work has been diminished by an enthusiastic and warm "Disneyfication" in the popular mind so that Swift scholar Daniel Cook from the University of Dundee deemed it necessary to write on the 350th anniversary of Swift's birth that the work was not in fact intended for children. My intention was to restore the biting edge and problematic critiques that have proven the original's worth as timeless and thus still "timely" literature. Knowing that we would be attracting the broadest possible audience by being located in the world's most visited location, Times Square, my hope was that Gulliver's Gate could communicate with each audience member on their own level. In particular, I hope it would resonate with the visitors based on their own appetite for cultural expression and complexity, without alienating anyone with either an overly saccharine sense of wonder, or on the opposite extreme, daunting high-brow sophistication and critical commentary. By allowing visitors to enter and control a world in miniature by walking through the figurative "Gate" the experience represented, we wanted to shift the passive reception of reading. The intention was to move the recipient towards an interactive position of performative acting in a real and augmented space that both reflects and distorts their own reality. The world, presented as a model, is capable of revealing systems and patterns that are "invisible" in our full-scale world. These are unperceivable, because they are too large to be perceived, too omnipresent to allow for an encapsulating view or too closed off behind limited access that keep us at arm's length. We partnered with a dozen other companies on four continents to design and fabricate the football-field size model of the world, each presenting a part of their home and heritage to share with our visitors. Our aim was to delight visitors from all over the world of any age, education, or level of sophistication, and reveal our cultural commonalities and differences. Moreover, our models were intended to show the audience that that which divides us, ever present and distinct, is not necessarily greater than that which unites us. The basics of human interdependence and existence crop up in every built space around the planet. It can present comedy, tragedy, disaster and joy in miniature, reveal the "secret" sides of society, that which is hidden, forgotten or celebrated by repetition and aggrandizement. We can see what different societies around the world value and emphasize as we loom above them, peering down, enjoying, judging, recalling and discovering.

Reflecting on my own experience, I can see how Gulliver's voyage embodied a struggle to understand each of the alien cultures he visited, which can be compared to the competing interests of an entrepreneurial venture. Even as a small organization, we represented cultures with varying values: financial, technical, creative, educational, administrative, etc. Being

Photo 5.2 Control Room
Image courtesy of Pascal Perich: pperich.com

charged with the development of content, the "language" of visitor engagement my team believed would be the most impactful experience, had to be constantly translated for the other groups. The technical staff had to materialize ideas within the physical space, make all the elements work together on a constant and dependable basis. The investor group was constantly looking to minimize expense and maximize return, so the excitement of the content and the logistics of the technical solutions could actually be achieved with the funding that could be allocated. In the book, Gulliver's time in each land required acquiring a new language so as to both comprehend the culture he was witnessing, while simultaneously explaining his own, in order to find a way to exist within it, as a shockingly distinct outsider. Assuming that acquiring the language of a culture alone is enough to overcome stark differences is a mistake. Again and again we see how Gulliver, a phenomenal polyglot, begins to speak the language of the cultural natives yet is incapable of finding a safe and stable place within their culture. Translation is not assimilation, a different level of understanding must be achieved, and it takes more time than gaining a language.

Superiority Can Distort Morality

In the original book, Gulliver's exploration culminates in his sojourn in a land ruled by horses, where he discovers his aspirational paradise in this supremely rational culture, free of all vice, lacking even the language to describe it. The natives instead manifest a complete and perfect xenophobia, a total lack of empathy or any emotion that would allow them to violate their sense of the proper order of things. All negative or inferior behavior is cast in the light of the Yahoos, the other, who are under-evolved humans, debased creatures they keep as slaves and beasts of burden. The ruling Houyhnhnm cannot conceive of the redemption of the other, even as it is embodied by Gulliver, who, though human, is clearly different than the savage Yahoos they're accustomed to. Regardless of every earnest effort by Gulliver, which they may even admire, they still cannot overcome their deep-seated prejudice. Though rightfully idealized by Gulliver as peaceful and wise, these evolved horses occupy a righteous utopia, guided by their complete inability to tolerate difference or flaws of any kind. In such a "perfect" world, where the concept of lying has no label – instead it is referred to as "to say that which is not" there is no space for fantasy, imagination or indeed technology, as innovation and creativity seem to be decidedly lacking, and perhaps unnecessary.

As Gulliver states, they are not proud of this mentality or cultural quality, they:

> ...who live under the government of reason, are no more proud
> of the good qualities they possess, than I should be for not

> wanting a leg or an arm; which no man in his wits would boast
> of, although he must be miserable without them.

The inhabitants are here revealed as radical fundamentalists, with no reflexive or critical awareness, as they are simply horrified by that which is different than they are. Indeed, Gulliver's characterization of the Yahoos lacks any sympathy or redeeming qualities, he loathes them as deeply as the ruling class of horses do, and seeks to hide how very closely he resembles them under his clothing. Finally, they see no alternative but to banish Gulliver because of his resemblance to the other humanoids, the irredeemably primitive and barbaric Yahoos. Gulliver feels no sense of outrage or self-preservation at being exiled, he continues to love and admire the Houyhnhnm as they force him off their island. He doesn't fight the threat of a potential death at sea in the small canoe he has to build for himself, rather brutally, out of the skins of Yahoos, using their children's hides as sail and tallow rendered from their bodies as waterproofing. Instead of harboring resentment or reacting against their rejection of him as irredeemable and unacceptable, his reverential attitude towards them makes it nearly impossible for him to tolerate his fellow human beings when he arrives back home in England. He has been thoroughly brainwashed in his aspiration for a "perfect" moral state, as the absolutism the Houyhnhnm have come to represent in his mind occludes his ability to differentiate his own family and fellow countrymen from the Yahoos. For him now all are equally imperfect and odious, when compared to the supreme rational beings he worships.

When seen in the light of corporate culture, another lesson that might be relevant is an awareness and even wariness of the dominant ethos of a company, especially one that is one-sidedly mission-driven to the exclusion of other approaches and value-orientations. We have seen that the "superior" performance and "nature" of a successful entity, like a purpose-driven profiteering organization, causes ruthless and discriminatory acts to be overlooked or justified due to their "necessity" in the face of the "greater good" that the company's successful operations bring.

An extreme and absolute viewpoint can evolve into a micro-culture of fundamentalism, marked by a shared sense of distinction from others. It is possible, though, as with the Houyhnhnm, that there may not even be a language that acknowledges this separation. It may manifest itself more in a lack of openness or curiosity for other cultures, a driving sense of rivalry that lacks admiration or openness to learning.

Each of the worlds that Gulliver traveled to was distinct and complete, in some senses admirable, in others absurd, or even odious, though this aspect of the culture might not have become clear to Gulliver himself. This is the case in particular as he prides himself to be more of a cultural sponge, absorbing and describing the culture and language he

Photo 5.3 Facade
Image courtesy of Pascal Perich: pperich.com

immerses himself into, rather than maintaining self-awareness, a sense of self-preservation and individuality.

Though he does recognize some of the aberrations and absurdities of the lands he visits, he always tries to fit in, conforming to the most challenging transformations of society. This happens first, where he is a giant in Lilliput, and second, where he himself is Lilliputian in comparison to their scale. The third context is the land as the floating island of Laputa, where the inhabitants are so lost in their own deep thoughts they have to be struck to be roused back to perceiving reality, and exhibit no curiosity whatsoever about Gulliver's culture, never asking him any questions. Their over-intellectualization ruthlessly rules their lives, and its bastardized form becomes true tyranny in Lagado, the capital city. This, the next land he visits, is governed by the flying island of Laputa at a distance that amplifies the convolutions dictated by their great insight. Interestingly, this pairing is a satirical view of London's lofty rule and subjugation of author Jonathan Swift's native Dublin. The tyranny of the colonial culture is meted out by the academics housed in the Academy of Projectors. These are those who, having "learned" from the luminaries housed in Laputa sometime before, continually invent new methods and issue directives that are untested, impractical and ultimately disastrous on all aspects of society. As opposed to what Gulliver perceives to be the perfection of the Houyhnhnm, the Projectors are immediately offensive and offer no justifiable reason to be given the slightest regard. Yet they determine the course of culture and have the complete faith of the masses. This represents another strain of the same sort of fundamentalism as the pure rationalism of the Houyhnhnm, but much easier to detect and

THE WISDOM OF OTHERS

resent, the siren song of innovation for its own sake. The cliff's edge for excessive innovation in a company is the point where complexity takes its place, raising costs and hindering growth, a phenomenon the majority of global managers confessed to in a survey conducted by Bain & Co. that was published in the *Harvard Business Review* in 2005.

Gulliver's sad guide through this world is a disgraced governor who has stuck to the old ways despite the ire that draws from the populace. It is his undoing, he loses all position and respect by declining to "innovate" with the latest dictate of trend, another valuable lesson taught in satirical tones. The established conventions of an organization should not to be discarded lightly, one must remain aware that the routinized practice or tradition of any organization may have earned its stable acceptance through its utility, not stagnation. At the same time, fundamental beliefs that keep us from questioning conventions are also potent blinders, regardless of their origins. Thus, it becomes essential to find enough critical distance to evaluate the assumptions that they advance, lest one inadvertently joins in a collective alchemical effort to turn feces into gold, the mission of one of the more outrageous Projectors.

Each land Gulliver entered recognized him as both a threat and potential leader because of his deeply ingrained difference. In a leadership role we must approach organizations with a balance of respect and awareness of their cultures and practices, as well as a balanced criticality of our own limitations and strengths. We are in some senses foreign, and in some of the same cloth wherever we land. Conforming, changing and transforming represent a delicate balancing act for operating effectively.

We can be wary of Gulliver's moral indignation and outrage at the cultural realities he instinctively reacted against as new disastrous circumstances arose. We can also admire his nimble diplomacy which saved him on multiple occasions, impressing the leadership and dominant hierarchy. He was a novel contributor to the societies he entered, but whenever we interact with an organization, we must turn our original contributions into fruitful collaborations that do not run so contrary to their existence as to bring about our own destruction. Perceiving the limitations of any organization's tolerance for change or difference represents a crucial means of interacting with it productively.

Beware the Allure of Pride

Back home among his people, Gulliver struggles to renew his acceptance of humanity, brutally lumping together criminals and professionals, sinners and public servants. He admits being able to tolerate them all, save his greatest and irreconcilable revile for "a lump of deformity and diseases, both in body and mind, smitten with pride." Anyone so foolish as to love themselves unquestioningly, "immediately breaks all the measures of my patience; neither shall I be ever able to comprehend how such an animal, and such a vice, could tally together." Here perhaps Swift is breaking with his solemn oath to satire and truly attacking the object of humanity most in need of reform. How can we, so flawed and failing, be pridefully enamored of ourselves? As Gulliver struggles with and achieves a measure of acceptance for humanity, despite their inadequacies in relation to his idealized Houyhnhnm, Swift forcefully inserts a message of self-awareness and criticism. This calls forth the fatal flaw so often cited in classic literature from mythology to Shakespeare, namely hubris. Such crowing not only deserves disdain, but also alerts us to the false image being projected by the guilty perpetrator. We must ask, does he (or she, even?) truly admire themselves with such passion as to be blinded by their own shortcomings? Or, is this personage a great deceiver, ruthlessly presenting their distorted individual version of "truth" to protect that fragile facade of perfection? Let us see ourselves as a work in process, hoping perhaps even for progress, a manifestation of our striving and earnest aspiration, and not a delusion of pure, ostensibly laudable accomplishment.

The narrator does not seem capable of turning his disdain of human pride into a critical lens to evaluate the horse-people he deifies. While he has built up an enthusiastic repulsion for his fellow citizens, he is blind to the shortcomings of those who have scorned him. Do we, at work, or school, fall for hero worship or calling for heroic leadership that blinds us both to the flaws of those we admire, as well as the positive strengths and attributes of our colleagues, or those we stand above within the established hierarchy? When seen from the outside through a well-crafted corporate image, competitors and market leaders can take on proportions beyond reproach. This is especially the case, when judged in isolation through the limiting lens of business reporting, consultancy, journalism, social media or other communications media which all have their strengths and failings, and must be viewed with a similarly critical regard.

Providing wisdom can sound like platitudes, truisms that ring disingenuous and hollow, perhaps that is the reason satire was a favorite form in the Enlightenment when Swift advanced it as a new kind of writing, critiquing the establishment, exposing the accepted prejudices and practices he found odious. Rather than to moralize, he satirized, and his attacks resonated both in the specific context in which they were applied, but also beyond, when those conditions were no longer present, but the fundamental concern had found a nasty new form. He became like the trickster or court jester who subversively uses jokes and barbs to instruct, instead of directly speaking out critically. If we use that kind of "instrumentality" as a guideline for the dissident delivery or indirect "mediation" of wisdom, perhaps we can avoid pedantic preaching and seed wise thinking and acting more effectively. That is not to say that satire is necessarily a productive approach to take, it may lose you more allies than

THE WISDOM OF OTHERS

it wins over, or may fall into cynicism. Rather, being open to various narrative forms can help transmit a message that you've not been able to share otherwise.

As an exercise in communication, try coming up with an instance where you had a message, or piece of wisdom that as a leader you wanted to convey to others but were not successful in getting across. Then, experiment by crafting it as a very brief message in multiple different forms that draw on one of the many forms shared in this book: a satire, a myth, legend, folklore or fable, etc.

Can you see how twisting your message into a tale may make it resonate? Communications courses are replete with calls to tell a story, and within this book you are being treated here to many forms of wise storytelling from across the ages. You can adapt them into your own thinking, and discussions, reframed by the context you're operating in. Communications courses and textbooks emphasize the high audience engagement created through the use of storytelling; the diverse set of stories you are reading throughout this book are all excellent fodder for your own presentations. Do not be just a reader, be an author, co-creatively engaged in harnessing the power of narrative expression and communication. Just as you find many texts from many sources here, you also can recall examples from your own personal history, cultural background and work experience that can resonate if you choose them wisely. Try making them your own, both to learn from, and to inspire others.

Gulliver's Travels, like other great works of literature, should not be subjected to a reductive interpretation that simplifies or popularizes its message. Rather, it is essential to recognize that it has remained vital to readers over the centuries through the complex, caricatured range of expressions of humanity, and our collective follies. Revisiting the book as the theme for a commercial enterprise challenged me to question myself as to whether I was able to see what I was creating in others' eyes. Would the ideal intent of reaching varying audiences on varying levels be clear and achievable? Given the practical compromises forced upon us as an entrepreneurial venture, could the organization succeed as the book had, on multiple registers simultaneously? When we draw on lasting works from our cultural past we gain a deep set of potential tools for evaluation. By turning to established sources of wisdom and culture, we can gain a shortcut to applying them to our own situations as practical wisdom. The great works that outlast their own era are too robust in their hard won roots to be quickly exhausted in application, as long as we remain open to the messages they carry, though they may seem foreign in our initial reading of them.

There's a great lesson in taking the time to learn the logic, the calculations and the operating assumptions of each world required to make any organization, young or old, large or small, function. We honor great works by learning from them, and applying their lessons in the challenging new situations we face. The tragedy of Gulliver's comedic journey is that he moved in such a bewildering circle of experiences that when he arrived back home for good, he could no longer accept the familiar. Rather than gaining the wisdom to reflect on the strengths *and* weaknesses of each culture, he becomes less tolerant of difference and more enamored of perceived superiority. You're holding in your hands a vast compilation of thought and experience, each of which requires a new kind of translation on your part as a student of the histories they draw upon. The highly varied narratives harnessed in this book, that of folklore, legend, fairy tale and so on, offer instructive guidance to us if we can change our own pace and frame of reference to theirs, and then patiently learn to let them speak to us in their own language. Broadening our frame of reference to include time-tested sources of wisdom can help make us wise in our own time.

As a responsible leader, you can strive to develop a longer-term, sustainable focus for your organization and a more beneficial outcome for the various stakeholders and audiences you impact by speaking their language and working with their culture. Sustainability cannot be a recipe, or ruled by your subjective inclinations. Rather it must be tailored to the complex particularities of the situation at hand. There are guiding principles that can be brought into relevance, but not absolutes or rigid rules

Photo 5.4 Russia Access Hatch
Image courtesy of Pascal Perich: pperich.com

that can be force fit onto any circumstances we encounter. Like Gulliver, you must learn the language, win trust and favor in order to be granted the opportunity to solidify the organization as it faces destabilizing challenges. If you become a destabilizing force that's too great for the local conditions, blind to the actual elasticity of the operation and its various partners and audiences, your most passionate, well-meaning efforts might force you into exile.

Note

1 The quote comes from the Latin epic poem, *The Aeneid*, written in 19 BC, by Vergil. The quotation refers to the end of the Trojan War when the wooden horse the Greeks are hiding inside is brought inside the walls of Troy, leading to a sneak attack and the fall of the city. The Sinon is the Greek warrior who lets himself be captured and pretends to turn on the Greeks for abusing, offering the wooden horse to Athena as a sacrifice guaranteeing the protection of Troy. He therefore stands as the archetypical traitor and is, on the contrary, consummately "untrue and a liar."

Swift puts these famously false words in the narrator's mouth knowingly, adding another satirical barb that places the story definitively among the other false travel tales Gulliver decries.

References

A New Dictionary of Quotations from the Greek, Latin, and Modern Languages: Translated Into English, and Occasionally Accompanied with Illustrations, Historical Poetical, and Anecdotal, with an Extensive Index, Referring to Every Important Word. (1869). Philadelphia: J.B. Lippincott & Co. Retrieved from https://books.google.com/books?id=_fVPAAAAMAAJ&dq=recalcitrat&source=gbs_navlinks_s

Aspinall, K. & Gottfredson, M. (2005). Innovation Versus Complexity: What Is Too Much of a Good Thing? *Harvard Business Review*, November issue. Retrieved from https://hbr.org/2005/11/innovation-versus-complexity-what-is-too-much-of-a-good-thing

Damrosch, Leo. (2013). *Jonathan Swift His Life and His World*. New Haven: Yale University Press.

Jones, J. W. Jr. (1965). Trojan Legend: Who Is Sinon? *The Classical Journal*, 61(3), 122–128. Published by: The Classical Association of the Middle West and South, Inc. (CAMWS)

Millhauser, S. (1983). The Fascination of the Miniature. *Grand Street*, 2(4), 128–135. doi:10.2307/25006539

Swift, J. (1826): *Gulliver's Travels*. London: Jones & Company. Retrieved from https://books.google.com/books/about/Gulliver_s_Travels.html?id=ta1uaL7RF5gC

Vosoughi, S., Roy, D., & Aral, S. (2018). The Spread of True and False News Online. *Science*, 359(6380), 1146–1151.

6

A TALE FROM THE AH-AH COUNTRY

Elen Riot

When I was a child, a singer would come to my mother's kitchen and sing a "gwerz" for me. "Gwerz" is the name of complaints in Cornwall where I come from. One of my favorite songs is that of the sorcerer, "Ar Sorcerez", because she is so mysterious and so knowledgeable. As soon as the voice is silent, the sorcerer seems to vanish in smoke.

This is how the song ends:

– So so, Marianna, you are sentenced to death	– O arsa 'ta, Marianna, bremañ pa'h oc'h barnet,
this egg, tell us how to keep it from hatching.	Petra zo dleet d'ober 'vit na brodufont ket?
– Put the serpents in a field and build a fire around,	– O lakaat en kreiz un park, ober tan'n dro dezhe:
the earth shall open and take them in turn.	an douar a zigoro a lonko anezhe.
But this fire, make it burn large, make it burn hot	Ha me ho ped, mar graet tan, graet ma vezo tan frank,
For if but one escapes the sky will be on fire.	Mar achap hini 'nezhe, 'tevo ar firmament.

(In Markowicz and Morvan, 2010: 26: my translation from the French and Breton)

Even when you catch a sorcerer and burn her, as she has long disappeared in smoke, there might always be eggs left behind hatching. Anthropologists who study magic tend to insist that it is meant for action: magic grounds choices about future actions in the experience of the present (for instance Marcel Mauss in *Sociologie et anthropologie* (1950: 116) and Claude Lévi-Strauss (2008: 596 note 1) in *La pensée sauvage*). So, This reminds me of the story of a tribe in the Himalaya mountains I recently organized a show about. They are called the Ah-Ah. Their story is quite fantastic: it

A TALE FROM THE AH-AH COUNTRY

is a tale of appearance and disappearance. It makes you question what you see and your most familiar representations. Some say it is just a daft, local variation of the great epic of King Gesar of Ling, but I think it is more than just daftness.

Once there was a very old tribe called the Ah-Ah and they lived on the outskirts of the Himalaya. As nomads, they had a few horses, and they made a living by selling their services to four kings as mercenaries. The four kings were always at war with each other since their kingdoms shared borders along the Silk Road. Meanwhile, the Ah-Ah were sometimes able to attack caravans and get away with it because there were so many robbers around. No one could really figure out who robbed whom. This is precisely why the Ah-Ah were called the Ah-Ah. They were experts at vanishing. No one could predict when they appeared and when they disappeared. The men rode horses and wore shiny armors whereas the women bred kids and yaks and made butter. All of them very much liked to put it in their tea to keep their spirits high, especially during the cold winter nights in the mountains. The women would help the men drink most of the tea and put the rest of the butter on their face. It protected them from sunburns and local suitors.

One day, all the men disappeared. Some say they may have been struck by lightning during one of their looting expeditions. Some say their camp at night was flooded by a lake at night. Other versions of the story are more original: they claim men were attacked by a gravid tigress and that she ate them all. Tigers, eagles and bears certainly took a toll on the Ah-Ah food supplies, which was why they had to keep on the move all the time. After waiting and waiting for the men to return, the women decided to do something. As they were wont to in such cases, they sat by the Rapid and sang. There came a very old woman who appeared coming down the stream from the mountains high up in the sky above. She sure knew a lot about plants and stars but is that what you want to hear about when you are really hungry and scared to death? Besides, because she had lost her teeth, it was quite hard to make out what she said. She said the men were gone for good, and if they wanted to survive, as they were starving already, the Ah-Ah should take the last horses and attack a caravan like the men did. "Ah-ah, the women said, let's just pretend we are men and attack the caravans at night, so no one will see us. The kings' men are such fools, the men said." At this, the old woman shook her head and said: "Ah-Ah, let us be thankful for the fools. But for them, the rest of us could not succeed." She added they should always keep on the move. As the women asked for some charm or a magic, she declined. She told them to follow the Rapid and watch out for the shadows. She added: "Beware the poison of arrogance." This was a part of an epic they all knew, the tale of King Gesar of Ling, so they all thought if the old woman did not have charms to trade, at least she had tales of trade to tell. They gave her pancakes and milk, and off they went to attack the First King army.

1. The Poison of Arrogance

Before they left the camp, the women drank from the barrels the men used to drink from before battle. Suddenly, they all felt full of spirit. The women went on the road, they went and went until they finally came across what they thought was a caravan: a fire burnt in the darkest of nights. As the Ah-Ah attacked, the First King's soldiers (for it was them who had attacked the caravan) were taken aback. In fact, they were so surprised they laughed at the small smelly shadows which kept falling down from the horses (and one donkey). "Ah ah ah ah ah, watch out for the urchins' attack." The women's pride was so hurt they started yelling at them in their language, and the soldiers stopped laughing and froze to death because they knew that language. Finally, one of them said: "Why, they are no urchins at all, they are the ghosts of the Ah-Ah we killed." And they all shacked and trembled on their feet until they could flee to their fortress in the depth of night. Only one man remained after them with the horses and the women kidnapped him because he had been sound asleep all along. He was a very big and fat Dobdob[1] who was the cook of the First King's men. In his despair, all he could do was eat all the food.

2. The Trap of Doubt

The Ah-Ah came back to their village with strong horses, armors and only a very small bag of barley. They were frightened, frozen and hungry. They were also angry at the men for bragging so much: their enemies were not such fools after all. To soothe them, the other Ah-Ah prepared a meal and they ate all the little barley they had (the cook proved a very good cook). They were anxious because they had to plan a second expedition very soon. Now they had to overcome their fear. Soon, they sat by the Rapid and sang a song. They also lit a fire near the Rapid and they prepared pancakes and milk. The old woman reappeared, descending on her canoe from the green, green stream of the Grand Rapid which was shiny like the back of a snake. After she listened to them, she told them they would be great warriors if only they could rely on surprise.

The Ah-Ah did not quite grasp what she meant by that. They asked the old woman about her idea of being always on the move. They said: "We want to build a fortress, one like the four Kings have." The old woman pointed at the Rapid, and she said they all still had to abide by its rule. "Beware the trap of doubt" she added. They all knew the Rapid was always utterly unpredictable when it flooded. She added they could always carry the fortress in their caravan, one that may never be equaled in real life.

At this, the women shook their heads: "Ah-Ah, maybe she has a point." That may have had to do with the fact that they knew the song and they all started humming and singing. That may have had to do with their realizing that they could surprise soldiers by really learning their skills since they thought they were just miserable urchins. They managed to get the fat man to train them, as he was very bored and starving. They soon became skillful with arms. They still felt clumsy, but one of them pondered. "Ah-Ah," one of the Ah-Ah sighed, "that kept the man from eating." And they all knew, although they were in doubt, they had to do something. The Ah-Ah left for a new campaign and came back to the village in a rapture: they had won the battle against the second king's army. They recaptured the women they had left dancing before the men. They now had plenty of food as well as more horses and weapons. Besides, the women who had been detained now knew a lot about the third king's trade plans as the second king's party was planning to loot their caravans.

3. The Ambush of Hope

Although the Ah-Ah had been advised to be careful with the food so it would last longer, it disappeared very fast. Initially, they blamed the man for it, then they discovered the women who had been detained by the second king's men and some of the women who had been training to ride a horse were pregnant. The rest of the women assembled and they were very angry. They could hardly sit by the Grand Rapid and sing the same song together. They lit a fire by the Grand Rapid and they prepared milk and pancakes. The old woman appeared. She saw they were about to tear each other apart and so she said: "Ah-Ah, but this is the way things should go. Otherwise, for lack of men, no seeds will be planted and the tribe will disappear. This is why you should all behave like a gravid tigress." Gravid tigresses are known for being so ferociously angry all the time so they are utterly unpredictable. One of the reasons that makes her so impressive is her extreme beauty and her extreme displays of anger. "Ah-ah," the old woman said, "this is the virtue of appearances. Why do you think the eagle is the king of the sky and the tiger is the king of the mountains?" None of the women knew why. One of them said she thought the bear and the lion were the kings of the mountains instead. A long debate ensued. To cut it short, the old woman concluded: "They can all be kings. And they are all kings because they take care of their fur and teeth so they are always white and shiny." So, the women took heed of that advice and they bathed using the scents and ointments they had been looting and they put on the beautiful adornments from the caravans of the first and the second kings. They also shared old men's clothes and jewels they had never felt they could wear. When they looked at themselves in the mirror of the Grand Rapid, they thought they really did look like gravid tigresses. Saying "Where are the urchins now?" they were full of hope they could mesmerize such mesmerizing men. It is quite unfortunate, however, that they did not remember the old woman's last warning: "Beware the ambush of hope."

As the battle took place, the third king's men were first so mesmerized they could not move an inch. They were faced with each other, they were all dressed in such splendor that they did not manage to hit each other. They were all afraid to tear or stain their precious attires. On both sides, the garments were utterly magnificent and they all kept saying: "Ah-Ah" with the other camp echoing: "Ah-Ah". So at last, at dusk they were able to regain some composure as their bright costumes disappeared in the dark. Besides, at that point, they all felt they needed a good night's sleep. During the night, many alliances were formed and they decided they would attack the fourth king together for he was a horrible tyrant. At dawn, when the two parties were still yawning, down came the army of the fourth king, and it decimated them all, taking away their horses and dress. These soldiers had not fallen under the spell, for they were quite uncouth boors. The Ah-Ah had just fallen in the ambush of hope. However, as the few surviving Ah-Ah were on their way home in a wood, one by one, the fourth king's soldiers came to see them. They asked if the Ah-Ah would be ok to kidnap them, as the word had gone among men that the Ah-Ah were very nice with men and they had no king to serve. "You are so smooth and elegant and all, and you see, all we need now, after so many battles, is a little refinement in life." "Ah-Ah", the Ah-Ah said sadly, for they were very tired, and badly bruised. Finally, the Ah-Ah said they would be ok but only if they would bring their food with them. So, no sooner said than done, and this is how the Ah-Ah went back to the camp with no hope left, but (a little) more food and many more men.

4. The Arrow of Uncertainty

The Ah-Ah's victorious expeditions had brought them fame. There came some explorers who were looking for the Himalayan Amazon tribe. Although many expeditions tried to find the village of "the Amazons", all of them failed because the Ah-Ah were nomads and so they had no village. Finally, after years and years, an expedition managed to get kidnapped by the Ah-Ah. They set up in the Ah-Ah camp and took pictures. The Ah-Ah loved both looking at themselves in the mirror and having pictures taken of them. Yet they did not forget to light a fire by the Rapid and prepare some pancakes and milk. For the truth was, the more they listened to the explorers, the more they suffered the pangs and arrows of uncertainty about who they were. There came the old woman, on the back of a very large wave down the Grand, angry Rapid. Before the anthropologists shooed her away with their shouts and camera flashes, they sang a song together and she warned them: "Don't worry so much about who you have to be and what you must look like, just do what you have to do. Beware the arrows of uncertainty."

After the old woman was gone, the experts set to work on the Ah-Ah culture and traditions. The folklore expert said that their tales were a variant of King Gesar, and so were their dress patterns. He advised them to go back to the original version of the poem and get rid of the decadent variants inspired by the animist superstitions of their old shaman. That made them "utterly unpredictable", which he interpreted as the sign of a weak culture. Observing men seemed to have gained the same rights as women; the political economy expert said if they were true Amazons then they should behave as such and he mentioned Virgil. He had his guide translate the episode he knew by heart and show them pictures of true Amazons.

The doctor expert who had come here to explore the nature of hysteria said the tribe was collectively hysterical, including men, which was a revolutionary finding. They collectively behaved like a "gravid tigress". He experimented a cure on the Ah-Ah. They were all forbidden from leaving their tent at night and instructed to recite King Gesar so he could take notes. At this point, the poor Ah-Ah remembered a song the old woman had sung at the occasion of her last visit:

The snow lion exists nowhere.
King Gesar is nothing but
A phenomenon that appears to fabricating minds,
Material proper only for poetic composition.

(Choepel, 1978: 33)

As a result of the quarantine, all Ah-Ah fell very ill because of the fancy costumes they had to wear in winter. At that point, part of the camp they had settled in was flooded by the nearby Rapid. The rest of the Ah-Ah got really angry. They sat by the Rapid and decided to go up in the mountains. And that very night, they disappeared. So, the explorers decided to go back home with their belongings. The collections shipped at the time were kept by one of the explorers' family who used it for masked balls. But the last generation decided there was more to it than just folklore, they developed the photographs and organized a show and an auction for the costumes. After that, a large roadshow toured the museums of the world. It was entitled "Rediscovering the Aÿnat Tribe" (the organizers thought the name "Ah-Ah" did not sound so good). They built global partnerships with investors with the ambitious project of building an Ah-Ah Shamballa resort for Amazon Women Leaders in the spirit of King Gesar. It was to be located nearby the new dam on the Rapid and the

Silk Road. When the entrepreneurs made the trip to the Himalaya, they lit a fire by the Rapid and down came an old woman who appeared on her canoe from the mountains. They asked her if they could buy her pancakes and milk so they could taste the local food, but she did not have any. "Look at this old urchin" one of them said. Another replied: "She is a shaman." And the others answered: "No, not, she is the old Ah-Ah's sorceress". Still, they found the woman, the ghosts and the angry spirits quite quaint. They loved the idea of replacing electricity by the tantra of shamanic spells. They decided to invite famous NGOs to a meeting near the Rapid. At that point the power plant went off. "This was utterly unpredictable" said the local Sherpa. He was the friend of the local contractors who had built the hydroelectric dam for the power plant. The local authorities who had hired the contractors and not checked the dam facilities had hired him for the job. The engineer who had been the expert for the dam (and had underestimated the risk of flood) was his stepfather. They all knew the contractors had not been very concerned with the risk of flooding the valley. To go back to the beginning of the story, all had left a serpent egg in the field and now it was about to hatch. As they waited for the electricity to come back, the people in the room started laughing and asked for spirits to show their tantric power. And in the dark, a little voice said: "Ah-Ah, where power plants fail, shamans fail as well."

Interpretation of the Four Episodes

The Ah-Ah disappeared long before their valley did. The story does not tell where they went, rather it tells you what they managed to escape from. There are further important findings that also have to do with strategy and leadership. In the beginning, the Ah-Ah Tribe is left in a sorry plight since all men have disappeared. The tale is inspired by the Himalayan Epic illustrating the life of King Gesar of Ling. King Gesar, who is born with no parents and grows up as a very ugly child, grows to become a powerful horseman and a king. Most of his victories on the four neighboring kingdoms are based on tricks and cunning rather than strength. We read the four episodes of the Ah-Ah as a folkloric variant of the teaching of King Gesar.[2]

Episode 1. The Poison of Arrogance and the Urchins' Tricks

One important figure is the old woman who can be identified as "a trickster" figure in folklore. This mythic figure has magic powers. In the logic of myth[3], it is impossible to tell if the Ah-Ah are good or bad, and if the old woman herself is good or bad. What matters here is survival. In matters of survival, what counts is how to deal with external control and gain some power when faced with a series of critical situations.

A TALE FROM THE AH-AH COUNTRY

The Ah-Ah are faced with unpredictable circumstances as nomads and wardens: they need to deal with the four kings' armies. The old woman tells them to apply the lessons they learnt with the Rapid. It is "utterly unpredictable". This force is what Victor Segalen wrote about in his encounters with rapids during his trip in the Himalaya at the same time as the explorers in the story:

> These are distinct elements: scattered gestures. All this, swirls, whirlwinds, increased speed, comes to condense at the extreme in this admirable Crisis of the Life of the River which is a Rapid. It is a not in the stream, a decisive moment, a complete tragedy where the exposition, its crisis and denouement take place in the same setting, and the denouement is a happy and victorious fate. At the heart of the Rapid the River carries to the extreme its qualities of violence, its resources, its guile on the mountain. The Rapid is the apogee of its violent qualities. Each threshold it embraces and envelops, each projection is a leaping trophies. And still the river seems to be unaware of its passing. Each obstacle can be as ancient as the river itself: it is a long slope, a threshold, rocks knows here by the Genius of the River long before the large oscillations of the embouchure, long before the regulation of the torrential course. But sometimes as in the most beautiful, purest of all, the Sin Long T'an, "New Rapid of the Dragon", it is a newly born obstacle which the River has not yet eroded. It is a hill sliding on its base and precipitated by the rains in the valley.
>
> (Segalen, 1983: 836, our translation)

"The poison of arrogance" makes one assess the situation by deciding not to see the danger. The Ah-Ah think they are bold when they call the first king's soldiers "fools" and go to battle full of drink. Yet they win when they use the unexpected situation: the fact that their enemies believe they are urchins (and laugh) and then they are ghosts (and flight). This is how they learn to ride the river, and ride their horses, in the face of experience. This has to do with the nature of strategic choices (Rumelt, 2011) and the role of practical wisdom.

> In Aristotle's words phronesis is a "true state, reasoned, and capable of action with regard to things that are good or bad for man." This means: "Phronesis goes beyond both analytical, scientific knowledge (episteme) and technical knowledge or know-how (techne) and involves judgments and decisions made in the manner of a virtuoso social and political actor. (...) phronesis is commonly involved in social practice, and that therefore attempts to reduce social science and theory either to

episteme or techne, or to comprehend them in those terms, are misguided."

(Flyvbjerg, 2001: 2)

What the old woman reminds the Ah-Ah is therefore to keep adapting their practical wisdom by learning. Yet, to feel the urge to learn more when aware of a looming danger, one often has to overcome a phase of doubt.

Episode 2. The Trap of Doubt and the "Utterly Unpredictable"

Initially, the Ah-Ah are not skilled warriors. Yet they were skilled in other fields, such as living nearby the Grand Rapid. They were also masters at disappearing. In the 1900s, an explorer, Alexandra David-Néel, described local habits in Tibet: "*There are many ways people can make themselves get out of reach.*" One of them is by looking like the people nobody wants to see:

Sometimes poverty is responsible for the ragged garments worn by the dobdob, but he often deliberately tears his monastic robe, to look- he thinks- more terrible. (...) However costly the material maybe, the dobdob kneading butter in his black hands, spreads it all over his new clothes. These strange fellows consider that nothing can be more elegant than a robe and a toga which has become as shining as velvet and stiff as armor, by the careful and constant application of dirt and filth.

(David-Neel, 1971: 110)

The Ah-Ah women used to be skillful at fleeing danger by disappearing. When they realize the kings' men are dangerous, they want to use that technique again, yet the old woman makes them aware that their situation has changed: now they also have to face danger. The old woman helps the Ah-Ah woman recognize that they need to learn new orders of things as their role is changing. They must overcome the feeling that they are breaking the rules:

Order implies restriction; from all possible materials, a limited selection has been made and from all possible relations a limited set has been used. So, disorder by implication is unlimited, no pattern has been realized in it, but its potential for patterning is indefinite. This is why, though we seek to create order, we do not simply condemn disorder. We recognize that it is destructive to existing patterns; also that it has potentiality. It symbolizes both danger and power.

(Douglas, 1966: 1)

New orders of action are combined with old, unpredictable ones, such as the Rapid. They are also very difficult to detect to outsiders, such as the king's soldiers: "Clearly the observer is in error when he decides that nothing has changed because a number of traits of the 'little tradition' are still extant. But the error is not only pardonable, it is almost inevitable" (Hirschman, 2013: 38).

At one point, the Ah-Ah think the way to do that is to build a fortress, like the kings did. But the old woman reminds them they still are the people of the Grand Rapid: they need to be on the move, so their fortress has to be a mental one. They need to build "a crystal fortress".

The Ah-Ah overcome their doubts by listening to the old woman who makes it clear they can only survive by learning new skills although, so far, only men would be learnt in such matters.

This is where the old woman may be acting as a leader, as illustrated by Hirschman:

> (...) charismatic leadership rests to a considerable extent on the leader's ability "to accentuate the sense of being in a desperate predicament," presumably regardless of whether this sense is justified by actual events. Yet, accentuation, exaggeration, and forceful articulation of prevailing attitudes and perceptions cannot be the only basis for leadership. Another is surely the ability to overcome and transcend some of these attitudes.
>
> (Hirschman, 2013: 44)

In the face of imminent dangers, the Ah-Ah need to react by learning new skills. The old woman displays two forms of transformative leadership tapping on both skills and charisma:

> Through our indirect approach—ascertaining first some "average" attitudes and perceptions and then defining leadership in terms of deviations from the norm—we have, in fact, come upon two contrasting components of leadership: skill, on the one hand, and charisma, on the other. Skill requires a stronger-than-average ability to perceive change, while charisma is based in part on a stronger-than-average refusal to do so. The charisma and the skill requirements of leadership, thus, are often at loggerheads, and the most effective leaders are likely to be those who can somehow accommodate both.
>
> (Hirschman, 2013: 45)

The old woman does not need to explain the situation when she appears. The Ah-Ah are always on the verge of disaster. Living near the Grand Rapid means it can always flood and carry them away. Yet, the old woman tells the Ah-Ah that they are the kind of people who have always lived (and survived) by a Grand Rapid, and so they have built skills. These transformative skills should teach them to ignore the fact that women do not go to war where they live. Only by building new skills can they face the situation. So in a struggle for survival, the Ah-Ah completely forget the very rules that may have forbidden them from access to such knowledge.

Episode 3. The Ambush of Hope and the Gravid Tigress

The Ah-Ah were feeling they could use their new skills as warriors when they realize some of them are pregnant, which makes them more vulnerable when they fight. The old woman tells them to use their reputation and their costume to compensate. As they change their dress, the Ah-Ah realize that they too can use appearances to make an impression. This is part of the warrior's skills. The Ah-Ah hope their new wardrobe will help them win men's favor with no fight. However, fortresses and dresses are very fragile shelters.

Still, the old woman teaches them that armors and other objects can be carried like burdens (men's attire for war) or they can be used like assets because they fit the situation. The same can be said of power. It should always be more than just an attribute: a form of action carried on by people who use it to make strategic choices as they are always challenging and challenged by other parties. The French philosopher Pascal writes, in his *Three Discourses to the Prince*, that the power of a man over others has to do with illusions since he is never more than "a legitimate usurper" dependent on the desire of others:

> To enter into the true knowledge of your condition, consider it in this image. A man is thrown by a storm onto an unknown island, whose inhabitants were at pains to find their king, who was lost; and bearing a strong resemblance in body and face to this king, he was taken for him and recognized as such by the whole population. At first, he did not know which part to take; but he resolved himself finally to lend himself to his good fortune. He received all the respects offered him and let himself be treated as king.
>
> (Pascal, 1955: 165)

However, the Ah-Ah learn not to expect too much from it as they can be mesmerized by men just as men can be mesmerized. If this situation is possible for one man, it is because no other power is more legitimate:

> Do not imagine that it is by a lesser accident that you possess the wealth of which you happen to be the master than that by

A TALE FROM THE AH-AH COUNTRY

which that man happens to be king. (...) Is it not by a thousand accidents that your ancestors acquired and preserved it? (...) It is only from this encounter with chance that you were born, by the whim of laws favorable with respect to you that puts you in possession of all those things.

(Pascal, 1955: 166)

As illustrated in Hans-Christian Andersen's tale, *The Emperor's New Clothes*, a dress is but an impression made on oneself and others. The roles are agreed upon socially: some rule, others don't. There also is a form of transmission that makes power legitimate in time. An Ah-Ah warrior in battle is dressed in an armor which is an assemblage of items of clothing which were temporarily passed on to the warrior. It is a temporary role going with a temporary costume. As Marilyn Strathern, an anthropologist, illustrates in her analysis of Papua warriors in New Guinea:

(...) the dancer's attire is an assemblage, put together there and then from many sources. The crucial analogy is between the clan as an assemblage of men and each man as an assemblage of men (his relations with others). I photographed Ketepa before the dance began; in the same way as the feather plaque recapitulates the kinds of attachments found in the decorations as a whole, Ketepa's assembling recapitulates the act of gathering ornaments in the first place.

(Strathern, 1999: 35)

The fact that power goes with appearances, and impression management, should not give the Ah-Ah any hope that this will protect them. This should encourage them to see themselves as transient in a group faced with specific circumstances. This transient, accidental situation is illustrated in a movie by Akura Kurosawa (1980), *Kagemusha, Shadow Warrior*, where we see a beggar take the role of a dead king and win battles. What makes the beggar and the Ah-Ah good in their role as leaders is their ability to be aware of that timely situation and make the right decisions instead of carrying power like a mere burden. The old woman helps the Ah-Ah by reminding them of traditions they have known for a long time. They acknowledge their songs are just as strong as armors because they share them. Instead of being passive listeners and spectators, the Ah-Ah become actors of their own tale.

Episode 4. The Arrow of Uncertainty and the Beginner's Mind

The expertise of the explorers on them makes the Ah-Ah uneasy. This may explain their sudden disappearance. They do not want to become museum fetishes. Anthropologists here act like bad consultants, who want to enforce their methods and inoculate a people with what experts think is their authentic culture. To accept the formula and accept to act as a caricature of oneself would mean, as Alvesson and Spicer formulated it: "You don't have to be stupid, but it helps" (Alvesson and Spicer, 2016). Therefore the Ah-Ah's resistance is a proof of lucidity and strength.

In the story, expertise more or less corresponds to the "synoptic ideal" of policy making for leaders. Braybrooke and Lindblom note that the synoptic ideal opposes facts and values as "separate compartments" when important choices are made: "(choosing) among alternatives after careful and complete study of all possible courses of action and all their possible consequences and after an evaluation of those consequences in the light of one's values"; as a result it makes you think you can solve a problem: "(...) ideally one treats the policy question as an intellectual problem; one does not look upon a policy question as calling for the exercise of something called 'political forces'" (Braybrooke and Lindblom, 1970 : 40).

Action requires using practical reason skills, and it is quite different than solving a math problem. Because no ready-made formula exists, it is more like what the old woman describes as "the beginner's mind" in an echo of Sunryu Suzuki: "In the beginner's mind, there are many possibilities, in the expert's mind, there are few" (Suzuki, 1970: 21).

The Ah-Ah face situations where they cannot tame or control the elements. They learn quite fast that such knowledge shows (only) to the learned eyes. Here we may want to point at the role of experience in progressively building up the practical skills needed to face unpredictable situations. The learner is first a novice then advanced beginner, competent then proficient performer and finally expert. He goes from applying the rules to appropriating the skills so he no longer needs to apply the rules. "In normal, familiar situations, real experts do not solve problems and do not make decisions. They just do what 'works'" (Flyvbjerg, 2001: 17). The old woman knows when to appear and when to disappear. In the end, the Ah-Ah learn this skill as well. They no longer need someone else to tell them how to react to unexpected circumstances. They also know that they cannot go back to the initial situation when they were under control, when they depended on men. Their silence is wise, in the sense that they are phronetic by responding to each situation in appreciating its specific nature. Their decision is a collective one. It seems they finally understood how to adapt their reactions to the situation: in front of the poison of arrogance, the trap of doubt, the ambush of hope, the arrow of uncertainty, surprise is not everything, but it counts for something, practical skills also count for something, dress and impression management counts for something. Finally, distance counts for something:

The momentum lies with alternatives to the dominant scientistic social science that unreflectively seeks to apply the models of the natural sciences to the social world. (This) (amply demonstrates) the power of a phronetic social science to contribute to the revitalization of democratized public decision-making.

(Flyvbjerg, Landman and Schram, 2012: 296)

When you no longer see any way to be loyal or to exert your voice, it may be a good way out to disappear (exit) (Hirschman, 1970), like the old woman and the Ah-Ah after her. One way of disappearing is by telling stories, which make people fantasize and see the world in a different light. By telling stories, one can make imaginary things happen, such as the emperor's new clothes in Andersen's tale. One can also make imaginary people appear. This is what Gedun Choepel mentions of the hero of the King Gesar epic: he is but "a phenomenon that appears to fabricating minds", a "material proper only for poetic composition". In the end of the story, before she disappears, the old woman even takes a distance with this magic and the shaman role she is assigned. Her acknowledging that her audience considers the magic of the shaman as a complement operator to technologies shows a distance from the traditions and superstitions people from the "under developed world" are supposed to have kept. By assuming she is "not quite a shaman" (Pedersen, 2011),[4] the old woman mirrors her visitors who may be lacking experience in both technical and local knowledge to build their "Ah-Ah Shambala" and become true "Ah-Ah". Their tantric center for women leaders also points at the problem of relying on roots, culture and traditions as a guidance for strategic leadership.

This leads me to the implications for leadership of my story.

Implication for Management and Leadership Education

The Ah-Ah tale is related, for me, to the role of folklore, culture and traditions with regard to individual and group identity. As part of a group of visual artists, I "invented a tribe" and this invention led to a roadshow in several French museums. For me, it was a real-life experiment, an occasion to test that, when faced with an official show, in arts and science institutions, such as museums, most people tend to believe what they see. They do not spontaneously exert their critical thinking and practical reason to make up a mind of their own. Part of the answer for this is that they respect a form of authority that has to do with past traditions and expertise. Yet another part of the answer might be less legitimate: people fail to pay enough attention to discriminate the nature of the reality presented before their eyes. So, in the age of mass-media communication and impression management, my goal was to question the power and the influence of official sources of expertise in building widely shared representations of reality. As all of us should be in a position to make informed choices and judgments, this led me to try and fabricate a tale that used "fake folklore" to introduce my views on how to deal with reality.

As visible in several studies (Anderson, 2006; Hobsbawm and Ranger, 2012), traditions are social constructions. Accordingly, they tend to correspond to acceptable and useful contemporary representations of the past, rather than an accurate "tale of the origins".

For several authors, this should leave room for multiple versions of history in a post-colonial world (Clavir, 2002 ; Simpson, 1996).[5] This approach sports a positive view of "world culture" in its diversity. However, in many cases, different views of the same past tend to conflict. Therefore, cultural relativism may not be a solution (Lévi-Strauss, 2008): when different versions of the same story conflict with important choices at stake. The credo that if different versions of the same story exist then people will be able to accept them all and not try to impose their own views seems quite delusional.

For instance, in the case of famous prehistoric sites, experts are concerned that the official story of the site is more oriented towards attracting additional tourists than towards providing valid information to the general public (Badone, 1987; Fairclough, Harrison, Jameson and Schofield, 2008; Gazin-Schwartz and Holtorf, 1999).[6] Misrepresentations as contained in popular versions of past history[7] may influence people's identity towards resentment and revenge, as illustrated by the influence of the movie *Braveheart* on Scottish pupils (Arnold, Davies and Ditchfield, 1998) or by Anti-French accounts of the age of "Collaboration" in Brittany conveyed by popular culture (Morvan, 2005).

The first four parts of the Ah-Ah history aim to provide a guide to help people exert their practical reason. The last part of the story is quite different in purpose. It is also a fabrication, but it is not based on the "Ah-Ah museum show" experiment. This time, it takes its origin in several fieldworks, I did, studying cultural heritage projects in relation to public policies. This last part, for me, is complementary with the four parts of the "guide" because it challenges the role played by public institutions in empowering all people. When looking at heritage sites and shows in public museums, one may raise questions as to their willingness to help the general public exert its practical reason and critical sense. My view is that although it may be materially difficult to broadly share all versions of the same past reality, public institutions have a major responsibility in making that possible. Consequently, they should provide educational tools so that people are in a position to engage in fact-checking. Even in a context of entertainment, one should be able to take position and exert one's critical judgment about real-life situations (Faubion, Guyer, Boellstorff, Strathern, Deliss, Keck and Smith, 2016). Unfortunately, this is rarely the case because institutions' goals are often contradictory. For instance, such institutions like the UNESCO are traditionally engaged in providing "salvation" and remediation to the cultural heritage, especially when it is endangered because of wars (Van Krieken-Pieters, 2010).[8] Yet, sometimes, despite the importance of what is at stake, they may prefer to collaborate with private sponsors because of budgetary constraints, also as a result, a gray market of heritage goods may develop. In other cases, they may be tempted to downplay the political dimensions of the past (Barnard and Woodburn, 1988; Clastres, Hurley and Stein, 1977; Leacock and Lee, 1982)[9] in an effort to compromise and promote "at all costs" local economic development via cultural tourism.

What, then, would be the alternative to relying on culture and traditions for a wise and sustainable leadership?

As opposed to culture, the allusion to the archetype and "the magic of the trickster" in the tale is a metaphor for the need to be open to the reality of experience. It is not a plea to rely on supra-normal forces, but rather on practical wisdom. The problem of the eggs of the snake hatching in the field, the ones Marianna mentions in the gwerz, requires plowing the field. But the allusion to "magic" refers to the need to use one's practical wisdom in situations of strategic decision-making, where neither the eggs of the snake or the field materialize. It is difficult to process this from a distance, yet we should not reduce it to combinations of pawns on a chessboard. In such situations of strategizing practices that are different than those of habitual routine, the practitioner needs to deal with the "utterly unexpected". Graeme Guthrie's (2017) provides practical descriptions of such in situ strategic decision-making in our times. In his book, "*The Firm Divided*", he shows a constant conflict over control in corporate governance. The board of director tends to monitor or motivate the CEO, but at the same time increasingly delegates this task to financial analysts and large shareholders and thus to capital markets.

To be ready and prepared, one can train to deal with such open situations beforehand. During training sessions, educators observed that, when experts are involved in game-plays, they tend to discover new, complementary forms of intelligence that help them build relations with others and react to the specificity of their environment: "They (...) appear (...) to be (...) drawing on their own innate intelligence and creativity" (Holliday, Statler and Flanders, 2007: 388). When faced with such specific situations, with no prior training it entails that all actors are paying more attention to each and everyone's emotions and embodied experiences of the environment than in more stable contexts (Küpers and Weibler, 2006: 369). So a better understanding for each other is also grounded in experience. Still, I believe for this to happen, one has to be ready to sit by the Rapid and sing. With this, I refer you to the splendid lines of Victor Segalen that I quoted in my story. The Rapid makes itself felt, because it is irresistible: nothing and no one can prove to be as powerful and as dangerous at the same time. Rather, one needs to appreciate the Rapid aesthetically. Both the old woman and the Ah-Ah are shaped by a Rapid. Its songs stay with us just as the charm of the Rapid does not leave our ears and eyes. In a similar way, knowledge in action has to be enacted to make sense for the actors in a sensual way, because senses make sense (Küpers, 2013) and:

> (the) basic levels of consciousness – although unfolding at different rates – can be seen as fluid, flowing, overlapping waves in an overall spectrum of consciousness and can be used as a 'scale' to measure all the lines. The 'lines of development' co-determine a human being's capacity to perform successfully in various circumstances.
>
> (Küpers and Statler, 2008: 386)

As this tale has shown, being under the influence of strong sensations and emotions may make choices and wise judgment more difficult to articulate, possibly because these are so deeply felt that they fit better with images and imagination than with words. It may also be difficult to accept it as it is directly connected to practical wisdom, instead of going in another direction. Once accepted, this difficulty, taking stock of a situation characterized by uncertainty and risk, may increase collective leadership and make all group members more ready for major transformations (Bathurst, Jackson and Statler, 2010). I hope my story offers a way to express this possibility. It shows collective leadership in the face of circumstances and not as the expression of a nature talent; just as when Marianna reveals where the eggs of the snake are, it does not mean she can make or unmake them.

Notes

1 Dobdobs in Tibet are fighting monks, as illustrated by Tashi's testimony collected by Hugh Richardson (1986).
2 Another well-known variant of the epic is that of Chogÿam Trungpa, and it is very much inspired by the Zen wisdom.
3 As illustrated, among many others, in the "story of Lynx" by Lévi-Strauss (2008).
4 During a fieldwork in Mongolia, this anthropologist, Axel Morten Pedersen, noticed that after the downfall of the Soviet Empire, public services did not work well. People would go back to "shamans", but, in a world where nothing seemed to work properly, it was only fair that shamans did not work either. Just as public services were "not quite" what they used to be, the shamans were "not quite shamans".

A TALE FROM THE AH-AH COUNTRY

5 Simpson calls that "bones of contention" in the case of archeology, whereas many accounts tend to be satisfied with the material reality of "a bone is a bone is a bone".

6 For instance, Fairclough et al. (2008: 524) point at the limits of "interpretive narrative archeology" in the case of the popular site of Stonehenge. They think "new age" versions may be limited in terms of truth-value although it may be more adequate to promote tourism.

7 Apparently, there is no limit to what folklore can legitimize. In one case-study, entitled "the last refuge of the fairies" (p. 255) in East-Sussex, Gazin-Schwart and Holstorf describe a woman as she actively reconstructs time and space in reference to fairies as real presences for people who follow her tours as a guide.

8 To be more specific about what I mean by "global and local tensions", this paper is a case-study illustrating the legitimacy problems involved in preserving and restituting their cultural heritage to countries at war such as Afghanistan, when private foundations are commissioned by international bodies such as the UNESCO.

9 All these authors write about "primitive worlds" of hunters-gatherers, and still they focus on political economy, whereas most accounts of "ancient civilizations" tend to downplay the complexity of these issues as if primitive ages were simpler because their norms and rules were identical to that of "nature" (whatever one means by that word).

References

Alvesson, M. and Spicer, A. (2016). *The Stupidity Paradox: The Power and Pitfalls of Functional Stupidity at Work*. Profile Books, London.

Anderson, B. (2006). *Imagined Communities: Reflections on the Origin and Spread of Nationalism*. Verso Books, New York.

Arnold, J., Davies, K. and Ditchfield, S. (1998), *History Heritage. Consuming the Past in Contemporary Culture*. Donhead Publishing, London.

Badone, E. (1987). Ethnicity, folklore, and local identity in rural Brittany. *Journal of American Folklore*, 161–190.

Barnard, A. and Woodburn, J. (1988), *Property, Power and Ideology in Hunter-Gatherer Societies, An Introduction*. Oxford Berg University Press, Oxford.

Bathurst, R., Jackson, B. and Statler, M. (2010). Leading aesthetically in uncertain times. *Leadership*, 6(3), 311–330.

Braybrooke, D. and Lindblom, C.E. (1970). *A Strategy of Decision, Policy Evaluation as Social Process*. The Free Press, New York.

Choepel, G. (1978). *The White Annals*, translated by Samten Norbu. Library of Tibetan Works and Archives, Dharamsala.

Clastres, P., Hurley, R. and Stein, A. (1977). *Society Against the State*. Blackwell University Press, Oxford.

Clavir, M. (2002). *Preserving what is Valued, Museums, Conservation and First Nation*. University of British Columbia Press, Canada.

David-Neel, A. (1971). *Magic and Mystery in Tibet*. Dover Publication, New York.

RIOT

Douglas, M. (2003 (1966)). *Purity and Danger: An Analysis of Concepts of Pollution and Taboo*. Routledge and Kegan Paul, London.

Fairclough, G., Harrison, R., Jameson, J.L.H. and Schofield, J. (2008). *The Heritage Reader*. Routledge Publishing, London.

Faubion, J.D., Guyer, J.I., Boellstorff, T., Strathern, M., Deliss, C., Keck, F., and Smith, T. (2016). On the anthropology of the contemporary: Addressing concepts, designs, and practices. *HAU: Journal of Ethnographic Theory*, 6(1), 371–402.

Flyvbjerg, B. (2001). *Making Social Science Matter: Why Social Inquiry Fails and How it Can Succeed Again*. Cambridge University Press, Cambridge.

Flyvbjerg, B., Landman, T. and Schram, S. (Eds.). (2012). *Real Social Science: Applied Phronesis*. Cambridge University Press, Cambridge.

Gazin-Schwartz, A. and Holtorf, C.J. (1999). *Archeology and Folklore*. Routledge Publishing, London.

Guthrie, G. (2017). The Firm Divided: Manager-*Share*holder Conflict and the Fight for Control of the Modern Corporation. Oxford University Press, Oxford.

Hirschman, A.O. (1970). *Exit, Voice, and Loyalty: Responses to Decline in Firms, Organizations, and States*. Harvard University Press, Cambridge, MA.

Hirschman, A.O. (2013).Underdevelopment, Obstacles to the Perception of Change, and Leadership. *The Essential Hirschman*. Princeton University Press, Princeton.

Hobsbawm, E. and Ranger, T. (Eds.). (2012). *The Invention of Tradition*. Cambridge University Press, Cambridge.

Holliday, G., Statler, M. and Flanders, M. (2007). Developing practically wise leaders through serious play. *Consulting Psychology Journal: Practice and Research*, 59(2), 126.

Küpers, W. (2013). The Sense-Makings of the Senses – Perspectives on Embodied *aisthesis* & Aesthetics in Organising & Organisations. Ian King and Jonathan Vickery (eds). *Experiencing Organisations – New Aesthetic Perspectives*, Series: Management, Policy & Education (pp. 33–56). Libri, Oxfordshire.

Küpers, W. and Statler, M. (2008). Practically wise leadership: toward an integral understanding. *Culture and Organization*, 14(4), 379–400.

Küpers, W. and Weibler, J. (2006). How emotional is transformational leadership really? Some suggestions for a necessary extension. *Leadership & Organization Development Journal*, 27(5), 368–383.

Leacock, E. and Lee, R. (1982). *Politics and History in Band Societies*. Cambridge University Press, Cambridge.

Lévi-Strauss, C. (2008). *Œuvres, Bibliothèque de la Pléiade*. NRF, Gallimard, Paris.

Markowicz A. and Morvan F. (2010). *Anciennes complaintes de Bretagne*, Editions Ouest-France, Rennes.

Mauss, M. (1950). *Sociologie et anthropologie*, Presses Universitaires de France, Paris.

Morvan, F. (2005). *Le monde comme si. Nationalisme et dérive identitaire en Bretagne*. Editions Actes Sud, Arles.

Pascal, B. (1955). Trois discours. Louis Lafuma (ed.) *Opuscules et lettres*, Editions Aubier-Montaigne, Paris in Marin, L. (1988). Portrait of the King, trans. Martha M. Houle (pp. 164–171). University of Minnesota Press, Minneapolis.

Pedersen, M.A. (2011). *Not Quite Shamans: Spirit Worlds and Political Lives in Northern Mongolia*. Cornell University Press, New York.

Richardson, H. (1986). *Adventures of a Tibetan Fighting Monk*. Tamarind Press, Bangkok.

Rumelt, R. (2011). *Good Strategy/Bad Strategy: The Difference and Why it Matters*. Profile Books, New York.

Segalen, V. (1983). *Equipée*, Editions Gallimard, Paris.

Simpson, M.G. (1996). *Making Representations. Museums in the Post-Colonial Era*. Routledge Publishing, London.

Strathern, M. (1999). Property, Substance and Effect: Anthropological Essays on Persons and Things. Athlone Press, London.

Suzuki, S. (1970). *Zen Mind, Beginner's Mind*. Shambhala Publications, Boston.

Van Krieken-Pieters, J. (2010). Hidden Afghanistan in the Musée Guimet. S. Labachi and C. Long (eds). *Heritage and Globalization* (pp. 79–92). Routledge Publishing, London.

7

LAOCOÖN, LEADERSHIP AND WISDOM

Robin Holt

Laocoön is an odd and oddly persistent figure in western thought. He appears as a minor character in an ancient Mediterranean tale that has been re-told in countless ways. I have chosen three of these. First comes Virgil's *Aenid*, an epic rendering of how the city of Troy fell and the wandering it set in train. Here we are introduced to Laocoön who as a priest is a leading figure in the city who fails to persuade the citizens to keep the wooden horse outside the city walls. Second is a passage of artistic expression that begins with an Ancient Greek sculptor who fixed Laocoön's violent end in stone and which reaches an apogee in a response to this sculpture by the German Romantic writer Gotthold Ephraim Lessing. Lessing uses Laocoön's story, and more significantly also considers the way in which the story is being told – the medium of expression, in this case stone – to expose his readers to a basic insight: when making knowledge claims – as surely all leaders are wont to do – it is the medium of expression, as much as the content, that governs their veracity, and that the aesthetic power of different media to move an audience must be protected from cross-appropriation. Third, I have chosen an etching by William Blake, which is created in critical response to the idea of a classical ideal, and which plays deftly with the intimacy between knowledge, vision and moral duplicity of reason.

In this company of three versions of the tale expressed in three different media (text (poetry), stone (sculpture), image (montaged etching)), I discuss the resonance of Laocoön for thinking about leadership. The chapter itself is set up as a kind of montage of three sections that are deliberately kept free from one another's narrative, but which of course talk to one another across their distinctiveness. The myth of Laocoön has a basic continuity of character and event, but these are rendered very differently, as through different media the myth leaves and then re-visits itself, so to speak, creating new perspectives as it unfolds.

As Text

From Virgil we learn of Laocoön as a member of the priestly caste, a leader in Trojan society, who is attempting to persuade the Trojans not to take the wooden horse into the city:

Then Laocoön comes running, followed by
A throng of others, and as he runs cries out
In an anguished voice, 'O my poor fellow Trojans,
What is this madness? Do you really think
The enemy has gone? Do you really think
The Greeks give guileless gifts? Do you really think
Ulysses is such a man? Either Achaeans
Are hiding inside this Thing or else this is
Some kind of war machine against our walls,
Or it's designed to look down over them
And see into our houses, or else it's made
So they can descend upon us from above,
Or there's some other trickery inside.
Trojans, don't trust this Horse. I'm afraid of Greeks.
Beware of gifts from Greeks.' This said, he turns
And with great force he hurls his mighty spear.
It strikes the beast in the belly and shaking stays,
And when it stays, there is, from deep within,
A reverberating hollow moaning sound.
And had the Fates permitted us to do so,
And had our minds not been so self-deluded,
We would have used our steel to open it up,
And see into the Argive hiding place,
And Priam's citadel, Troy, would be standing

But at that moment a loudly shouting crowd
Of shepherds from the countryside appears,
Bringing into the presence of the king
A youth whose hands they'd tied behind his back.
This stranger, who is resolute in his purpose
Either to die or else to bring about
The opening up of Troy to the Achaeans,
Had so contrived to situate himself
That the guileless shepherds, encountering him, would seize him.
From all around a mob of Trojan youths
Come running here to see this captured Greek,
Reviling him, pressed close around him, taunting.
Now listen and hear what treachery the Greeks

Are capable of, by hearing what this Greek
Was capable of, for, as, unarmed, he stood there,
Looking helpless, looking desperate, looking around
At the Phrygian crowd that was gathered looking at him,
He cries: 'Alas, alas, what land is there
Where I can go where they will take me in?
What will become of me? I have no place
Among the Greeks; and the Dardanidae
Cry out on me for vengeance, seeking my blood!'
Hearing him wail like this, our impetus
For violence against him is quieted down.
We urge him to tell us who he is and what
Information he has, to give to us:
'You are our prisoner now, what is your story?'
After awhile, seeming less fearful, he speaks:

...

'O king, whatever it is that happens to me,
I'll tell the truth, nor will I deny that I
Am Greek by birth; I tell you this once.
Though Fortune has fashioned Sinon for misery,
She cannot make Sinon a liar. The fame
Of Palamedes, son of Belus, may
Have reached your ears. Because of his refusal
To participate in the Ilian adventure,
He was, though innocent, by false report
Brought down to death by the Pelasgians-
Who mourn him now that he is lost to the light.
My father was his kinsmen, who, though poor,
Sent me when I was young to serve with him.
While he was powerful still, a prince whose voice
Was respected in the councils of the king,
Our family's standing and repute were strong;
But when, because of Ulysses' subtle contriving
(As is well known), he left the upper air,
Then I was left alone to labor through
My shattered life in the darkness of my grief
And anger over the things that had been done
To my innocent friend and patron. 1did not keep
My anger to myself, or my vows that if
I ever returned in triumph to my Argos,
I would exact revenge. My words were heard,
And I was feared and distrusted by many who heard them.
This is how it began, and it is how Ulysses

138

LAOCOÖN, LEADERSHIP AND WISDOM

Contrived against me by spreading dark rumors about me,
And seeking confederates in his conspiracy
To bring me down. He didn't rest until
He enlisted Calchas as his instrument.
But why am I telling this story to ears to which
It is unwelcome? What are you waiting for?
If you regard all Greeks as all the same,
And if its enough for you to know I'm Greek,
Then take your revenge on me, have done with it,
For this is what the Ithacan would desire,
And what the sons of Atreus prize.'

Then we are ardent to hear his story and
To understand it, ignorant as we were
Of such Pelasgian wickedness and deceit.
And so the dissembler continues the story, trembling,
And speaking with dissembling deep emotion:

'The Greeks were weary of protracted war,
And anxious to weigh anchor and depart,
Longing to find their homes. Would they had done so.
But too many times there were great storms at sea
That kept them back from going. And, just at the moment
This horse you see, built out of wooden planks,
Was finally completed. From great clouds loud
Thunder sounded all across the sky.

What could this be? They sent Eurypylus
To consult the oracle of Phoebus, and
When he returned from the shrine he brought these words:
"Danae, when you set sail for Ilium,
You pacified the winds with the blood of a virgin,
Slain as sacrifice. When you aspire
To return from there, you must pacify the winds,
With the blood of an Achaean sacrifice."
A cold shudder ran through the hearts of all
In the listening crowd when they heard the oracle.
"Who is it for whom the Fates are readying death?
Who is it Apollo calls for?" And then there's tumult,
When Calchas the seer is dragged into their midst
By the Ithacan demanding that he tell
What the gods desire. In the crowd there were many who said
That it was I whose death had been foretold,
And silently they waited for what they knew
Was going to come to pass when the seer spoke.

139

HOLT

Five days the seer is silent in his tent,
And five more days; and would not say words
That would send someone to death; and then, at last,
Yielding to the Ithacan's loud insistence,
He ended his silence with words that spelled my doom.
It was I who was to be sacrificed at the altar.
The crowd received his utterance with approval,
Each one of them accepting the exchange
Of another's death for his own relief from fear.

And now the day too horrible to imagine
Had come upon me. They were preparing the rites,
The salted meal to sprinkle on my head,
The fillets to bind my brow, making me ready.
But there was a moment when, being left alone,
Somehow I broke my bonds, and got away,
Escaping from my death. I hid myself
In the sedgy mire at the edge of a muddy lake,
Hoping to be unseen till they sailed away,
If that was going to happen. I knew I had
No hope of ever seeing my country again,
Or seeing my father again, or my sweet children
I so desired to see once more. I knew
That it might come to be that the Greeks would exact
Retribution, by their deaths, oh wretched ones,
For the crime I had committed by my flight.
But I beg, in the name of the gods on high,
The powers who know the truth and will sustain it,
If anywhere in the world among mortal men
There's an unstained purity of faith, have pity,
Have pity on one whose sorrow is undeserved.'

In response to his tears we spare him, and, more than that,
We pity him. It is Priam, the king, himself,
Who commands that he be freed from his constraints,
And speaks to him with welcome and with kindness:
'Whoever you are, now you are one of us;
Forget the Greeks; now they are lost to you.
But you must answer this question I ask:
What is the reason they raised this giant Horse?
Who is it who made it? Why was it made? Is it
An offering to supplicate a god?
Is it a war machine? And when he ceased,
The other, who had been so well instructed

140

LAOCOÖN, LEADERSHIP AND WISDOM

In Pelasgian deceit, raised up to the heavens
His hands now free from their bindings and cried out,

'Witness, eternal inviolable fires above,
You stars, you altars, and you evil swords,
You fillets of the gods I wore when they
Prepared me for the sacrificial altar,
Grant me the right to be released from all
My sacred vows of allegiance to the Greeks,
Grant me the right to hate them, the right to bring
All secret things that are hidden in the dark,
Out into the light. I am no longer bound
By any laws of the country that I came from.
If what I tell you keeps you safe,
Then keep me safe as you have promised me,
In equal exchange for what I bring you.

The hope and confidence of the Danaans
Depended on Pallas's help. However, impious
Tydides and Ulysses the contriver
Together ravished the sacred shrine of Pallas,
And slew the guardians of the citadel,
And with their bloody hands seized her holy image,
Touching the fillets of the virgin goddess.
It was from that time and act that the strength of the Greeks
Was broken desire, their hopes collapsed, and they
Were angrily dispelled from the heart of the outraged
Goddess. Hardly had the sacred image
Been placed in the camp it was brought to, over the seas,
Than Tritonia showed the signs that this was so.
Fire blazed out from the effigy's upraised eyes,
Sweat poured over its limbs, and, *mirabile dictum*,
In lightning flashes the goddess herself three times
Was seen with spear and shield, and vanished again!
The prophecy of Calcas from his shrine
Was that these signs are signs they must take
To the sea and go, that Pergamum can't be conquered
By Argive weapons unless they return to Argos
To find new omens, carrying back with them
In their curvèd ships the effigy they had stolen
And brought with them from there. And now as they
Are gone before the wind to their Mycenae,
They go to recover their forces and their gods,
And after they have done so, then, unexpected,

They will return. Thus Calchas reads the omens.
Because of Calcahs's admonition the Greeks
Have made this giant effigy to atone
For the insult to the gods and in penance for
Their disastrous unholy sacrilegious act,
The violation of the Palladium.
Calchas told them to make the effigy
Enormous, to raise it up to the skies so high
That it couldn't be gotten through the gates and drawn
Within the citadel walls where it would be,
According to their ancient sheltering faith,
Guardian of the safety of the people.
If by your hands there should be any harm,
To this offering of Minerva, utter ruin
(O may this omen turn back upon the seer!)
Would then come down on Priam and the Phrygians;
But if by your hands the effigy could ascend
Into the citadel, then Asia would
Be able to take the war to the walls of Pelops,
And doom would then descend upon Greek children!'

Thus, by the guile and art of perjured Sinon,
We believed him, and therefore we became his captives,
Under compulsion of his tricks and tears,
We whom neither Tydides nor Larissean
Achilles, nor ten years, nor a thousand ships,
Could ever bring to our knees.

...

But then there is
An event even more frightful still, that comes upon us
Unprovided unforeseeing souls.
Laocoön, chosen by lot to be
The priest of Neptune, was in the act of performing
The sacrifice of a great bull at the altar
When, lo, I shudder to speak it, over the tranquil
Quiet sea that lies between the island
Of Tenedos and the mainland, there comes a pair
Of giant serpents swimming toward us, their
Immense coils writhing as side by side they make
Their steady way through the waters and head for shore,
Their breasts held high, impelling the waves before them,
Their blood-red crests held high, the rest of their bodies
Following along on the surface of the water,

LAOCOÖN, LEADERSHIP AND WISDOM

Their great sinuous backs coiling behind them;
We can hear, as they come, the sound of the foaming water
Their bodies displace; we see how with bloodshot fiery
Eyes, they gaze at the shore as they approach,
Licking their hissing mouths with their quivering tongues.
The blood drains from our faces at the sight,
As we shrink back. They reach the shore and dreadful they
Move without swerving toward Laocoön.
Then first each one of the two enwraps the little
Body of one of his two sons in its
Enfolding embrace, and pastures upon its limbs.
And then, as Laocoön is rushing, armed
To try and come to the aid of his dying children,
They seize him and bind him in their giant coils,
Twice coiling around his waist, then twice again,
Their scaly coils coiling round his throat,
Their heads and necks held high, victorious;
He struggles with his hands to get himself free
From the knots they wind around him; his priestly fillets
Are drenched in his bloody gore and the serpents' black venom.
The clamor of his horrifying cries
Rises to the stars like the loud bellowing
Of a bull, half-killed, who has broken away from the altar
And from the misjudged blow of the ritual axe
Aimed at its neck. And then the pair of dragons
Slither away and seek the shrine of fierce
Tritonia, and shelter there beneath
The feet of the goddess and her circle shield.

Then, when the people see this, there is a strange
Terror that shudders through all their hearts and they
Turn to each other and say that Laocoön
Deserved what the serpents had done to him, because
Of what he had done when he had hurled his infamous spear
Into the body of the sacred oak,
And so profaned it. This is the general cry:
'We must take the effigy to the goddess's shrine
And supplicate her divinity for forgiveness.'

And so we open up the city walls
And expose the battlements, all working together
To make this happen, fastening gliding wheels
To its giant feet, and ropes around its neck,
As halters with which to draw it to the shrine.
The fatal machine, pregnant with arms, begins

143

To climb our walls. Around it boys
And unwedded girls, joyfully singing hymns
And joyfully touching the ropes by means of which
The Horse begins to move. It climbs up through
The opening walls, and, once this is done, it rolls
Menacing into the central city – O
My country, O my Ilium, home of the gods,
O all-protecting, glorious battlements
Of Troy! Four times as it is moved, it halts
At the city gates, and four times then there is
Within the horse the sound of armor clashing,
Yet blind with fury and not knowing what
It is that we are doing we keep going
Until we have enshrined the monstrous Thing
In the citadel itself. Cassandra is there,
And even then cries out in prophecy
Of the doom that was right now coming upon us,
But by a god's command her voice was never
To be believed by Trojan ears. And we,
Unhappy people, on this our final day,
Festoon the town with celebratory garlands.

...

(Ferry, 2017: 37–46)

In these sections from the second book of Virgil's Aeneid the siege of Troy reaches a watershed. After a decade of fighting, the Greeks and their ships have, apparently, departed. The Trojans stand and ponder the empty shoreline; they really want to believe the Greeks have surrendered. Vanity creeps into the pause, aided by the crafty Sinon, whose cunning talk nudges them to the conclusions they so want to reach. They suppose their enemy has turned tail and gone home. Perhaps they have been worn down by conflict, their resources and resolve spent, their bodies hollowed-out, and their failure to win over Troy become a source of disappointment for their goddess and protector Athena. Sinon encourages them in their unspoken speculations, but suggests the fault lay back in time, to a moment of grave offence, which only now had become apparent, in the weariness of drawn out and bloody siege. Sinon suggests the Greeks finally realised their transgression, and so, accepting their punishment, they would return home vanquished, leaving in their dismal wake an offering whose immensity might expatiate their sin. In apology and tribute they build a wondrous wooden horse – her animal.

The Trojans, also exhausted, are all too ready to believe the admixture of Sinon's comment and their own faulty argument. They observe a coastline emptied of their enemy, they listen to an account of an army's departure, and imagine the motivations for building the wooden horse and leaving it behind on the beach. Bringing these sources of evidence together they reach a conclusion: after years of siege, skirmish and slaying, to which bloody repetition generations have been sacrificed, Troy has won, perhaps not in the forceful way they might have envisaged and wished for, but still. The Greek phalanxes have dissolved into the horizon leaving the city open to live and trade once more. Buoyed by their collective reasoning the Trojan leaders order the horse to be taken into the city, recalling Sinon's gentle insinuation that any city containing the horse would find immortal favour. The horse underscored the city's success and enhanced its longevity.

There has been, though, a voice of dissent (one underscored by Cassandra, forever doomed to be heard but ignored). It comes from the priest Laocoön who has been performing rites with his sons for the god Apollo. Laocoön – whose name means "he who takes care of his people" – councils the Trojans with the disciplined skepticism of a wise reasoner: leave alone what you cannot know and be suspicious of human judgement and its self-enhancing entailments. He is not persuaded the Greeks would just leave and thinks the horse looks wrong, perhaps just a little too still, as though it were holding its breath. He wants to investigate its insides, attempting to expose the ruse, and so takes a spear and starts to thrust at its wooden sides, urging the Trojans to think with the kind of cunning he suspects is embodied in this huge and improbable "gift".

Beware of Gifts from Greeks

Athena was looking upon Laocoön with some concern: the horse had been created at her instigation (through Odysseus, who, with his soldiers, was packed tightly into the speared belly) and in having worked so hard to help bring about this moment, she was fain to see it slip away. So she acts swiftly, compelling two serpents to spring from the sea and throw themselves at Laocoön and his sons, entwining and strangling the two unfortunate young boys, and then encircling and dragging their father back into the wine dark depths from whence they had been divinely summoned.

The Trojans watch in awe as this human source of doubt is swallowed entire. Still convinced the horse marks the Greeks loss of divine favour, Laocoön's watery dispatch seems to further warrant Sinon's tale. The immortals, for whom little goes un-noticed, had clearly been vexed by Laocoön's profanity in spearing an offering to a goddess: no wonder his attempt to try and divert the efficacious spring of divine will met such swift and brutal retribution. Even more reason to bring the horse into the walls and set it in front of the goddesses temple, to show no affront was meant.

With the objection removed the Trojans were left free to sleep with their self-willed importance awhile, until the wooden belly of the horse split open from within, and their city was rent utterly, from one side to the other, its life spilling hotly into the dark dust of the night.

Etymologically, tragedy is associated with the wailing of a goat – (*tragos*, goat, *aoidiā*, song) being sent in sacrifice out from the safety of the city walls and into the wilderness to atone for sins.[1] The Trojans' tragedy is a playful inverse of this, in which an already lifeless horse is brought into the walls within which Paris, Helen, Priam and Achilles were set to die, or be abused and taken as slaves. The Trojans had shown the hubris of a self-scripted sense of collective desert, and this was the consequence. They had expected the world to come and willingly open up to them because it was they who had been more diligent and dexterous than their enemy. To deserve something is to feel as though you have earned it somehow, it is an expectation warranted by your own character and to which the future must be abeyant. It was a "natural" feeling for those who have nurtured and organized their faculties in such ways as to feel they deserve praise and the boons of praise. In this case, as in many, these feelings of naturalness were marred with error.

Laocoön plays the role of a truth teller – a parrhesiast – a figure which for modern ears has been resurrected from Ancient Greece by Michel Foucault and used to remind us of how sometimes were are compelled by the feeling of truth. In Greek tragedies the parrhesiast was he or she who could not contain their awareness of a truth so apparent that it had to be told, no matter the consequences for themselves. In most myths the parrhesiast role was given to a slave, woman, prophet or outsider, typically a liminal or powerless figure, and the audience for this truth was power itself embodied in a leader who refused to listen. Cue tragedy, which lay in the necessity of refusal: being more powerful a leader would only indulge council, and was free to ignore what felt uncomfortable. Leaders had to be, and appear to be, strong and a change of heart indicated weakness: even patience was conflated with dithering. Authority has a single source and by definition those who feel the need to tell truths that run contrary to those preferred by a leader are authoring an alternative source of power.

Laocoön is not a slave, he is a leader, but of a priestly and so perhaps other worldly nature. His suspicion was to trespass into the world of everyday affairs in which his spiritual knowledge carries less authority than other more worldly figures. As is the fate of many parrhesiasts, his truth-telling ends with death. He was aware that to cope with the ungovernable and unknowable allegiances to which the gods were privy one must act cautiously and flexibly. You cannot just assert things, so he attempts to find evidence and to envisage how things might be otherwise. Yet he failed to sense the collective weariness and the willingness of others to believe what they wanted to hear. Virgil works hard in the text to persuade of this, detailing a passage events laid down in an "if… then…" chain of cause and effect, surrounded by an affective atmosphere of happy exhaustion and credulity.

From the text we learn that leaders, too, can be parrhesiasts, and that the truths they feel compelled to speak are often meant to go unheard. Even when Laocoön provides evidence of his claim his advice is not followed. It is a lesson of caution: in making knowledge claims – for example, analyzing a state of affairs and presenting the results as the basis of, and warrant for, a sound decision – the urge for clear and unambiguous statements belies what is always a contested and open scene of interpretation. The leader cannot rely on the evidence and analysis of a state of affairs to persuade others to follow along. Laocoön's single incision into the horse should have been convincing had others listened to the evidence. But they were not wanting to listen, they were diverted by voices, they were relieved and happy to have come through the war, all of which feeling conspires against Laocoön. Odysseus' trick held fast: cunning, it seems, is stronger than reason alone, for it knows when to act and when to withdraw, knowing how to operate on the back of events rather than attempt to assail or direct them (Zundel and MacKay, 2014). Virgil's text narrates how those who are cunning (metis) absorb events and work with them, by sleight of hand, without resentment or expectation that things last, aware that at any moment accident or immortal witchery can intervene: '[m]agic precisely means that no one can be worthy of happiness and that, as the ancients knew, any happiness commensurate with man is always hubris; it is always the result of arrogance and excess' (Agamben, 2007: 20). Against these machinations human effort can be charming, graceful, irascible and eventful, but also often puny, and never really in command.

As Sculpture

Unearthed in Rome in the early sixteenth century, and made perhaps in Rhodes between 200 BC–30 AD, the sculpture of Laocoön and his two sons has been held in almost peerless regard ever since. Götfried Lessing chose the sculpture to show how the visual arts (sculpture, painting) use one set of spatial signs (colours, figures) and the written arts (prose, poetry) use a different set of temporal signs (sounds and words). By extension, the signs in space have one subject matter (objects of coexisting parts and wholes) and the signs in time another (objects whose parts and wholes are consecutive). These signs (or what Lessing calls "means of imitation") are the limits of the medium and in turn the medium limits what can be conveyed.

Photo 7.1 Laocoön and his sons, or *Laocoön Group*. Marble copy made from second century BC Greek 'original'. Found in 1506 at Baths of Trajan
Source: https://commons.wikimedia.org/wiki/File:Laocoon_Pio-Clementino_Inv1059-1064–1067.jpg

The poetry of Virgil works with sounds articulated over time (and the story of Laocoön is told thus), whereas the un-named sculptor of Rhodes works with spatial volume, planes and weights in stone. It was, argued Lessing, because of this fundamental difference that the sculpture depicts the spatial form of agony inscribed into the contortions of a human body, and not the sequential effects leading up to and from the pain rendered so bleakly in Virgil's narrative. Poetry works by one sign following another, in imitation of one object succeeding another, creating the temporal sequence of a narrative, whereas in sculpture one sign was placed alongside another in imitation of one object being alongside another, the spatial parts of a whole that is immediately "there". Poetry has time and hence history woven in, sculpture has space and hence is always read in the present.

LAOCOÖN, LEADERSHIP AND WISDOM

For Lessing, these divisions of medium along the axis of time and space must be respected. If poetry or prose get spatial they can either lose coherence (as in modernist writing experiments with breaking sequential grammatical codes) or tighten to the point of dogmatic idealism (become little more than hymnal propaganda). And if sculpture becomes temporal (for example the kinetic mobiles of Naum Gabo) it achieves a lightness and elusiveness that loosen presence to the point of invisibility – it cannot signify anything. The visual and verbal arts must respect the proper limits of their mediums: writers do not sculpt and sculptors do not tell stories.

The distinction, though, cannot be taken too far. Indeed for Mitchell (2017; 1984) the distinctions evoked in the Laocoön are so fragile that he reasons Lessing himself must have been aware of them, and was deliberately playing with them. No sooner is poetry accorded the status of a temporal medium then its reliance on spatial form becomes apparent – both because events happen somewhere and are enacted by very present material things and immaterial symbols, and the poetry itself can occupy sculptural form in its shape and rhythm, acting, as Voltaire suggested, like a painting of the voice. Likewise, the moment sculpture is refused the role of storytelling, its capacity to evoke events, motives and expectations is made all the more apparent. Indeed so overlapping and indirect are these mediations that it becomes a moot question whether isolating them makes any sense at all (Rancière, 2013: 156–157).

When we look at the Laocoön group we do not sense another's pain directly, but do so by stretching quite naturally into already existing expressions of pain with which we have become familiar. And in doing so we might also start thinking of the limits of using the word pain – can a sculpture feel pain, or a wooden horse whose belly is punctured by a spear, or is it just a human experience?

So why not accept both Virgil's words and the sculpture as spatio-temporal, only differing in emphasis, one more visual while the other aural? What is to be gained from the attempt at separating the mediated differences of spatial bodies and temporal actions? The answer, Mitchell (1984: 105) argues, is a normative one of taste: *time is not a proper medium for sculpture* (so it should avoid allegory, aphorism and narrative), and *space is not a proper medium for poetry* (so it should avoid adjectival descriptions of static moments). The problem *is precisely that* poems can be speaking pictures and sculptures can be allegories, and this should be stopped, or at least acknowledged and resisted: whilst they can take on the privilege of the other, they ought to adopt a "policy" of mutual forbearance.

Lessing justifies this policing of expression as an enlightened act. If we discipline artistic practice into being configured by its medium alone, it cannot then properly be limited by political or religious interference: it is free *because* it refuses itself a wide range of representation. Lessing

149

wants to insist on this abeyance to the representational limits of different media because in being made distinct one practice cannot be governed by the criteria of another. And here comes the differently mediated lesson for leadership: art is one practice, the leadership of commercial and public organizations another. They can coexist, but always according to their own criteria, aided, thought Lessing, by a common grounding in communicative reason. Lessing is worrying not so much about contamination (after all, artists have and will continue to experiment in different mediums, and leaders with different forms of persuasive expression) but over what Rancière (2007: 39–40) calls a "dialectic reading" in which any separation of practices is itself understood as the operation of an instrumental form of rationality. This form of reason – the management of affairs – can permeate, alter and exploit the unnatural and powerful facility of art to lend prominent durability to the most fleeting of human experiences (think of sculptures depicting heroics of battle leaders then assuming political office). For Lessing, if art is subject to such managerial ministrations it ceases to be art, because the sole concern of art is the expression of the beautiful and sublime from within its proper medium; it should not be used to promulgate theologies, ennoble the aspirations of tyrants or camouflage social failings (Lessing, 1836: 16). Lessing's reading of the Laocoön becomes an attack on all those who would enlist art for their political, social and economic benefit, typically, for Lessing, nations like France and Spain whose arts were little more than a barrage of gilded propaganda and unseemly cross fertilization. Also guilty was the Roman Catholic church at whose very centre, in the Vatican, the Laocoön group was sitting. Observe how a moment of pain has been grasped in beautiful harmony, and with such a vivid and illusory force, and one can feel how viewers can be completely swept away in a florid swirl of sensory emotion and symbolic suggestion (Lessing, 1836: 29–30), at least for a while. Viewers can become stupefied, losing the rectitude and reasoned sympathy from which well-ordered and well-led societies were to be formed. Used instrumentally, the artist and poet have a power to attract and even compel irrational and "improper" thoughts and feelings in creator and audience alike, evoking vivid and provocative associations, whose illusory power crowd out truth (Lessing, 1836: 165).

Mitchell (2017) takes Lessing's argument further still, for not only is this allegorical visual art potentially deranging, it also detracts from the great, more superior art of the word (and so of text). Laocoön's scream is frozen, as is our imagination in its apprehension: we witness the moment of pain, but lack completely the context that Virgil gives us, and the critical awareness this instils in us as we attempt to read the event against its historically lit and socially structured setting. In the poetry we gain a sense of the priest's civic and paternal dedication, his increasingly urgent skepticism, his willingness to act with what Kant called maturity, his bravery and the tragedy of being overtaken by events. This awareness makes the scream more terrible still for it embeds it in the growing unity of his unfolding life: a sensation stripped from a whole history of actions lacks the rich complexity that Virgil restores as a tragic event.

Lessing's reading of Laocoön, then, sets in train an awareness of the medium of expression. It admits to the affective power of sculptural form, and warns those who aspire to be guardians of the consequences of using such imagery to seduce others. Sculpture (and we might then extend this to many different material forms, such as corporate headquarters, or symbols) can instill feelings that crowd out reasonable and critical sentiment to the point where a people can be more readily corrupted by vested interests. If it is one's interests, perhaps this is for the good, but lacking the narrative work of text it will always be an ungrounded and unreliable support. Sculptural form alone obliterates the complex run of events by which human lives are acted out. Virgil is aware of his power as a poet – he has language in which allusions, crystallizations, ironies, contraries and associations can be made to show characters acting, and how this action through time amounts to the building of character (ethos). The symbolic power of form is always weaker than reasoned argument, and reasoned argument is weaker the more the leader refuses timely and historically occasioned self-critique.

As Montage

Where Virgil works with time aided by space, and the sculpture with space aided by time, there is a third rendering of the Laocoön myth in which time and space vie with one another as equals: William Blake's engraving. For Blake, argues Mitchell (1984: 111–112), the job of the poet-illustrator, the writing artist, was to create a myth in which space and time not only co-habited, but did so to one another's mutual enhancement.

William Blake's engraving of Laocoön was taken from a cast copy of the sculpture held in the Royal Academy in London. Blake finds in the Laocoön group an embodied distillation of classicism that irks him, utterly. Unlike Lessing, he is unimpressed. Not by the artistry, but by its having been taken up by the establishment and considered a model worthy of emulation, part of a cannon to be learned rote and emulated without question. The Laocoön's sculptural power was immediately evident to Blake as to many others – from the contorted curves and gestures of shock and pain emerge a sense of the fundamental grammar of the human body. The message being taken from the form, though, was a slavish one of how to uncritically apprehend and appreciate classical culture. Classical culture was venerated as that from which we have fallen and toward which we should once more strive. The Laocoön group shows us the way. Though many believed the group had attained a perfection that

Photo 7.2 William Blake Laocoön 1826
Source: Copy B copyright © 1998 William Blake Archive

was only matched by Michelangelo's daring homage, for Blake the group was inferior precisely because of its being confined by, and understood as promulgating, timeless, humanist values associated with idealized proportions, with virtue and with proper social orders.

If one was really serious about what was timeless and infinite, better to see it in a grain of sand than in academic fashion.

Blake, like Lessing, suspects sculpture of defrauding reality by parading around as its better; as though with art the human can improve upon nature through a civilizing and disciplined attentiveness to appearance and the essential forms lying within. The painter or sculptor is an illusionist presenting the audience with the possibility of new worlds to whose grandeur and intensity casts the everyday world in a state of perpetual deficit. Lessing wants to confine the artist, so as to protect art and prevent politics from exploiting the undoubted power of image and word. Which is also a form of ordering, albeit one warranted by enlightened principles.

Blake's montage cannot abide this mediating, stabilizing order embodied in Laocoön. His vision is of an unstable, fluxing reality animated by contraries and lit from open and often half-dark horizons. There is no ideal form, either human or natural, by which our actions ought to be convened, save that of the imaginative struggle for visions that work to *transform* whatever is being produced: there are no end points, only multiple and varied imaginative production. Spatial unity gives way under the pull of different temporalities, and history becomes a patchwork of uneven association in which chronology has little place.

In Rancière's (2007: 43) terms, where settlement starts imagination stops, and Blake's work bristles with this awareness, notably his montage. It claims our attention, then disappears, a concealment that pulls you in further. It is a proto-form of what Rancière (2007: 46) calls a 'sentence image'. This kind of image not only presents itself as a combination of text and imagery but also loosens the representative ties between text and image. Are the curvaceous text lines images? Are sentences to be read literally or metaphorically, and is the conjunction with the image providing a contrary? Can the spaces between the image and text carry meaning? Blake is showing how aesthetic form can open a "sublime gap" through which the form gives over to yet new forms which are both unbound and chaotic and yet somehow in a distinct shape. Thereby the chaos is given a profoundly affecting clarity, it is neither madness nor spectacle.

For Rancière (2007: 56–59), this sublime gap of the sentence-image opens up the world in two related ways. First, as a dialectic form, the montage deliberately breaks narratives or pulls companion terms apart, so revealing one world within or behind another. The Laocoön etching presents us with a classic classical form. One that is assured in its anatomical command of the idealized human form and that was well known to an audience steeped in a tradition of appropriately reverential responses to antique perfection. The biblical motifs, Hebraic letters and bombastic political messages deliberately brush up against the image, taunting and cajoling as a cat might paw its prey. The aphorisms and conjectures gesture toward the world of hierarchical belief systems, thoughtless cultural imitation and commercial addiction that lie behind the orthodoxy of the Laocoön group, and which continue to sustain its eminence.

Why, asks Blake's etching, do we venerate this classical form? After all, he conjectures, it too is a copy, something Rome imitated from Greece.

Or maybe the original was not Greek at all, but a statue of the Hebraic god Yah with his sons Adam and Satan?[2] What is an origin, after all, and an original genius, other than a restricting and classifying genius in the making? Blake's text suggests our commitment to such values and ideals and to the mimetic ordering they set in train corrodes the way we sense the world. The corrosion comes when action, thought and events are evaluated against yardsticks. These are the evaluations that say, for example, that a sober, considered and amiable society based on commerce and manners is preferable to baroque excess. What might it be, asks Blake, to live beyond yardsticks?

Second, this giving over to new forms through the gap of the montage works by finding, in apparently dissimilar parts, forms of continuity hitherto unrecognized, a mysterious world where the "other" is also at home, whilst always remaining the "other". It is a whole whose mystery is its only ever being parts or fragments, all of which refract a unity without reliance on historical succession or creative origins. In Blake's Laocoön montage, this uneasy unity comes with the curving, insinuating lines of text in which he attempts to bring the mind into community with the body, love into community with sexual pleasure, impressions into union with vision, and the mortal with the immortal, without comparing or reconciling them.

Blake uses Laocoön to show us the deadening forces of reason which he understood very broadly as a combined production of memory (collectively gathered as the prejudices of tradition and habit), law (that which constrains expression and action through silent, generalizing and headless forms of regulation) and identified physical sensation (the obviously and immediately empirical). Under reason we live lives of division, and our nature becomes one of dividing – of dividing the world ideals from that of their orthodox imitation, of dividing one practice from another, and in turn divide ourselves continually: into different cultures, nations, groups, corporations and belief systems. We divide good from bad action, beauty from ugliness, vulgarity from refinement. And we divide one sense from another. The upshot is a life held in alignments of fearful symmetry. By contrast, the montage is a plea to re-connect across these divides, to find communion in difference, to find wisdom though an excess of possible meaning brought about when we drop the binaries and marry heaven to hell, the male to female, or innocence to experience.

It is from such a marriage of text and imagery that Lessing's fragile binaries of form and text and space and time begin to break up: "Without Contraries is no progression. Attraction and Repulsion, Reason and Energy, Love and Hate are necessary to Human existence." So in his Proverbs from Hell, Blake (1908) attempts to ambush those for whom contraries amount to error. But the ambush is a small one. He works alone, and acknowledges reason as a new and powerful form of cunning,

LAOCOÖN, LEADERSHIP AND WISDOM

not the lively responsiveness of Odysseus, but a divisive sophistry which, in his own visionary world, he embodies in the god figure of Urizen (your reason) who suggests how it should be to lead with wisdom Blake (1908):

AND Urizen read in his Book of Brass in sounding tones:—
Listen, O Daughters, to my voice! listen to the words of wisdom!
Compel the Poor to live upon a crust of bread by soft mild arts:
So shall [you] govern over all. Let Moral Duty tune your tongue,
But be your hearts harder than the nether millstone;
To bring the Shadow of Enitharmon beneath our wondrous Tree,
That Los may evaporate like smoke, and be no more.
Draw down Enitharmon to the Spectre of Urthona,
And let him have dominion over Los, the terrible Shade.
Smile when they frown, frown when they smile; and when a man looks pale
With labour and abstinence, say he looks healthy and happy;
And when his children sicken, let them die: there are enough
Born, even too many, and our earth will soon be overrun
Without these arts. If you would make the Poor live with temper,
With pomp give every crust of bread you give; with gracious cunning
Magnify small gifts; reduce the man to want a gift, and then give with pomp.
Say he smiles, if you hear him sigh; if pale, say he is ruddy.
Preach temperance: say he is overgorg'd, and drowns his wit
In strong drink, tho' you know that bread and water are all
He can afford. Flatter his wife, pity his children, till we can
Reduce all to our will, as spaniels are taught with art.
(*Four Zoas,* Night VII, Revised Version, ll. 109–129)

Blake fears that leadership is little more than this. Urizen's advice has won out, and its cruelties hidden by morals, by pomp and, above all, by the shutting down and closing off of the sublime gap through which contraries might come to enrich peoples' lives.

Laocoön, Wisdom and Leadership

The three versions of the Laocoön offer their own montage in relation to practical wisdom and leadership.

As Text

As a text, Virgil's tale of the tragic fate of Laocoön and Troy testifies both to the limits of evidential reasoning and the risks of collective myopia.

155

The Trojans are desperate for their victory and only too quick to interpret the absence of their foe as a well-earned victory. The priest demurs, and his warnings go unheeded, they are untimely and tell of a truth others do not want to hear.

Desperation, exhaustion and vanity are fertile soil for exploitation. Through cunning – *metis* – Odysseus and Athena reveal an opportunity into which they spill with wall-splitting brio. Cunning matters, and matters more when leavened by a doughty awareness of how fate and chance will also have their say. The textual story of Laocoön reveals an intimacy between leadership and cunning that often goes unacknowledged, perhaps because by definition it cannot really be pinned down and conceptualized save in tales like those we have in myth.

In leadership cunning cannot be relied on (on his serpentine travels homeward Odysseus manages to lose a lot of his men, and is enjoined to life-twisting fate way beyond his control) but in the events surrounding the downfall of Troy it works far better than the retrospective reasoning used by the Trojan leaders. Odysseus knows that humans are not equipped to stay within the certainties from which the gods are minted, but that they believe themselves to be so, creating an illusion open to manipulation. Odysseus finds the Trojans to be exemplary here. They may believe themselves to have properly read a situation of which they appear to be in control, but while believing this, it is events that are in control of them. Laocoön's entreaty that they stop and spectate on themselves awhile is lost to the excited babble of relief, giving way to pride. In enjoying the prospect of their success they do not want to remember Odysseus' cunning or Athena's implacable opposition. They lose their sense of wariness because they are no longer watching themselves. Without spectating on itself, a people are found headless and heedless. It is not a question of setting direction, but of appreciating the present from as many perspectives as are possible, hence cunning, which avoids elevation. The elevated lose hold on everyday events in which their fate is held. A lesson for leadership surely? Aim for the ground and refuse the temptations of loftiness.

Further lessons emerge from Laocoön's attempt to tell the truth. Wisdom is the experience of letting truth in; but is less about stable verified fact and more the sense of exposure. Laocoön experiences this exposure in two ways. First, as a skeptical figure Laocoön embodies a kind of scientific mode of inquiry. He is suspicious of the Greeks bearing gifts, and looks to ground his suspicion by examining the horse's belly. Laocoön is a priest of Apollo, god of truth, and his devotion to truth is borne along in a flow of skepticism by which doubt he seeks to find secure ground. As a figure he embodies the importance of seeking evidence, but also of why evidence is often insufficient. As his spear splinters the wood, groans are audible, yet the Trojans fail to acknowledge their senses, or at least hear instead the overriding sounds from the approach of a "captured"

LAOCOÖN, LEADERSHIP AND WISDOM

Greek from whose mouth the ruse continues to be spun. In his devotion to factual investigation Laocoön's fate also emblematizes its inevitable limits: evidence is often competing, and can be ignored, indeed it is almost impossible to disentangle from the habit and emotion by which it is evaluated. Perhaps, being practically wise, leadership might be better configured in awareness that the evidence is nothing beyond the event of its being spoken and heard, and these events are multiple and open.

Second, as a figure possessed by a truth that demands to be heard: Laocoön struggles to embody what is truthful. He is not a philosopher in possession of reasoned information, nor a pedagogue wanting to teach right from wrong, nor even a prophet attempting to guide a flock of believers. As a priest he might be all these things, but in this one event around which he is the active force he is a parrhesiast, someone who feels the truth so irresistibly that it compels him to speak, as a leader. From birth he has been named as he who cares for his people, it is his fate to make the attempt. The audience is at a loss, his fellow leaders especially fail to listen, and the city, like Laocoön, dies. The story reveals our very human tendency to not see what is there to see, it reveals our tendency to conceal. Further still it shows us the failure of Laocoön himself to realize this tendency, and his pain is not just felt physically and for the loss of his family, but is also felt as a failure. He is the failed leader, the one who wants to care for his people by showing the truth behind the illusion but fails because the desperation and compulsion are so strong. He offers his audience little room for manoeuvre; he does nothing to goad or seduce them into thinking his way. His is a brave but perhaps, practically speaking, stupid speech, lacking the cunning of the more successful leader Odysseus, whose embodied truth lies within the illusion, coiled and ready to spring.

As Sculpture

Lessing's endeavour to distinguish the arts from one another, and art from politics and commerce, is undertaken because he is aware of what profound affect form can have. Form does not sustain life, but can make life worth sustaining, and equally can corrupt and restrict such life by being enlisted in dogmatic idealizations. Lessing wants to keep art separate from leadership for fear its atmospheric power to move an audience will be abused. The association is a subtle one, for, as Lessing makes us aware, the skill of the Laocoön sculptor is in withholding a representation of the moment of utter grief and pain sufficiently to draw the audience in, and leadership might similarly cue itself up with such a well-managed and calculating emotional appeal (Rancière, 2013: 160).

Such an association is dangerous because the appeal of leadership should not, in the enlightened eyes of Lessing, be confined to feelings of awe, delight and distraction. Such use of form is configured through logics of instrumental reason in which an elitist, Guardian class seeks to impose its views on others, enlisting them in the service of specific interests. For many this is leadership, yet it is conditioned on the premise that a leader is already and always aware of the organizational form they wish to preside over and to which opposition is treated as both threat to be avoided and obstacle to be overcome. What began, perhaps, as the desire to investigate and know is converted into a refusal to listen (Rancière, 2007: 114), and the beguiling forms of which art is capable can be enlisted to make this refusal all the more plausible. Lessing makes us alive to the demands of this refusal, one that restricts human action to the point where life itself can be snuffed out.

As Montage

Finally, under the generative force of Blake's montaged Laocoön, good leadership can only ever be a process of indirect communication realized by nudging and harrying and provoking others through asides and conjectures and suppositions, playing with contraries. All a leader can do is to form the present order through the encouraging of productive contraries, and this forming is not at all of the kind attributed to the deliberation of a sovereign agent designing strategies for social and economic structures such as nation states or industrial conglomerates.

What Blake implies in his montage is that all leadership is suspicious. Somewhat in the spirit of Hardt and Negri's (2000) *Empire* which posits a post-national global order of procedures without centre or central control, Blake's refusal to accept the classical primacy of the Laocoön group, or even its authenticity, impels us toward a self-sustaining world of temporary alignments in which the body (personal and collective) successively attempts to bend with circumstance without relying on Guardian classes to act as guides. It is a montage that questions the need for ideals, especially the seductive ones of humanism embodied in classical forms like the Laocoön group. What appears decent is far from it.

Though Blake is referring to the sculpture, Laocoön himself becomes a figure of deep ambivalence here. He is someone who falls in with the orders of reason; following Blake's definition, Laocoön appealed to memory (as a priest he invokes tradition) to law (of the gods) and to evidence (he investigates). And in limiting himself to this he fails. He perhaps should have been more cunning, under-informing his people, toying with their sensibilities, being less direct. Cunning, though wise, is also rare, and whilst embodied in Odysseus proves effective (in a very roundabout way), it can, in others like Urizen, become oppression.

Blake's montage seems to be suggesting something else than just cunning is needed. It shows a condition of circulating orders in whose company leadership almost becomes synonymous with a kind of nomadic resistance to the rules, norms and prejudices that quite naturally take hold in peoples' lives (Blake and his wife were constantly moving from neighbourhood to neighbourhood, impelled and imperilled in equal measure by his eccentricity). The montage is not preaching outright hostility to these orders. There remains conscious ordering of sorts in the montage, and certainly in his other works such as the *Marriage of Heaven and Hell* we find the poet struggling enthusiastically to create ordered form, only they are ones which could have been many other forms and which, imaginatively, also transform, in ways that draw others alongside awhile, without this being at all a unified, organized body of divided parts.

If leadership were to learn from this condition of forming as montage it would become something noisy, and leaders, as Jacques Attali (1984: 124–126) noticed, tend to shut noise down. Noise is an irritant and distracting. What leaders tend to want is sound, the smooth, settled sound of things held in order. Before giving in to this tendency, however, they might ponder, wisely, on how without noise they are nothing: Attali uses a musical example:

> [T]he orchestra leader did not become necessary and explicit until he was legitimated by the growth in the size of orchestras. He was noise first. Later he was symbolized in abstract signs, at the culmination of a very long process of the abstraction of regulatory power.
>
> (Attali, 1984: 66)

The conductor no longer makes noise, for to do so would be barbaric. The conductor corals and harmonically institutes those who do make noise, demanding they look up in unison and comply with the directions that impose order. As with musical leaders, so leadership generally. Prompted by Blake, wisdom entails a return to noise, but not wholesale, for then chaos bulges and bursts without restraint. It is more akin to what Attali calls a dropping of the baton and a falling in with events and assuming the others, those labelled followers, will also fall in. In such a mutual falling in, 'the necessity of power no longer needs to be established. Power is; it has no need to impose itself; and the technique of conducting evolves from authority toward discretion' (Attali, 1984: 66). Blake's wisdom is a calling toward such discretion, an awareness of when to let Lent or Carnival take hold, and to then hold on for the ride.

Acknowledgements

Thank you to University of Chicago Press for permission to quote from the translation of the Aeneid by David Ferry.

Thank you to the William Blake Archive for permission to reproduce the Laocoön Copy B.

Notes

1 The etymology of tragedy is mysterious. *Tragos* (he-goat) and *aiodiā* (song) seem agreed upon, though some suggest grape and the grape harvest – *trygos* – another possible source. The nature of any ritual involving the goat is also unknown, and the possibility of its being an expulsion from a place and so a proto form of the cloth tied to the scape goat then sent into the wilderness in Jewish culture I took from a prompt in Tom McCarthy's novel *Satin Island* (2015).
2 Lessing (1836: 57–68) also speculates on the difficulty of attributing a common origin, wondering whether Virgil was influenced by the poet Pisander, and if Virgil's own reading was a remodelling of what was found in Greek tradition in which the children but not the father were mauled by the double-folding serpents.

References

Agamben, Giorgio (2007) *Profanations*. New York: Zone Books.
Attali, Jacques (1984) *Noise: The Political Economy of Music*. Translated by Brian Massumi. Minneapolis: University of Minnesota Press.
Blake, William (1908) *The Poetical Works of William Blake*. Edited by John Sampson. London, New York: Oxford University Press. Sourced from Bartleby. com, 2011. www.bartleby.com/235
Ferry, David (translator) (2017) *Virgil: The Aeneid*. Chicago: University of Chicago Press.
Hardt, M., & Negri, A. (2000) Empire. Cambridge: Harvard University Press.
Lessing, G.E. (1836) *Laocoön or The Limits of Poetry and Painting*. Translated by William Ross. London: Ridgway & Sons.
McCarthy, Tom (2015) Satin Island. London: Jonathan Cape.
Mitchell, W.T. (1984) 'The Politics of Genre: Space and Time in Lessing's Laocoön', *Representations*, 6: 98–115.
Mitchell, W.T. (2017) 'Why Lessing's Laocoön Still Matters' in *Rethinking Lessing's Laocoon: Antiquity, Enlightenment, and the 'Limits' of Painting and Poetry*. Edited by Avi Lifschitz and Michael Squire. Oxford: Oxford University Press.
Rancière, J, (2007) *The Future of the Image*. Translated by Gregory Elliott. London: Verso.
Rancière, J. (2013) *Aisthesis*. Translated by Paul Zakir. London: Verso.
Zundel, M., & MacKay, D. (2014) 'Exploring the Practical Wisdom of Metis for Management Learning', Management Learning, 45: 418–436.

8

HOW YOU WANNA GO?

Learning from the Unfortunate Rake

Matt Statler

For Mark Brennan

Memento Mori: Introducing ... the End!?!

In 1928, the influential New Orleans jazz ensemble Louis Armstrong and His Orchestra had a hit with "St. James Infirmary", a song about a man whose girlfriend has died. The man tells about going to the hospital to view her pale, lifeless body. Standing in a bar, drinking to ease his pain, the man describes the circumstances he hopes for his own eventual death.

Even as he prays for his girlfriend's well-being, he struggles to accept that she has gone. He confesses his love for her, albeit rather vainly in reference to his own character, and he asks his unnamed interlocutor – you – to help him in the future by preparing his corpse for burial. He wants to look nice, and he wants to secure a good reputation in the memory of his friends.

What does the death of a loved one mean for our lives? How should we live, knowing that one day we too will die? This question, this scene, this character, this sentiment, and this tune echo across millennia and continents. In 1960, Folkways Records collected nineteen variations of what Kenneth Goldstein referred to in the album liner notes as the "Rake cycle" of songs, providing a background and context for Armstrong's hit. This oral narrative folk tradition has been traced back to Dublin in the late 1700s, and it has been carried on and transmitted by innumerable folk musicians whose idioms have shaped the lyrics as well as the tune. The confluence of Irish and Scottish, Spanish, French and African musical traditions in early 20th-century New Orleans shaped Louis Armstrong's particular sound. But whatever the variation, this folktale deals with someone who, faced with death, reflects on the meaning of life.

What significance does this tale have for the practice of leadership in contemporary organizations? In this chapter, I develop an interpretation of "The Unfortunate Rake" that considers the images of success propagated in business schools by business students in view of the catastrophic threats currently unfolding in the Anthropocene Age. I frame the practice of leadership in reference to series of philosophical considerations about death and the affirmation of life. The chapter closes with a set of implications for contemporary leaders, including learning from the muses, engaging in collective action, and adopting an attitude of restraint.

Images of Success: Who is the Rake?

An Ambivalent Figure

The term 'Rake' abbreviates the original 'rakehell', which dictionaries tend to define as 'hellraiser'. In other words, the Rake presents the figure of a young man whose life includes excessive indulgence in pleasure. And more than just pleasure, the Rake engages in the types of pleasing activities that stimulate negative moral judgment and yet also evoke or merit careful aesthetic portrayal and appreciation. The Rake was a familiar stock character in late 17th-century theater productions in London, providing comic entertainment as well as a tragic counterpoint to the virtues of other characters. In this sense, the Rake is deeply ambivalent: compelling our attention, and eliciting our judgment.

Arising from this older dramatic and literary tradition, the Rake cycle of folk songs appears as part of the institutionalization of Christian morality within English society. It draws on people's fascination with excess, extravagant spending, libertinage, and intoxication, while it discourages listeners from engaging in such behavior. At first glance, the song serves the moral, pedagogical purpose of encouraging people "not to do as I have done" in the words of another variation made famous by Woody Guthrie in 1941, Bob Dylan in 1962, and later by the Animals in 1964, "The House of the Rising Sun".

And yet, other variations of the tale change the identity of the protagonist. The Folkways album includes the Rake alongside others, including: trooper, sailor, young man, bad girl, fair darling damsel, prostitute, cowboy, gambler, carman, lineman, lumberjack, skier, longshoreman, worker, freshman student, and professor. I assume that most readers of this textbook can identify with one or more of these figures. These variations indicate the flexibility of the narrative – the Rake appears as an indeterminate cipher that could conceal or reveal anyone.

These other variations in the song cycle also differ in terms of how innocent or blameworthy the figure is with respect to his/her fate. In some instances, the narrator's judgment is heavy-handed, and the moral of the story seems clear: fellow listeners, we should all condemn the lascivious thrill-seeker. Yet in other cases, the narrator speaks more sympathetically about a protagonist who is innocently suffering a fate foisted upon him/her by other people, or by circumstances beyond anyone's control. In these instances, the moral of the story remains for us to decide: how would we react or behave if we were in similar circumstances?

Pending moral judgment or decision, the common theme woven through all variations of the Rake cycle is that the protagonist is young, and has been living life successfully without reason to anticipate that it will soon end. The Rake cycle thus begins with an image of success, a person who lives and enjoys life, a life lived well, a good life.

Living the Good Life

Contemporary research in the fields of philosophy, psychology, and economics provides various accounts of the good life. Key concepts include: happiness, utility, thriving, flourishing, self-actualization, resilience, well-being, *eudaimonia*, etc. Each of these concepts merits further study, especially since they are associated with practical wisdom. But in the context of teaching and learning about leadership in a business school, one term that captures a broad range of values and aspirations is *success*.

In the Fall of 2017 at NYU Stern School of Business, my faculty colleagues and I asked all 600+ senior undergraduate students enrolled in thirty different sections of a course called Professional Responsibility and Leadership, *what is success?* In my section of twenty-four students, I gave them the opportunity to use LEGO bricks to build models of success. They then took turns holding up their models and describing them to the rest of the class, introducing themselves to each other and beginning a process of inquiry and dialogue about leadership, organizations, and the good life. After they had all presented, I asked them to take pictures of their own model, to post that image in an online chat forum dedicated to the class, and to write out a short description of it. I additionally asked that, once everyone had posted images and descriptions of their own models, each student should read all of the descriptions and post at least three comments in response to their classmates' images of success.

My students are all young people well-positioned to enjoy the good life – they are intelligent enough to be admitted into an elite business school, diligent enough to be enrolled in a senior capstone course, resilient enough to have survived at three years in the decadent tumult of New York City, and lucky enough to anticipate a 95% job placement rate upon graduation. Their responses to the question *what is success?* merit consideration in reference to the Rake.

As would perhaps be expected, some of them did write about money and the exercise of power:

> "Success is often measured by the amount of wealth an individual can accumulate throughout his or her life. In modern culture, it is not only important to be successful, but also to be able to display it. ... The most successful people in today's society are viewed as those with the most wealth."
>
> "It is about the freedom, the lack of barriers to see the world when and how you want ... the epitome of being a 'master of the universe'."

Written at a time when public trust in business as an institution remains at a historic low, these words could easily trigger moral condemnation. But only these two students mentioned material wealth at all – other students wrote about success in terms of fulfilling experiences and flowing with change:

> "Ultimately, I find that the greatest successes can come from meaningful experiences, when we are able to enjoy the process and celebrate each step..."
>
> "As life progresses and one encounters the different elements that shape success, the wheel will continue to spin and transform the way one perceives success – which is ever-changing with the passage of time."
>
> "...[T]he idea of success will change as we keep on living life. What may seem extremely important to me now may not be my priority in ten years, which is the reason I have left that platform completely empty right now."

Far from being ego-driven hedonists, these students appear able to see beyond themselves and consider the range of human experience and the phases and horizons of life. Other students focused specifically on the importance of gaining understanding:

> "In order to achieve success one needs to remain open-minded. Without an open mind, it becomes impossible to progress, as one never truly encounters and thinks about things from a perspective other than his/her own."
>
> "It is about achieving emotional fullness, trusting the guidance of your path, enjoying and appreciating what life gives you, as an intelligent human being."
>
> "After an entire life of self-reflection, I believe success comes from within, and is the fruit of the drive to understand not only ourselves, but the world around us."

Later in the semester, I prompted all the students to consider the political, economic, technological, and ecological systems that provide the conditions for success, so I know that they would now recognize how difficult it might be to maintain an open mind when living in extreme poverty, or to understand the world in the middle of a civil war or a natural disaster. They might concede that 'emotional fullness' has its own material underpinnings, yet their definitions of success frame materiality as means to a higher end or purpose.

But interestingly, the theme most prevalent in all the students' comments characterized success in terms of interpersonal relationships, especially friendship:

> "Friendships and relationships are the backbone of success, and nothing means success more to me than this idea."
>
> "I believe that success is not achievable without a network of people supporting you, helping you, believing in you and celebrating with you."
>
> "While monetary success and the like are appealing, having a fulfilling relationship with my parents and sibling as well as significant other and friends mean so much more."
>
> "Specifically, my success is feeling functionally valuable to coworkers, emotionally valuable to friends and family, and simply valuable to myself."
>
> "A meaningful connection can be created between mother and child, boss and employee, artist and stranger, teacher and student. Success is subjective, of course, but I think that this element of human connection is one common thread that we can all include in our definitions."

Far from triggering moral condemnation, these words written by business school students seem positively endearing. I imagine that their families and friends would feel good reading them. I certainly felt good as their professor, since the students appeared attuned to the subtlety of interpersonal relations, and reflective enough to recognize how their own well-being is entangled with the well-being of others, making my job easier from the outset. Aristotle – whose works most of my students have not and will not ever read – similarly recognized that any individual, in order to experience true '*eudaimonia*' (translated as happiness, utility, flourishing, etc.), must exist within a flourishing 'oikos' or home, and within a flourishing 'demos' or community, and within a flourishing 'polis' or city. More recently, the famous Grant Study, conducted at Harvard and tracking individual happiness and well-being over a period of more than seventy years, has provided additional evidence to support the notion that the good life depends more on the quality of our interpersonal relationships than on anything else (see Mineo, 2017).

So then, who is the Rake? For the purposes of this chapter, the student in a leadership class appears as the Rake, defining the good life in terms of establishing and maintaining good relationships with other people. In the following section, I consider why, in the cycle of songs, the Rake appears as tragically 'unfortunate'.

The Inevitability of Death: Why is the Rake Unfortunate?

Cut Down in my Prime

The Rake is unfortunate because, however successful he may be or feel, he is about to die. And while the precise cause of death differs across the many variations in the cycle, the most commonly attributed cause is syphilis. In Louis Armstrong's version of the tale, the narrator has just viewed his dead girlfriend's body. Implicitly, he knows that what killed her will soon kill him, and he knows that it is because they loved each other. In the first version of the tale included in the Folkways collection, which Goldstein claims is "sufficiently close enough to the original ballad to warrant its use as a starting point for an examination of the whole family of related parodies and recensions" (1960: 2), the Rake laments:

> And had she but told me before she disordered me
> Had she but told me of it in time
> I might have got pills and salts of white mercury,
> But now I'm cut down in the height of my prime.

Thus the tragedy of this folk narrative for students in a leadership class hinges not so much on the medicine used to treat syphilis in 19th-century England, as on the point that the same human connections enabling us to experience happiness and well-being can also lead directly to our downfall.

Of course, each of my students, all students everywhere, and every living being will die sooner or later. As time passes, individual living beings pass into and out of existence. In an essay called "That to Study Philosophy is to Learn to Die" (1580), Montaigne writes:

> Aristotle tells us that there are certain little beasts upon the banks of the river Hypanis, that never live above a day: they which die at eight of the clock in the morning, die in their youth, and those that die at five in the evening, in their decrepitude: which of us would not laugh to see this moment of continuance put

into the consideration of weal or woe? The most and the least, of ours, in comparison with eternity, or yet with the duration of mountains, rivers, stars, trees, and even of some animals, is no less ridiculous.

And yet, a premise of Montaigne's essay – and this chapter – is that we do not typically view our fleeting existence as ridiculous. Instead, the inevitability of our death, "if it frights us, 'tis a perpetual torment, for which there is no sort of consolation" (1580). I dwell on the conditional "if" in this quote, but Montaigne's claim prompts an initial, albeit counterintuitive question: if death is inevitable, why does it provoke fear or sadness in the first place? Why would death not be one of many commonplace, unremarkable, or even banal features of our human experience, like cleaning our teeth or scratching an itch? When it happens, we would accept it and move on: why not?

It is difficult to answer this simple question without making broad pronouncements about life itself. Do not all things that live seek to survive rather than perish? Indeed, if suddenly all living creatures were to become indifferent to the continuation of their own lives, would life not come to a rather hasty end? We might presume that the basic impetus to survive may be 'mute', lacking conscious awareness of itself, or driven by some other, unknown animating force. Yet still, in view of the many animal and human behaviors that appear to involve deliberate and careful preparation for the future, we can hardly deny the apparently natural drive to live and thrive, rather than die.

Evolutionary theorists would concede, however, that the mechanisms of natural selection and adaptation are far from perfectly efficient. Moreover, many human traits and behaviors may be interpreted in reference to objectives other than distributing one's genetic material to subsequent generations. People feel attached to things they care about, and these feelings draw on memories as well as cultural narratives. They constitute our identities, and they motivate our efforts to strive, to imagine and to think rationally about the future and take actions to realize our desires and aspirations. These feelings additionally shape how we evaluate individual and collective efforts to survive, and how we judge the character of individual people whom we think of as 'leaders'.

But irrespective of our judgment, ultimately all efforts will fail – astrophysicists describe the eventual end of the universe in terms of 'heat death', anticipating a future point in time when all of the energy generated by the big bang will eventually dissipate, and entropy finally wins. However we might feel about this inevitability, we cannot deny that in the meantime a great deal of human energy is devoted to making sense of life and death and trying to deal with the fact of dying.

A Story of Our Time

The narratives that help make sense of death most familiar to students in a leadership class are likely spiritual, religious, or theological. Speaking about the Protestant Lutheran Christian tradition in which I was personally raised, the story is that when our bodies die, our souls do not. If we have been baptized in the church, sincerely sought God's forgiveness for our bad behavior, and accepted Jesus Christ as our one and only savior, then our souls can rise to heaven where they exist eternally by the grace of God. In my experience, such narratives can provide consolation to the bereaved, as well as guidance for how to act while alive. What greater relief than the assurance that our dearly departed is now in heaven, a much better place than earth? What greater sanction for non-compliance with the church's doctrines than the threat of eternal torment in hell? Of course, other religious traditions frame the circumstances surrounding death differently. Accordingly, anyone raised or educated in such a tradition can reflect similarly on the stories about life and death that they were told as children as well as the stories that they tell themselves now.

But beyond religion, there are many other secular narrative traditions in and through which people reflect on dying, and try to make sense of death. Again, personally for me the ancient Greek and Roman philosophical tradition of stoicism has been particularly compelling, with its emphasis on discernment, acceptance, and equanimity in the face of death as well as all suffering. Also personally influential for me is the musical genre of the blues. The following section of this chapter addresses these concepts more directly, weaving them into an interpretation of the American blues tradition in which the Rake cycle of songs can be situated.

As I gesture toward these ancient and contemporary religious and secular narratives as part of this interpretation of the unfortunate Rake, they appear particularly poignant in our contemporary historical time period: the so called Age of the Anthropocene. This term has been introduced in recent years by scientists to describe our current geological epoch, in which the planet is shaped by human activity. Geologists offer different kinds of evidence to support this claim, including everything from the presence of radioactive nuclear isotopes, to the layer of carbon soot residue, to the large-scale tunnels and excavations generated by mining operations. While none of these factors alone focuses our attention on death per se, biologists are increasingly recognizing that human influence is triggering an extinction event across the globe and throughout the biosphere. Elizabeth Kolbert's book *The Sixth Extinction* (2014) gathers and presents evidence of this event – which began several thousand years ago with large fauna and is now impacting smaller fauna as well as terrestrial and marine flora – and it attributes causality to human influence.

In this sense, any contemporary consideration of death (no less than life) must include consideration of entire ecosystems, the 'natural capital' that provides the material basis for our economic systems, including the institutions of business, society, and especially government as well as the flows of information, goods, and services throughout the globalized world. The most recent World Economic Forum's Global Risks Report (2017) provides a striking snapshot in which senior executives, policy-makers, and government officials appear to believe that the most catastrophically disruptive trends (including political, cultural, and environmental factors) are also becoming increasingly more likely.

So then, just as we may be in our prime, savoring the benefits of technologically advanced civilization, we may find ourselves confronting the prospect of ecological collapse, and with it, the end of humanity as we know it. And like the Rake, our tragedy is that we have collectively brought this fate upon ourselves and the entire dying planet.

Montaigne urges us to waste no time in reflecting on the situation, writing in 1580 that:

> They go, they come, they gallop and dance, and not a word of death. All this is very fine; but withal, when it comes either to themselves, their wives, their children, or friends, surprising them at unawares and unprepared, then, what torment, what outcries, what madness and despair! Did you ever see anything so subdued, so changed, and so confounded? A man must, therefore, make more early provision for it[.]

Following this line of thinking, the 'unfortunate' circumstance of the Rake cannot be dismissed as a speculative, esoteric matter best considered by philosophers or clerics, or as a technical problem properly addressed by engineers in an ecomodernist fashion. Instead, because the fate of humanity hinges at least in part on the day-to-day decisions and actions of each of us, we should all "make more early provision for it".

Life Facing Death: How You Wanna Go?

I Ought to Know

Blind Willie McTell sings a version of the Rake ballad called "The Dyin' Crapshooter's Blues". In this version, the protagonist is a gambler named Jesse who has been shot by the police, and the narrator has carried him home and is nursing him while he is "sick from the shot". As Jesse's death approaches, a "gang of crapshooters" gathers around his bedside.

Whether mourning the death of a loved one, anticipating our own death, or recognizing the catastrophic risks confronting humanity in the Anthropocene Age, the question arises, how should we live?

We could of course ignore death's inevitability, focusing on other matters. In the passage quoted on p. 169, Montaigne describes how this approach can sometimes work for people until they are confronted with the death of a loved one, and then because they have not prepared themselves, they are outraged and experience more extreme suffering.

In a recent best-selling book, *Being Mortal* (2014), a surgeon named Atul Gawande describes how death has been framed by modern medicine as an event that happens not in the home, but in an institution such as a hospital. He emphasizes that while the technological advancements in the field of medicine have made this the best time in human history to enjoy old age, the institutionalization of death (together with the consolidation of the power to avoid it in the figure of the scientist-doctor) may have the effect of intensifying the fear and suffering experienced both by the dying and the bereaved. Following this line of argument, even as life expectancy rates have risen, and infant mortality rates have fallen, our fear of death has intensified because we think of it as a problem to be solved by experts. In other words, we suffer death more when we try to ignore it.

So if instead we choose to follow the advice of Montaigne and Gawande and consider death carefully, and in so doing, change our relationship to it, what then? Surely, one possibility involves depression and nihilism. Yet another possibility exists, and we can identify it in reference to the example of the Unfortunate Rake.

Rolling Along

Roger McGuinn, founder of the influential folk rock group The Byrds, recorded a version of the Rake cycle and released it on a 2004 album called *Stories, Songs and Friends*. He calls his version "Gambler's Blues", and picking up where the "Dyin' Crapshooter" left off, he includes lyrics to describe how he wants to go.

While singing, the narrator is not yet dead, and he anticipates that his friends will survive. Since the narrator is the Unfortunate Rake (and not the fop, another stock character in Restoration comedy), it follows that their friendship involves having fun together, enjoying life as much as they can. For the Rake, the good life involves having fun together with friends, and when anticipating his own demise, he affirms their lives together and expresses his desire to have fun in the future. Nietzsche's phrase describing this attitude is: *"amor fati"*:

> My formula for greatness in a human being is *amor fati*: that one wants nothing to be different, not forward, not backward, not in all eternity. Not merely bear what is necessary, still less conceal it – all idealism is mendaciousness is the face of what is necessary – but *love* it.
>
> (Nietzsche, 1974: 258)

The love of fate, of what is fated, the affirmation of whatever may transpire or exist extends beyond endurance and fatalism. Such an attitude may seem practically impossible to sustain on an individual level, especially when your beloved has died and you know that you are next. Rather than grasping for comfort from a story about the afterlife, contemporary theologian Mark Taylor interprets Nietzsche's claim as a critique of redemptive narratives:

> There is neither life after death nor any other world than this one. The challenge, then, is not to live a life of denial that supposedly prepares one for the next world, but to live the fullest life possible in the only world there is.
>
> (2018: 50)

What then is the 'fullest life possible'? According to my students, it involves understanding and community, and an attitude of acceptance as things change. According to Nietzsche, it involves living as if every moment would return again and again eternally, affirming it with joy:

> Did you ever say 'Yes' to one joy? Oh my friends, then you also said 'Yes' to *all* pain. All things are entwined, enmeshed, enamored – did you ever want Once to be Twice, did you ever say 'I love you, bliss – instant – flash' then you wanted *everything* back. – Everything anew, everything forever, everything entwined, enmeshed, enamored – oh, thus you love the world – you everlasting ones, thus you love it forever and for all time; even to pain you say: Refrain but – come again. *For joy accepts everlasting flow!*
>
> (Nietzsche, 1978: 335)

Recalling Montaigne's conditional "if it frights us…" from earlier in this chapter, we can now identify not only fearlessness or courage in the Rake who is rehearsing his own death in song, but joy. According to Jesse the dying crapshooter, the life that merits joyful affirmation includes:

Sixteen real good crapshooters
Sixteen bootleggers to sing a song

Sixteen racket men gamblin'
Couple tend bar while I'm rollin' along

With these words, the Rake affirms the life that is his, the fate that has befallen him, the relationships he has with his friends, and the activities he enjoys. Together, he and his friends 'raise hell as *we* roll along', where the Rake includes himself in their activity even though he will at that time no longer be actively participating. The Rake wants to die as he has lived, and yet as he lives, he sings the blues about dying.

Montaigne (1580) provides an interesting account of why singing the blues can alleviate the fear of death:

> ...to begin to deprive him [death] of the greatest advantage he has over us, let us take a way quite contrary to the common course. Let us disarm him of his novelty and strangeness, let us converse and be familiar with him, and have nothing so frequent in our thoughts as death. Upon all occasions represent him to our imagination in his every shape; at the stumbling of a horse, at the falling of a tile, at the least prick of a pin, let us presently consider, and say to ourselves, 'Well, and what if it had been death itself?' and, thereupon, let us encourage and fortify ourselves.

In this sense, a blues song that appears first as morose and depressing becomes exultant and thrilling – we who sing the blues are not dead! Montaigne continues: "The premeditation of death is the premeditation of liberty; he who has learned to die has unlearned to serve." Here, liberty is defined negatively in terms of the absence of servitude, but the point is that we who sing the blues realize how very much alive we are. We also realize how precious this time is, how important it is to live intensively. Montaigne again: "For anything I have to do before I die, the longest leisure would seem too short, were it but an hour's business I had to do." Thus in addition to positive affect (joy!), reflections on death can have the effect of motivating people to keep moving, keep rolling along rather than collapse in sadness and depression.

I recognize that the figure of the Rake, no less than the appeal to Nietzsche's life-affirming philosophy, could be easily misinterpreted as some kind of truly nihilistic hedonism, wherein YOLO ('You Only Live Once') becomes a justification for any kind of behavior with any kind of consequences. More broadly, the Rake might be criticized as a personification of precisely the socio-pathology that allows the richest .01% of the world's population to keep having fun while planetary ecosystems collapse. I believe, however, that the Rake's embracing, affirmative attitude toward death holds a series of important lessons for people who want to study and practice leadership in the Anthropocene Age. I outline these implications in the following section.

Jazz Band on the Tailgate: Of What Do the Muses Sing?

Leadership by the Muses

One important implication of the unfortunate Rake for leadership study and practice has to do with the medium in which this particular folktale has been cultivated, and the musical cultural tradition to which it explicitly refers. Though it draws on an older theatrical tradition, the Rake cycle occurs in *song*. Why would the Rake, or anyone else, want a song to be sung about him at his funeral? Again the traditional words:

> Six chorus girls to sing my song.
> Put a jazz band on my tailgate
> To raise hell as we roll along.

The governments of the Netherlands and New Zealand have jointly funded the development of a website called Theoi (www.theoi.com) focused on ancient Greek mythology and religion which includes original written accounts of the Greek traditions alongside extensively researched and annotated excerpts from the classical texts, with translations drawn from the public domain. The Mousai page begins by stating that "The Mousai (Muses) were the goddesses of music, song and dance, and the source of inspiration to poets. They were also goddesses of knowledge, who remembered all things that had come to pass" (www.theoi.com/Ouranios/Mousai.html).

The specific roles associated with particular deities varied over time – "originally, three were worshipped on Mount Helicon in Boeotia, namely Melete (meditation), Mneme (memory), and Aoede (song)", and eventually, the number grew to nine, and the areas of specialization included: epic poetry, history, lyric poetry, tragedy, choral dance and song, erotic poetry and mimicry, the sublime hymn, astronomy, and comedy (www.theoi.com/Ouranios/Mousai.html). If indeed memory, song, and meditation provide a basis for all knowledge, then I believe this list of the Muses and their specialties can be interpreted as a curriculum for leadership practice.

While the differentiation of the activities that happen by the Muses by the Greeks provides us with a starting place from which to develop a leadership curriculum, surely other ancient and contemporary folk traditions have alternative accounts of the various human activities that bring creativity and the imagination to bear on the practical challenges associated with living the good life. What we today call music or folk narrative shares key elements with other disciplines including not only what we consider the fine and performing arts, but also history, literature (including all manner of contemporary media productions), astronomy, etc.

These contemporary academic disciplines – and the folk traditions they arise from and reflect upon – provide the fabric for culture and society. They exist and extend far beyond any individual contributor, narrator, etc. And they provide us with sources of insight and chronicles of experience from people who we will never personally know. These sources go beyond popular culture or globalization to include the deep cultural and even ecological roots of rhythm and form. As we students and scholars of leadership participate in these practices, they can sustain and nourish us, and we them by sharing. The activities that occur 'by the muse' can enable leaders to emerge, and leaders can draw from and participate in them, changing them (or not).

Leadership scholars have focused in recent years on art and aesthetics (see Hansen et al., 2007), and this book contributes to this broader literature. Researchers have connected music with the ability to lead in times of crisis (see Bathurst et al., 2010). Yet more research is needed to interpret leadership practice in terms of song, melody, and rhythm. In order to describe these dynamics, we can draw on process ontologies of leadership (see Helin et al., 2014).

But pending future study, the particular contribution of the Rake cycle to this stream of academic research literature on aesthetics and leadership is to present *the jazz funeral* as a cultural practice in which organizations – i.e., jazz bands – emerge spontaneously as the hearse rolls along the streets of New Orleans.

Leadership as Collective Action

In the jazz funeral, leadership appears as a negative or contingent phenomenon, a need that emerges among people. Within formal, hierarchically organized structures, the formal position carries considerable force, surely. And sometimes leaders within formal organizations have distinct and unique responsibilities to guide others not just by setting an example but also by holding other people accountable to replicate the example. But even the exercise of leadership within the most hierarchical structure still depends on followership.

In this sense, leadership involves acting in a way that prompts others to act similarly, and the relationship is reciprocal: leaders and followers relate to each other through a role modeling logic of imitation, call, and response. Of course, mimetic imitation can involve all manner of life-denying cruelty. But it can also involve attunement to natural rhythms and cycles, and in the Anthropocene Age the need for such attunement is becoming increasingly undeniable.

HOW YOU WANNA GO?

But whether any of us are able to strike a balance with nature, the point of the jazz funeral as a metaphor for organization is that leadership appears not as an individualized phenomenon, but as plural, multiple, and distributed. This shift of conceptual and methodological focus has been noted by leadership researchers (Denis et al., 2012), and it moves us not only beyond the archetype of heroic pattern. Rather with this post-heroic orientation it moves also beyond mimesis and into the simulacrum. In the ballad of the Unfortunate Rake, who is the singer? As we sing the ballad, does the song sing us? Nietzsche addresses this phenomenon in *The Birth of Tragedy* using the religious vocabulary of his early work:

> Now the gospel of universal harmony is sounded, each individual becomes not only reconciled to his fellow but actually at one with him – as though the veil of Maya had been torn apart and there remained only shreds floating before the vision of mystical Oneness. Man now expresses himself through song and dance as the member of a community; he has forgotten how to walk, how to speak, and is on the brink of taking wing as he dances. Each of his gestures betokens enchantment; through him sounds a supernatural power...He feels himself to be godlike and strides with the same elation and ecstasy as the gods he has seen in his dreams. No longer the *artist*, he has himself become a *work of art*: the productive power of the whole universe is now manifest in his transport, to the glorious satisfaction of the primordial One.
>
> (Nietzsche, 1956: 22–24)

With regard to eudaimonia, happiness, pleasure, utility, fulfillment, positive emotions, etc., what is 'glorious satisfaction'? As noted earlier, there are diverse opinions about how to define these terms as well as about how these concepts relate to action or motivation. For leadership scholars, it makes a difference how we define such terms because they can help us pragmatically to organize people so that these positive experiences increase or intensify. And if they do not help us create glorious satisfaction, then perhaps they can at least contribute to our survival. But key questions remain: should we attempt to survive at scale, with ever more people? Should we attempt to survive at scale over time, extending humanity into the future? If indeed leadership appears as post-heroic, trans-individual, or collective practice, then which collective, acting as such for how long, and serving which purpose?

The Mediterranean cultures that gave rise to the Stoic tradition witnessed the rise and collapse of empires, but they had not yet confronted the resource horizon at the planetary scale. Now, we become aware of the global tragedy of the commons, with no further resource horizon other

than technological innovation (enabling more efficiency) or space exploration (providing more resources and/or *Lebensraum*). So how could we
claim to be having fun, affirming life, while foolishly wasting resources
and moving further into an ecocidal 'Age of Man'?

Things take time to change, and we are still living in the conceptual, political, and material systems that were constructed prior to the
Anthropocene Age. I believe that the key for leadership practice is therefore to participate in the process of adjusting and adapting these existing
systems. Additionally I believe that leaders should seek not to police judgments about what is bad, but instead, to question claims about what is
good. In the Anthropocene Age, leaders can raise critical questions about
what actions can contribute to human flourishing, questioning those
unsustainable actions that appear to erode the basis for it.

Leadership as Non-Doing

For the last several centuries or perhaps much longer, the familiar figures
of successful political leaders in government have engaged in activities
such as winning wars, conquering new territories, building and maintaining empires. In the context of business, the figures appear even more
consistently and clearly to engage in expanding a profitable enterprise,
developing and commercializing new technologies, motivating employees
to work harder for less pay, etc. In civil society, the figures of leadership
build coalitions, refine cultural identities, advocate for and achieve emancipation and justice for those who need it. We tend to associate or attribute wisdom to people who have been able to achieve such outcomes, and
we tend to presuppose a causal relationship whereby individual people
took actions that had identifiable results.

I believe that the Anthropocene Age has come about in no small part
because of the value placed on individual, rational action. Bruno Latour
dissects this value and claims that science, religion, and politics have all
colluded on a portrayal of the relationship between man and the world
that can no longer be credibly sustained (2017). We are not only acting
on a passive world, the world acts on us as well, and our existence is
always embedded in and entangled with other living beings and ecological systems.

In this context, wise leadership increasingly appears to involve the
exercise of restraint, affirming less rather than more, slowing rather than
accelerating, cultivating the past rather than creating the future, etc.
In this sense, wise leadership would appear to involve relatively more
non-doing rather than doing; marking the limits of knowledge rather
than extending them; shifting into a more circular and harmonious relationship with natural ecosystems rather than seeking to dominate them
through technology or organization; and thinking less in terms of linear

time moving like an arrow toward a redemptive apocalypse and more in terms of spiraling or recursive cycles of *songs*.

References

Bathurst, R., Jackson, B., & Statler, M. (2010). Leading aesthetically in uncertain times. *Leadership*, 6(3), 311–330.

Denis, J. L., Langley, A., & Sergi, V. (2012). Leadership in the plural. *The Academy of Management Annals*, 6(1), 211–283.

Gawande, A. (2014). *Being mortal: medicine and what matters in the end* (Vol. 36). New York: Metropolitan Books.

Goldstein, K. S. (1960). *The Unfortunate Rake: a study in the evolution of a ballad*. Washington DC: Smithsonian Folkways Records.

Hansen, H., Ropo, A., & Sauer, E. (2007). Aesthetic leadership. *The Leadership Quarterly*, 18(6), 544–560.

Helin, J., Hernes, T., Hjorth, D., & Holt, R. (Eds.). (2014). *The Oxford handbook of process philosophy and organization studies*. Oxford: Oxford University Press.

Kolbert, E. (2014). *The sixth extinction: an unnatural history*. New York, NY: Henry Holt & Co.

Latour, B. (2017). *Facing Gaia: eight lectures on the new climatic regime*. Hoboken, NJ: John Wiley & Sons.

Mineo, L. (2017). "Good Genes are Nice, but Joy is Better" *Harvard Gazette*.

Montaigne, M. (1580). "That to Study Philosophy is to Learn to Die" *Essays of Michel De Montaigne*. Translated by Charles Cotton, Edited by William Carew Hazilitt 1877. Accessed at: www.gutenberg.org/cache/epub/3583/pg3583.html

Nietzsche, F. (1956). *The birth of tragedy and the genealogy of morals*. Translated by Francis Golffing. New York: Doubleday.

Nietzsche, F. W. (1974). *The gay science: with a prelude in German rhymes and an appendix of songs* (Vol. 985). New York: Vintage.

Nietzsche, F. W. (1978). *Thus spoke Zarathustra: a book for all and no one*. New York: Penguin.

Taylor, M. C. (2018). *Last works: lessons in leaving*. Yale University Press.

World Economic Forum. (2017). *Global risks report*. www.weforum.org/reports/the-global-risks-report-2017

9

THE STORY OF MERLIN AS A TALE OF WISDOM

Wendelin Küpers

Introduction

For many, the figure Merlin appears not only as the paragon of a magician, but also as wisdom incarnate.

Imagine if we would ask a reincarnated Merlin – as representing an acclaimed wise figure – about what he would think is generally over- and undervalued today by people, economies and societies or organizations and in leadership: what would he answer?

How would he, as an archetypical figure, see the role and importance of qualities of wisdom in our contemporary world? Can we still resonate with what Merlin stood and stands for proto-typically, in relation to the capability to ask about and to do the right thing, at the right time, for the right reason? How could this exemplary figure help us to understand how and when we can choose the right means for attaining the right ends, nowadays, and for a tomorrow to come? Or how would he respond to the quests and questions about what the main obstacles are that prevent young adults and supposedly mature people from living in a way that is practically wise? What would he say and offer concerning the question why it makes sense to become wise, in a world that is so different compared to his past incarnations, but which still and even more calls for enacted practical wisdom?

The intentional proposition of this chapter will be that listening to and reinterpreting the story of Merlin may contribute to dealing with the current dearth of wisdom and the need to cultivate and learn the same, in particular in leadership and organizations (Küpers & Gunlaugsson, 2017; Küpers & Pauleen, 2013). Accordingly, the aim will be to listen to messages inspired by him and what he represents that offer wise advice in relation to nature and for our contemporary society and economy as well as our organization and leadership practices, marked by hubris and other unwise realities and practices. The latter ones include hyper-accelerated lives, hyper-corporatized pursuits of short-term growth and features of monstrous zombie-like hydras of hyper-capitalism or "capitalist monster-ology" (McNally, 2011: 2).[1]

In a time characterized by a lack of prudent reasoning and absence or underdeveloped wisdom of individuals, communities, organizations and leadership that are increasingly dominated by functional stupidity,[2] and amoral or unethical practices, there is a 'sage' message in retelling stories of proto-wise figures, like that of Merlin. Therefore, the starting point and guiding proposal will be that the legend of and stories about Merlin have important 'lessons' or inspirations for us and organizations, also in relation to their stakeholders. These possible insights and learnings will be explored, especially with regard to envisioning futures, prophecies, mentoring and counselling, especially for political leadership strategically (King Arthur, Camelot), institutionalizing value-based forms of governance (Round Table), and adventurous quests for integration (Holy Grail, Wild Man, Love Spell).

As we will see, in all his various forms and in many different ways, Merlin embodies and may inspire wise practices for our meandering journeys today and for sustainable moves towards tomorrow. But it is challenging to reinterpret what it means and implies to find wisdom with regard to Merlin in our personal and transpersonal quests and for lifeworlds of organization and leadership. We cannot simply follow or imitate an easy role-model or apply clear-cut templates with unequivocally transferable patterns.

Ambivalently, Merlin, and what he signifies, remains furtive, being both dark and bright, mysterious, enigmatic, thus elusive, full of conflicting identities and mixed messages.

Merlin is 'Other', and his otherness is based on his strange connections to a secretive past origin, ways of anticipating future foresight and acumen as well as magical influences, supposed supernatural abilities and subversive powers.

In a certain way Merlin is an axial figure, who symbolizes a transition from ancient pagan practices and the newly arrived Christian imperatives in Europe as illustrated by the Grail quest, undertaken by the Knights of the Round Table of Camelot. However, as much as he is centre-staged, he also is marginalized, revealing a contradictory portrayal and 'otherings', overruled by his passion, that have been connected to this rise and fall (Ying-hsiu, 2014).

What fascinates me, and others, is that he appears as a projective medium, who has provided a rich, imaginative diversity concerning his development as a fictional character over time, in different contexts and cultures. Being a complex figure and playing all kinds of roles in the past, he is offering imaginaries for our times and perhaps for a more sustainable future to come. Provoking and evoking, with his enthralling weirdness and secretive eeriness (Fisher, 2017),[3] and in all his varieties, Merlin appears as an embodiment and emblem for practical wisdom. This is a wisdom that is not just a reason-based individual capability, but resonates with and integrates pre-personal, personal and transpersonal dimensions.

All these qualities refer to an individuation process that – independent and critical of Jung's understanding – is situated between pre- and post-individuation in the sense of Merleau-Ponty (1995) as an inter-relational event of a post-foundational becoming. Moreover, this individuation may be related to Simondon (1995, 2007) as a meta-distable transductive amplification, or to Deleuze (1990, 2005) as a differentiating and inten-sifying involution (Alloa & Michalet, 2017). As such, Merlin provides a referencing folio or medium for considering not only propositional, explicit knowledge, but also presentational, implicit knowing, felt senses and an extended sense-making.

Studying him is like going backwards to move forward. It allows revis-iting and juxtaposing positions and contexts of pre-modern spheres, before the modern trajectories of materialist, utilitarian ideologies and post-modern relativism took prevalence. Retelling, reconstructing and reinterpreting the story and mythos or myth-making (mythopoeia) of Merlin can serve as a critical reference and valuable source for what wis-dom was, is and could be, especially in relation to organizations and leadership. Accordingly, the following once again invites us to hear about the narrative of Merlin. It will be a tale of wisdom and of a figure, who served as a proto- and arche-typical character of the same.

Merlin as Arche-Type

The adult Merlin fully exemplifies the Jungian archetype of the wise old man – young at heart – who appears in dreams in the guise of magician, healer, shamanic priest, wonder-worker, teacher, grandfather or any other

THE STORY OF MERLIN AS A TALE OF WISDOM

male possessing authority playing roles of mediation and integration. In general, an archetype refers to an exemplary proto-type or 'model' and pattern of behaviour and 'complex' that is a combination or clusters of emotional issues and dynamics, drawn from past, present and even the future.

Partly inspired by Platonic and Kantian ideas of (pure) forms and energetic a priori modes, for the post-Freudian tradition of Jungian psychology, an archetype is a collectively inherited subconscious image or archaic pattern of thought. Importantly, and ambivalently, for Jung the so-called sub- or unconscious is not only full of wild and destructive drives, it is also the source of creativity, spirituality and the capacity for more mature relationships.

As such, archetypes are universally present and offer potentials for individual and collective psyches, expressed as a constantly recurring symbol or leitmotif. Archetypes are collective in the sense that they embody the general characteristics of a thing rather than its specific peculiarities. As refined elements or generative forms, derived from the collective unconscious, archetypes can only be explored indirectly by examining expressions via rituals or in symbols, images, dreams or myths.

That is why they are articulated in revealing works of art, like paintings, or literature and mythologies. Being an inherited potential, or "active living dispositions ... that pre-form and continually influence our thoughts and feelings and actions" (Jung, 1954: par. 154; in Stevens, 2006: 79), archetypes can be 'actualized'. They are actualized, when entering consciousness as living images or manifesting in leitmotifs, enacted in behaviour or interaction with the outside world (Stevens, 2006).

> The archetype in itself is empty and purely formal, nothing but a facultas praeformandi, a possibility of representation which is given a priori. The representations themselves are not inherited, only the forms, and in that respect they correspond in every way to the instincts, which are also determined in form only.
>
> (Jung, 1954: par. 155, in: Stevens, 2006: 78)

As such, archetypes are somehow 'autonomous' and hidden or unfilled forms. They are transformative and transformed once they enter consciousness and are given particular expression by individuals and their cultures. Combining the universal with the individual, the general with the unique, archetypes are both: common to all humanity, but manifested in every individual in a manner peculiar to persons (Stevens, 2006: 79). Of course, history, culture and (inter-)personal context influence and shape these manifest representations and thereby give them their specific contents and developments.

Interestingly, "archetypes ... manifest themselves only through their ability to organize images and ideas" (Jung, 1954: par. 44). However, Jung emphasized that the archetype was not an arid, intellectual concept, but "a living, empirical entity, charged not only with meaningfulness, but also with feeling, thus is s a piece of life, a living system of reactions and aptitudes" (Jung, 1953–1978: par. 339). Accordingly, as a systems of images "it is connected with the living individual by the bridge of emotion" (Jung, 1961: par. 589, in Stevens, 2006: 80), and powerfully, it cultivates a readiness for action (Jung, 1953–1978: par. 53 see also Stevens, 2006: 80).

For Jung, the arche-typical actualization determines the degree to which the over-riding goal of individuation is achieved, thus how they are evoked, constellated and actualized proceeds in accordance with the laws of association, in particular the law of similarity and the law of contiguity in relation to complexes. These complexes are functional units, which make up the personal unconscious, just as the collective unconscious is composed of archetypes. Furthermore, the constellated archetype is always the primordial image that relates to the need of the moment (Jung, 1911–1912: par. 450, in Stevens, 2006: 86).

Relating to another most fascinating phenomenon, Jung believed that also synchronicity as the expression of an acausal orderedness is dependent upon archetypal functioning. Thus, archetypes are connected to those meaningful coincidences "in time of two or more causally unrelated events which have the same or similar meaning" (Jung, 1952: par. 849 in Stevens, 2006: 89).

With Jung, archetypes can be interpreted as a sort of mental therapy for the sufferings and anxieties of mankind in general. When individuation is achieved with the help of archetypes of wisdom and power along the path, the conscious and unconscious body-minds, with all their lights and shadows, are in resonance and the body-soul-spirit is at peace. Not at peace with this Jungian interpretation have been various fundamental critiques, including essentialism.[4] Nevertheless, different applications of archetypical approaches have been developed and employed also in relation to organization and management, showing its explanatory and interpretative value.[5]

Merlin as Archetype of Magician and Wise Man: Being a Multitude

According to the outlined Jungian interpretations, in Merlin specific archetypical patterns and images with particular intensive constellated form and contents can be discovered and realized. Merlin corresponds to the archetypal Gestalt of the magician and wise man, who in its mature form tries to integrate oppositions and inner splitting, for example concerning his bipolar shadows.[6]

The wise old man here represents the highest and wisest resources of the 'sub-conscious' and the spiritual, serving as medium for the

THE STORY OF MERLIN AS A TALE OF WISDOM

transformation of the self (Gollnick, 1990). "Merlin is a symbolic model of transformed consciousness: his movements and his utterances are highly amplified, even exaggerated, archetypified" (Steward, 1986: 227). "The Life of Merlin is an exemplary magical and spiritual life-pattern for the (trans-)personal growth of the (Western) psyche; it demonstrates clearly the feminine and masculine powers and polarities in a systematic development, leading to a continuing insight" (Steward, 1986: 408). With all these and further facets, Merlin is not a simple archetype or person(ality), but a multi-tude and compound of various, different qualities and multilayered dimensions that were projected or placed on him as a folio. Accordingly, over the passage of time, he was given all kinds of characters and played various roles. These roles ranged from wild man and Celtic shaman, foreknowing prophet, far-seeing druid and judicious judge, charming enchanter, heretic sorcerer or gaseous wizard. Thus, he re-presented all the major types of magician, functioning as an astute and imaginative seer, astrologer, cosmologist and proto-alchemist. As such he is one, who was moving at the cutting edge of old 'science', while his powers were convincingly 'real'. But he was also seen as an artfully poetic bard, and seductive or subversive 'wise-foolish' trickster, and tragic romantic lover, all outlined in the following sections. As an influential practitioner, he functioned as educator, mentor, king-maker and adviser or counselor, and political consultant. Practically, he served as engineer, architect and project manager, who shaped and shifted things, people and realities. Moreover, he was playing the roles of a travelling scholar and creative artist as storyteller; hence overall a singular, interstitial but culturally diverse character.

Being an 'in-betweener', Merlin's role was one of a sagacious conjuror, and mediating 'bridger' between this and other worlds, thus a this-worldly other, being capable of a 'transcendencing-in-immanence'. Being such a kind of transformative inter-mediator, he moved between inner-worldly and other-worldly spheres, 'in-betweening' or 'thresholding',[7] as one, who knows how to dance on the limen (Küpers, 2011a).

Like the character himself, his story is one, full of different interpretations, translations and transformations. Original texts about him have been reinterpreted, historicized and adapted. In this way, he and his accounts and narratives reflect and explore themes, interests and preoccupations of different times and *Zeitgeist*.

All these diverse constructs, with their patterns of continuation and further elaborations, but also discontinuities, modifications and instrumentalization, can be reconstructed.

Historically, Merlin, as Myrddin, was an original Celtic character, older than the famous Arthurian legend that is mostly associated with him.[8] Over time, this pagan character, with his many faces and shapes, was attempted to be Christianized and in particular morphed to fit a

Christian dualistic structure. In fact, the duality of the wild, natural and pagan against a caging Christian conversion make up the central elements of Merlin's depiction in art (Painter, 2016). As Painter showed, the surprising variety of representations and depictions in art are not only revealing the complex variety and expressions of power of wisdom. Rather, they are also a case of Christian appropriation of pagan symbols and tries at suppressing opposing spiritual ideas and practices as heretic.

Considering the prejudicial interpretation of Christian moralizing and its judgemental derision and projection, it will be important to retain and incorporate the other, also ambivalent, ambiguous and darker sides. Consequently, the challenge will be to preserve and reveal pagan qualities and his non-Christian back-grounds and imaginations.

Added to this, what needs to be considered are the vagaries of early medieval writers with their own inherent love of myth and legend, and the powerful kings, who paid them well in order to spread their fame. Alongside their heroic deeds, warlords wanted to be seen as cultured, educated and generous sponsors of music and poetry.

Furthermore, over time, varying agendas of all kinds of authors and authorities have used Merlin for specific political ends, vested interests and agendas or political games and intrigues. And taken that the story of Merlin emerged in the so called dark age, his tales were viewed as entertaining, de-lightful myths and legends embroidered to add colour to a colourless age. Accordingly, Merlin appeared in different forms, related to knowledge and power through the ages (Stewart & Matthews, 1995; Knight, 2009)[9] for more than 1500 years of cultural and literary history, from archaic times, to the global present, and now reaches out for a future to come.

So the figure of Merlin was invented and reinvented from the sixth century – Celtic Welsh, Irish, Scottish, British Bretonic Gestalt as Myrddin – through the middle ages, to renaissance, romanticism, the nineteenth and twentieth centuries, to the present. Using songs, poems and stories from Celtic origins,[10] in particular the medieval Christian Geoffrey of Monmouth became foundational, with his 'Vita Merlini' (c. 1148), this story was then processed by influential authors like Chrétien de Troyes and Robert de Boron through whom Merlin was popularized and became a Christian(ized) authority, representing a bridge between scholarly learning and clerical and/or political institutions and power regimes.

The mentioned authors, and other following them, were laying the base for the famous Arthurian stories and songs, or poems by the Anglo-Norman and Norman-French troubadours of the eleventh and twelfth centuries, then later refined by Thomas Malory's much read and studied 'Morte D'Arthur' (1485). Later romanticism used Merlin, for example expressed in Tennyson 'Idylls of the King' (1833–85) and many more forms of artful processing, in European Romantic movements.

Thus, stories of Merlin were not only Celtic and British, but spread all over Europe, especially in connection to the Grail legend (Goodrich, 2002; Goodrich & Thompson, 2001/2003; see section on Merlin and the Holy Grail). Merlin and Arthurian myths continue to be popular, not only as a 'Disneyfied' wizard for children, young-adult and fantasy incarnations or post-modern recastings of the wizard in film, and television. Also, interpretation of Merlin in the international New-Age spiritualism, usages in pop-culture (Petrovskaia, 2017)[11] or computer games show his popularity. He reached a very broad readership and audience as Gandalf in J. R. R. Tolkien books and the films, as Dumbledore in J. K. Rowling's book series as well as the recent BBC television adaptation of the legend 'Merlin' (Semper, 2015), again demonstrating his ongoing attractiveness and resonance.

As this brief overview has shown, Merlin is a constantly re-appropriated figure, alive as a restless spirit that 'incarnates' or is 'incarnated' in different contexts, for various interests, while reaching many people, time and again. This chapter has not the space for discussing in detail all the various ideological and narratological roles, neo-Celtic and other reinterpretations, with their influences and impacts, that Merlin has had in the course of 'his-story', through the ages. Rather than attempting to authenticate a historical or fictional figure, this chapter tells some aspects and episodes about a type, who is an embodiment and configuration of different qualities that have something to tell us today. Accordingly, the following retells only some selected events out of the compounded life of this enigmatic figure to hermeneutically explore possible meanings of wisdom. In particular those aspects that were chosen may offer messages for practical wisdom in our and a more sustainable society and economy, as well as in organization and leadership.

Origin and Destiny of Merlin

According to legends, our figure is incarnated as being born from a demonic father and a pious mother. In a proto-Christianized interpretation, an airy incubus, as a fallen angel, inseminates a virgin nun, who gives birth to a messenger, whose task will be to mediate between the world of humans and the other-worlds.

He grows up as a relentless 'wonder'(-ful) child of the amoral devil and the benign kind-hearted mother, thus carries both sides in himself, calling to live up to them. Being a demonic-earthly and loving-celestial being, he has inherited the knowledge of all past and the prophecy for foreseeing the future, as supposed 'super-natural' capabilities. This allows him to seduce and lead humans with understanding and vision, exerting power and empowering others to understand and enact (or not) the possible.

Merlin can only become the 'Wise Old Man' and carry out his responsibilities to King Arthur and the British people when during his childhood he has established his resonating connection with the 'earthly numinous' and the world of the spirit. As such he is situated between the profane and the sacred (Eliade, 1961),[12] between old Pagan Druidism and the new Christianity.

Growing up fatherless, he soon is given and takes tasks on to advise, counsel and mentor others, dealing with necessities and possibilities. Correspondingly, he appeared in relation to ancient British king Vortigern. The same wished to erect a tower, but each time he tried it would collapse before completion. For preventing this to happen and to continue with his project, he was told he would have to first sprinkle the ground beneath the tower with the blood of a child who was born without a father. As the young Merlin Ambrosius was thought to have been born without a father, he was brought before Vortigern. Instead of killing him, the king listened to the young man.

Let us listen into a possible dialogue between the Kind and Merlin:

> KING VORTIGERN: *So tell me Merlin, why can the towers not be built?*
>
> MERLIN EMRYS: (Questing the wisdom of the advisers of the king first then declared) *Your project of establishing these towers will fail. They are not supported upon the foundation, because two battling dragons live beneath. These are representing the war between Saxons and the Britons.*
>
> KING VORTIGERN: *So what shall I do then?*
>
> MERLIN EMRYS: *The tower and your kingdom will only stand when you allow me to advise you and listen to my prophecies also in relation to war and peace.*
>
> KING VORTIGERN: *Offer me your advice then?*
>
> MERLIN EMRYS: *Release these hidden underground dragons to fight one another ... I will now unfold to you the meaning of this mystery. The pool is the emblem of this world, and the tent that of your kingdom: the two serpents are two dragons; the red serpent is your dragon, but the white serpent is the dragon of the people who occupy several provinces and districts of Britain, at length. However, our people shall rise and drive away the Saxon race from beyond the sea. ... To you it is incumbent to seek other provinces, where you may build a fortress.*[13]
>
> KING VORTIGERN: *Elaborate and tell me what it means and what I shall do!*
>
> MERLIN EMRYS: *The Red Dragon represented the native Celtic inhabitants and defenders of Britain. They, although exhausted and appearing defeated will eventually rise up and repulse the*

> *White Dragon of the invading Germanic Anglo-Saxons. There will be the coming of a new king initiating a lineage of rulers who will reign before the Anglo-Saxons returned to rule over Britain ... You, king Vortigern are not destined to build your fortress on this site, and thus must seek elsewhere for a suitable one.*

Vortigern followed Merlin's advice and eventually settled on different grounds ... although he later dismissed his warning of a coming fray of an avenging bloodshed.

For the defenders of Britain, the prophecy of the two dragons was a powerful event, giving hope and inspiration for those who lived in those times to carry on the fight that was an important moment in the destiny of Britain.[14]

Merlin went on to make further, uncanny prophecies and broad visions concerning the future of Britain, beyond Arthur's time. Hence he functioned as visionary adviser, not only in terms of investments and crisis (conquering and civil war, famine, etc.), but also related to a corresponding mediator of conflicts, for a prudent political leadership that establishes policies and strategies for negotiations.

This early involvement in prophecies and consultancies are examples that show how Merlin sees unseen realities and renders implications explicit. Merlin knows to move between the visible and the invisible, also in relation to organizations and projects (Küpers, 2013a). Because for him, the invisible is visible, he is connected to old and new understandings of the magical. These imply also a deep comprehension of spiritualism and occultism that make sense of realities as mystical, allowing to find a 'Place of Enchantment' (Owen, 2004: 213; see also During, 2002). For this reenchanting emplacement, Merlin draws from ancient wisdom traditions that do not exclude a valorization of reason, but go beyond rationalism and 'materialistic' naturalism.

Lessons for Leadership and Organization

Historical figures and their archetypical characters and structures, like that of Merlin, are resonating with many of the vital issues that business leaders have to deal with. In management studies archetypes are typically used in four characteristic ways (see Kociatkiewicz & Kostera, 2012). This includes the capacity to reveal hidden aspects of organization (e.g., Bowles, 1993), and to translate values into more personalized forms, closer to experience (Carr, 2002). Furthermore, it includes being able to make sense of powers that are present within the organization as a potential, which may or may not be brought to life (e.g., Kociatkiewicz, 2008), and to inspire managers to be motivated and more imaginative (e.g., Hatch et al., 2006).

Being able to see under the surface, and understanding invisible forces, Merlin has access to knowledge that is not immediately apparent or commonsensical and makes constructive and creative use of it. In terms of leadership, his capacity to en-vision is also related to an attributed inversion of temporality he incarnates. Living backwards in time allows him to have in-, hind- and foresight, with visionary as well as transformational forms of leading acting in the present as ambassador for different imaginaries of futures, which was described as '*The Merlin Factor*'[15] in relation to organization and leadership.

What can be learned from Merlin here is that all visioning and imagination starts with creative perception that is sensing and seeing things differently. This then can be followed by making sense of how emergent patterns can inform future possibilities. All throughout this kind of processing, Merlin kept being in the presence, and thus accessing and employing inner sources of creativity as well as a sense of the possible, 'possibilizing' lives to become.

Related to organization, to be effective, the vision of the future must permeate decisions and actions, energizing, aligning and empowering all organizational members to make the vision real and going on moveable paths-ways towards it. But Merlin would insist that for accomplishing empowering and transforming levels, specific requirements are needed. Such understanding presupposes to use embodied senses and emotions, to think analogically and metaphorically, while reading life experiences for their meanings and know how to interpret, share and tell image-rich stories to communicate effectively. Accordingly, with Merlin we can learn about the role of embodied transformative metaphors and narratives that can be related and used for communicating, and shaping in the contextuality of organizational life-worlds of change and transformational leadership (Küpers, 2012a,b).

Merlin as Mentor and Counselling Adviser for the Arthur(ian) World

Merlin's prophecies, and various other stories, led to his inclusion into Arthurian legends. These entail the tale of Merlin as the one who is responsible for the mysterious birth of Arthur and who functions as king-maker. Over the years, Merlin was interspersed more and more through these tales of Arthurian worlds. The following first briefly shows his mentorship with Arthur, followed by connections to the trickster archetype, and then his establishment of the Round Table as well as guiding role for the Holy Grail.

Merlin is most known in relation to the prince and later king Arthur, with whom he is connected in a twisted fate and joint destiny. As hinted to before, Merlin uses his magic to arrange for the birth of Arthur via

THE STORY OF MERLIN AS A TALE OF WISDOM

romantic deception of King Uther. He arranged for King Uther to seduce Igraine by magically having him take the shape of her husband, Gorlois. Then, he took the child, Arthur, born of this union, and spirited him away for safety.

When the aged and infirm Uther is nearing his last battle, Merlin arranges the Sword-in-the-Stone contest, and magically pre-ordained Arthur to be able to draw forth the sword and thus became the true and rightful king. Merlin becomes Arthur's main teacher, counsellor and then architect of the Round Table (see next section), but later he slowly withdraws from the court.

Being a mentor for his protégé Arthur, Merlin served as a wise advisor and guiding facilitator. For this, he is teaching and coaching him as young prince and adult king. In this way, he becomes also a kind of parental figure, while giving royal assistance for political leadership and development of the kingdom. Merlin himself here takes on the role of a mentoring leadership (Whitney et al., 2000) for the future leader.

Accordingly, Merlin helps Arthur to learn things that he would have learned less well, more slowly or not at all, if left alone (Bell, 2000: 53). Like in other mentor–mentee relationships, a respected, seasoned person, here Merlin, engages with a more novice person, the less experienced or less knowledgeable mentee, here Arthur, to ensure becoming a responsible leader, who is achieving something of worth. His mentorship can be related to principles of human becoming that structure opportunities for co-creating meanings that are unique, while focussing on the relationship *between* persons. With Parse (1998: 34) these principles involve:

- structuring meaning multi-dimensionally as co-creating reality through the languaging of valuing and imaging;
- co-creating rhythmical patterns of relating as form of living the paradoxical unit of both revealing and concealing as well as enabling a limiting, while connecting and separating simultaneously;
- co-transcending with the possible as empowering unique ways of originating in the process of transforming.

Through engaging in mentoring, new understandings arise, values are clarified and new directions undertaken, while he is helping the prince to be a "leader-as-learner" (Antonacopoulou & Bento, 2018) in an ongoing search for meaning and enacting noble courses and the art of governing just and wisely.

Providing a "diligent loving presence" (Parse, 2002: 97), Merlinian mentoring is situational and co-creational, and while being unpredictable and ever-changing, it always connects the freedom to choose with responsibility for decisions and deeds. With gentle urgings, Merlin draws Arthur's attention to those issues and concerns in his life that will support him to actualising here his ultimate destiny as political leader. In a mentoring sense, Merlin conveys, mediates or acts as role-model for visions, values, virtues related to humanism, common good, well-being, restoring and keeping peace. This mentoring also comprised developing strategic capabilities and practical competencies for running the kingdom and its economy. Merlin taught Arthur to develop the male archetype of a king in its full and highest expression, while knowing about and avoiding the two bi-polar dysfunctional shadow sides of being a blustering tyrant or a scared weakling. Arthur needs to reconcile and integrate these shadows in order to become a mature king and to attain a proper kingship.

As much as Merlin tells Arthur the truth, even when its messages are challenging and difficult for Arthur to hear and accept, he warns him not to hide behind compliance with rules, as this might undermine intrinsically motivated ethical behaviour. The problem of fixed rules and procedures is that they actually allow an abdication of personal leadership, accountability and responsibility, especially if these abstract forms are not underpinned with a strong ethical culture. Merlin teaches that ethical behaviour means acting in a way that is congruent with one's own principles, value orientation and virtuous qualities, like honesty, respect, fairness or justice and equity in all interpersonal activities and for building a community with and service for others.

Possible further personal conscience values, like trustworthiness, conscientiousness, humility, vulnerability, patience, excellence and integrity, mercy, forgiveness and prosocial, even altruistic orientations have been probably part of the education. Moreover, what could be called self-determination values might have been integrated into the teaching. These include, for example, a refined sense of proper purpose, noble, aspirations, energetic motivation, passionate drive, perseverance and volition, courage, resilience and self-efficacy.

However, more important than teaching or preaching these values and virtues in isolated or imposed ways, Merlin invites Arthur to ponder about more existential questions and concerns in contextually and situationally specific forms.

Arthur learns from Merlin that while outwardly putting right principles and rules into real action, these outer realizations must come from a mature and healthy inner place, sensed deeply and thoughtfully reflected upon:

> MERLIN: *To cultivate a centring power within yourself allows you to take up the position at the centre of things, and maintaining order. This does not mean to believe that the world revolves around you, but rather that of your confidence, and decisiveness and integrity. This all gives you a supreme sense of balance,*

THE STORY OF MERLIN AS A TALE OF WISDOM

remaining cool, calm and collected, whatever happens, while executing with practical wisdom that is knowing of how to do the right thing, at the right time, for the right reasons.

ARTHUR: *That sounds challenging! How can I realize that?*

MERLIN: *You must always, on all your ways ask: why? whence? and whither? Who is affected or to be involved and for which purpose, being guided by what kind of values, which goals are set and forces and means mobilized* (see also Jung, 1975: 220).

ARTHUR: *You told me so much about all these values, virtues and principles. How can I live up to all of these standards and enact them properly in various situations?*

MERLIN: *Ask yourself the following questions (on your quest) and responding to them gives you the answer:*

- *What kind of person will I become if I do this? or*
- *Is this action consistent with my acting at my best?*

You see: It is all about an art of character (Landes, 2018) *for finding a habitualized duration and expressive being in and of the world. With such a character you can render trajectories as open movement of self-cultivation, and virtuous practice in relation to others. Thus all these virtues are dispositions and excellent traits of and for your character that need to be well entrenched in you.*

ARTHUR: *So knowing about virtues is not enough, but as a living character enacting them.*

MERLIN: *Yes, they need to go all the way down for raising up – that is you learn to perceive or notice, feel, desire or expect, but also value, choose, act and respond in qualified characteristic ways. To possess a virtue is to be a certain sort of person with a certain complex embodied mind-set, situationally responsive and responsible!*

- *When facing fear of important damages or losses, be courageous that is neither coward or reckless*
- *When sensual appetites and their pleasures overwhelm you, be moderate falling neither into chastity nor shrivel into prudishness*
- *For cultivating self-control, discipline, humility, exercise temperance, but know that self-reliance can harden into prideful stubbornness*
- *When there is a need for distribution of limited resources, practice justice*
- *When practicing resolution find a mean between spinelessness and obstinacy.*

191

- *As leader see loyalty of others and yourself as neither fickleness or blind obedience.*
- *For cultivating the art of leadership, never forget the appreciation of beauty, excellence, gratitude, hope, optimism, future mindedness, but also playfulness and humour, zest, and enthusiasm.*

So being virtuous, and having virtues, is then not only a discerning intellectual and virtue-oriented process of deliberating the means and reflecting the ends of contextually constrained actions. Rather, as a living and lived practicing and 'journefying' through this always involves sensing, perceiving, intuiting options, opportunities and choices with all its doubts, uncertainties, etc. which go with these. Even more, this practice is actually about realizing decisions and actions that display appropriate and creative responses under challenging circumstances through bodily and expressive ways of engagement, up to the smallest gestures.

Merlin may have also taught Arthur never to forget to inspire creativity in others as well as recognizing and honouring others for their achievements as a way to bless them in actions that are uplifting and edifying. And one last ad-vice he has and is giving Arthurian kings is that they should try to leave a legacy, by which their accomplishments become immortal, and to leave behind something that would remind subsequent generations of those deeds. Merlin himself left such legacy in the form of the famous Round Table.

Merlin and the Round(ing) Table as Proto-integral Leadership and for Instituting Governance

Merlin was the mastermind and instigating 'meta-leader' behind the Round Table as political architect of Arthurian reign and also associated to the cultic Stonehenge. In all these roles, he uses the already alluded archetypal or visionary imagination, through which it is possible to enter a reality beyond personal interests by positioning real imaginal beings in such a way as to surpass empirical existence (Casey, 1974, 2000). Moreover, Merlin is "Giving Voice to Place, Memory, and Imagination" (Landes & Cruz-Pierre, 2013).

The placed Round Table as part of the deep memory also of collective subconscious serves both as symbol and as a 'proto-practice'[16] for a different kind of leadership, organization and system of governance.

Based on principles of democratic participation, where everyone has a voice and is involved, the Round Table is a proto-form of wise leadership practice and institutional governance that is relational, inclusive, decentred and distributed (e.g. Denis et al., 2012; Bush, 2013). To establish a Round Table as an institution is to create a forum that is guided and enacts ideals, virtues and values of equality, justice and wise decision-making. Interpreted dynamically, as a process, it enables a 'round-tabling' of problems, issues, concerns and strategic decision-making, also as a much needed form of a different kind of leadership and organizational and societal praxis.

Leading in the spirit of the Round Table may be interpreted as an example of an integral 'Inter-Leadership' (Küpers & Weibler, 2008). Furthermore, it resonates with 'Leadership in the Plural' as co-creatively structured or emergent and as mutual or coalitional collective phenomenon (Denis et al., 2012). Like Denis et al. and others have described, Merlin would advocate such pluralizing leadership in arrangements of concentrated authority and sceneries concerned with channelling the forms of plurality that appear in diffuse power settings. As an alternative to great person-centred approaches, a post-heroic understanding of leading and managing organizations involves multiple in-dividuals and relationships that are situated in practice configured in terms of interactions among organizational members and stakeholders as enabled and constrained by aspects of their specific circumstances.

Merlin would find a soul mate in Mary Parker Follett, who in her 1924 book, 'Creative Experience', developed an early and fully processual perspective of a situational leadership. For her, such leadership is mediated by inter-relationships and interactions in organizations as dynamic and evolving.

Correspondingly, Merlin would agree with her reinterpretation of power moving from a *power-over* orientation towards a *power-with* understanding and practice as "a jointly developed power, a co-active, not a coercive power" (Follett, 1924; cited in Mendenhall & Marsh, 2010). Following her idea of circularity, where "power and authority continually shift and morph to match the situation as it evolves" (Bathurst & Monin, 2010: 120), and occurs when all actors, regardless of their status within the organization, understand the common purpose. Such understanding involves depersonalizing commands and repersonalizing relationships in order to achieve solidarity. In the spirit of a radicalized relational leadership theory (Uhl-Bien, 2006) and process ontology of inter-becoming (Küpers, 2017a), a 'Merlinian leadership' is transcending individual actors and becomes emergent, always created and recreated, out of an "undefined middle, the *in* of the between" (Wood, 2005: 1111–1112).

Leadership, inspired by Merlin, is more a movement in and over time and place, thus a situational event that is distributed in various ways. Distributed leadership matters, as it offers actualisable potentials and transpersonal possibilities of collective intelligence, but also corresponding practicalities (Harris, 2013a). This kind of dispersed leadership also implies "actively brokering, facilitating and supporting the leadership of others" (Harris, 2013b: 547), thus being radically socially relational.

With Cunliffe and Eriksen (2011), such inter-relational leadership, in the sense of Merlin, is a 'way of being-in-the-world' that not only 'refers' to, but lives and institutionalizes practical wisdom. The very Round Table is one form of institutionalization that helps to transform not only individuals and communities, but also structurally and systemically.

The Round Table is not only an institution, as such, but invites instituting practical wisdom, while serving for enacting democratic values (Rosanvallon, 2011) and valuable civic virtues. As medium for embodied, deliberative and political dis-course, the table, as institution and 'practice', enables people to find the proper course for organizing, responsiveness and integrative responsibilities (Küpers, 2012a). Today, this includes adequate forms of governance, transparency and accountability, in particular for corporations (Scherer & Palazzo, 2007). But as individual actors and agencies are gathering around the table to instigate and institute new ways of doing pro-jects, they need to deal with all kinds of constraints. Especially, they are forced to take up and integrate what is always already instituted as sediments that are causing captivating path-dependencies.

Today, such Merlinian Round Table leadership is one that includes corporate citizenship sustainability, responsive and responsible practices in relation to stakeholders, beyond instrumental 'Corporate Social Responsibility' and the business case (Kuepers, 2011c).

A leader and leadership practice in the embodied spirit of Merlinian 'table ronde' helps others, including members of organizations and their stakeholders (and thereby the economy, society and the planet), to keep their integrity and to flourish. Leaders in their relationships and systemic-structural leadership that 'round table' are mediators and media for well-be(com)ing (Küpers, 2005), for the 'good' of people and the 'common good' of more-than-human communities, including those of stones, plants, animals and ecologies.

Merlin Guiding the Quest(-ion) of and for the Holy (Inter-)Grail

The following section outlines some basic ideas about how Merlin initiated and guided the famous Grail Quest and his resonance with the trickster archetype. Closely connected to Merlin's relation to Arthur and his Knights, as well as the founding of the Round Table, is the story of the quest for the Grail. This Grail and its quest represent the realm of alchemical symbolism[17] and search for integration.

Historically, the Grail myth dates back to at least the twelfth century in Europe, and was transmitted in various versions, including French (poetic works by Chretien de Troyes), English ('Le Morte d'Arther' by Thomas Malory), German (Parsifal by Wolfram von Eschenbach's version, used as the base for Richard Wagner's 'Parsifal' opera) and others.

The myth surrounds the wounded Fisher-King Amfortas, who is the king of the Grail castle. He is in agonizing pain, and the kingdom suffers as a result. With his wound, as a symbol of disintegration, the Fisher-King remains unhealed.

As outlined earlier, the 'table ronde' represents a symbol for equality, unity and integration. The 'roundness' of the table expresses the rounding of a completeness that corresponds to the circle form as it symbolizes the most perfected of all forms. But in the finite world there is no perfection, and thus the table is not rounded yet. There are answers to be found and there remains an empty seat (siege perilleux). This gap stands as a symbol for an unfulfilled space, for an Other "ecart" as a kind of experience-enabling 'difference-spacing-openness' (Weiss. 2000). This écart is described by Merleau-Ponty as 'dehiscence', 'shift' or 'fundamental fission' or rupture. As such, it marks a constitutive and subtle difference in the fabric of experience, a 'separation-in-relation', beyond the traditional categories of identity and opposition. This dehiscencing appears as a kind of slippage or displacement, a distance, a stance of dis-stance that is allowing moveable 'standing states' of differentiation, singularization and integration. Metaphorically, it can be described as a revolving spinning pivot through which self and world and self and others in a non-fusingly and difference-maintaining way that overlaps in contact. Processing this écart expresses the continuity and differentiation among beings in the sensible world (Merleau-Ponty, 1995: 21). As both are a bond and an opening, this processing engenders a mutual connection and divergence of the Flesh.

The world is full of wicked, unsolved problems and dilemmas, lack of responses, and unanswered questions, in particular for the knights and the injured Fisher-King, yearning for compassion. Some main emerging questions that are calling for a quest related to ethical issues are, for example, how to integrate the evil, symbolized by Morgana and Mordred,[18] and how to find release, salvation and redemption, also in a pagan or secular sense.

Merlin announces that the open seat can only be taken by a knight who has found the Grail as symbol and practice of integration. However, some knights, and eventually Parsifal, try to take the seat and occupy the place illicitly, driven by self-interest and lack of compassion. In this way, they violate the order that was envisioned by Merlin, and thus the round splits. Consequently, only through the 'rescue' by the integrating Grail can this split be healed. The splitting corresponds to the suffering of those on the quest and in particular of the Grail-King himself, as a symbol of the Self, in which opposites are not yet 'united'. Accordingly, the task of the quest for the Grail is to integrate and thus to get beyond the dualistic positioning, like between good and evil, among other opposites. For getting such integrative orientation, feelings, thoughts and values need to be brought together for finding wise judgement and corresponding practices. Correspondingly, Merlin's Grail represents an instance of an archetypical judgement of emotion and value that is able to embrace shadows. Such an integrative Grail both requires and empowers a spiritual and material leadership in the world, bringing together particular interests and more general inter-est for the other and the common good.

Merlin as the mysterious instigator of Parsifal's quest guides him to attain an integral Self that is able to relate to himself, others and the world wholesomely. He helps Parsifal to go to find the Grail or better to say enables him to be found by the Grail with the right attitudes and responsive behaviour. Like in his mentorship to Arthur, here incarnated as Gournamond, Gurnemanz or Klingsor, Merlin teaches chivalric virtues, including courage, perseverance, faith, art of loving or 'minne', that enable him to respond with passion and compassion, and test all these virtues and values practically.

Moreover, Merlin conveys deeper knowledge to Parsifal so that he can become ready, open and mature enough so that the Grail can find or be given to him as grace or gift. The latter events can be interpreted as a sense of serendipity: an unplanned, fortuitous discovery; or also as experiencing zemblanity, that is, making unhappy, unlucky and unexpected confluences, occurring by design (Boyd, 1998).

Merlin knows and sensitizes those who are on the quest that unpredictable things might happen and emerging phenomena appear. This may include helping forces, but also hindrances as well as all kinds of ordeals or trials of resolve, that often occur in unexpected ways. As a message, this implies the call for questers to remain open and alert for irregularities, exceptions and other interruptions, while looking for the magic of unanticipated opportunities and chances.

In a first round, Parsifal fails to spontaneously ask a specific question to the wounded Grail-King Amfortas and thus misses the chance for becoming part of the Grail community and their new leader. With the disappearance of the Grail Castle, he has to continue his quest and it takes years of gruelling, rigorous battles and further quests characterized by futility and disillusionments. By this sobering or even disheartening experience, his arrogance and pride are beaten, undermined and humbled.

Ultimately, then, Parsifal is earning his way back to the castle and its community and can partake of the Grail and heal the Fisher-King. Again,

THE STORY OF MERLIN AS A TALE OF WISDOM

it was a Merlinian hermit who helps him to find the way and ask the essential questions.

PARSIFAL: *Merlin what question do I need to ask when I am in the Grail castle?*

MERLIN: *You need to show compassion, in particular in relation to the wounded Grail King. Ask him how he feels and what has caused his pain.*

PARSIFAL: *Yes, I will do so next time, when I meet the suffering Amfortas. What else shall I ask to the Grail Community, to show that I am worthy of joining them?*

MERLIN: *The essential question will be: "Whom does the Grail serve?" to which the answer is to serve something far greater than ourselves, thus moving beyond the Ego towards a 'higher' Self, and We. And for that, sometimes you need to live with this quest and this question rather than reaching for ready-made answers* (as a later bard Rilke described it).

Moreover, expect that over and over again, you will be called to the realm of further adventures.

In this way, Merlin guides 'Parsifalian' leaders on their quest and facilitates to ask the right questions and serve higher purposes by reconfiguring and transforming their centre of gravity of personality to actually moving towards some-thing, some-one and some-where more demanding and comprehensive. This may imply suffering, facing loss of control, but also fulfilling experiences in an integral way. In a Jungian interpretation, "Merlin is the Grail as a symbol of developing the self-archetype. He guides the way and is the way as a symbol of how the goal of psychological and spiritual transformation occurs" (Gollnick, 1990: 324). In a Junginan sense, "One does not become enlightened by imagining figures of light, but by making the darkness conscious" (Jung, 1967, in Jung, 1953–78: 265). Merlin has not only learned to embrace his shadow, but also functions as a proto-integrative figure. Representing an integral self, Merlin himself is or may become the hidden 'contents' of the mysterious Grail and serves as guide and mediator to gain access to the same, as it emerges through the alchemic mystery of transformation.

Offering immanent and transcendent functions, the Grail legend and Merlin's role in it can be viewed as a symbol of continuing incarnation designed not only to offset previous imbalances. Rather it also synthesize opposites and brings together the unconscious and conscious, the pre-reflective primordial and reflective mind-ful modes dynamically.

All symbols of the Grail, like the vessel or the stone, signify the integrated whole of a Self in the universe. This integrated Self is a transformative realization of 'earthly-divine' potential that is embodied right down into matter and being connected responsively and responsible to issues, tasks and ideas that matter. Being both incarnated earthly and spiritually, Merlin is the embodied spirit in and of the world. He is an incarnation of the arche-type that unites oppositional forces, pursuing the task of integrating dynamically 'bodily-spiritually', the light and shadow via an ongoing 'inter-betweening' process. Such 'non-arriving' integrative orientation allows seeing how order and disorder and all its subqualities are incessantly intertwined and that one does not exist without the other, including other-than-human beings.

Knowing this, he acts and non-acts as a free, sensual spirit, who makes sense of the dynamics of fate, destined also to allow, when necessary, the wicked to enable the higher good.

Lessons for Leaders and Leadership on the Quest

The Quest for the Holy Grail is not futile or in vain or a mission impossible! Rather it offers a processual understanding of enacted virtues of leaders and virtuous leadership. Virtues and character strengths being tested on the quest may deliver not only positive, effective leadership and organizational performance. An enacted orientation, especially when related to practical wisdom, generates benefits for the greater and common good. However, a Merlinian approach towards an ethos of virtues and virtue ethical practice for local and global leaders (Rego et al. 2012), on their quest today, is not prescriptive, nor a preached collection of normative and piously followed guidelines.

Enacting a virtue ethics based on Merlian vision can serve as a guide into the Millennium. But those realising such virtue practice are conscious about the danger of an excessive virtuousness' of a person-centred and heroic approach.

Besides virtuous leaders, today's quests need to integrate even more the interplay with other actors and agencies or institutions, of public life and civil society, as well as all kinds of stakeholders. All of them are called to work on values-based, virtue-mediated and wisdom-oriented, rethinking, reimagining and rearrangements of the existing order, especially capitalism. Guided by values, virtues and wisdom, such undertaking can make a difference for a more sustainable practice and praxis (Küpers, 2019) and contributes to fostering peaceful societies (Rego et al., 2012) and wiser ways of living convivially.

Enacting wisdom on the quest, as a virtuous and virtuoso practice of leadership, is an embodied intuitive (Calabretta et al., 2017) and reflective, morally committed doing (Kemmis & Smith, 2008). This implies that it is situationally based on well-founded reasons and realized by proper ways of leading and organizing that are rendering desirable effects and beneficial consequences for all, including plants, animals and eco-systems.

THE STORY OF MERLIN AS A TALE OF WISDOM

Accordingly, a wise Merlinian leadership and organization practice is one that achieves the right ends using the right means at the right time, and includes making prudent decisions and enacting them. Here, 'right' refers to the legitimate and ethical interests and concerns of multiple stakeholders affected by the decisions and subsequent actions. In the business and organization context today, this encompasses employees, managers, the organization as a whole, customers, suppliers and partners, and the wider local and societal communities and environment in which all are embedded. In a certain sense, Merlinian wisdom may be seen as a placeholder for 'something more', when transforming practices and a newly understood and enacted prâxis. While being oriented and informed by traditions, such transformed practices and prâxis is one for a world worth living in (Kemmis & Smith, 2008). In our neo-libertarian era, with its constraining regimes and detaching globalization, the reintegration of Merlinian wisdom practices and actions can remind us of our situatedness and our location in places and time. Being situated and emplaced in presence is where things really do happen to and by people. It is in the bodied here and now where events and leadership interventions render real impacts and conceivable adverse or enlivening consequences and effects for all on this fragile planet with its delicate life (Connolly, 2013), calling for a wisely committed '(g)localism' (Kemmis, 2012).

Merlin can teach us that a circumstantial and circumspective orientation of reintegrated and reinstituted forms of a wisdom-prâxis and wise practices and actions becomes even more relevant as today's organizations are positioned in increasingly complex, often paradoxical and dilemmatic settings individually and collectively. A prudent inter-connection between wisdom-integrating prâxis, practice and action mediates the cultivation of an integral 'well-be(com)ing' in organizations (Küpers, 2005) and serving the flourishing of its stakeholders. Instead of imposing formulae and rules or norms, a Merlinian inspired, integrated, 'proto-wise' nexus of prâxis, practices and actions incorporates the capacity for appropriate responsive processing, and dealing with constraints in the face of particularities, heterogeneities and imprecations. Taking the predicament of our current state of affairs, business and civic society can only ignore at their peril the cultivation of the art of wisdom in relation to sustainable living (Küpers, 2013a) that Merlin inspires.

Of course, also a Merlin of today would understand that a realization of and research on integrating prâxis, practices and practical wisdom in organization and beyond is and will be a challenging endeavour, entailing various tensions and ambiguities (e.g. Rooney et al., 2010). Nevertheless, it is a worthwhile and urgent transformative undertaking that contributes to more flourishing unfoldment within organizations and with regard to stakeholders, including those of social and 'natural' life-worlds and economic, political, cultural relationships and realities.

Merlin as Trickster

Not being a saintly sage, Merlin is connected to the Trickster archetype. In that role he challenges to move beyond the warrior archetype and to live in creative tensions with one another. The function of the trickster is to free and correct or compensate one-sided ossifications. These refer to irritating tendencies and manifestations of paralyzing congealments and deadening rigidifications of the collective and its subconsciousness. He is doing this by healingly opening up to and keeping open the a-rational depth and richness of other worlds and archetypical qualities.

Revealingly, as the mythical figure of the trickster, Merlin comprises contradictory traits, from wisdom to foolishness. Being a kind of trickster-like change agent, his liminal practices irritate by introducing disorder and opening up for new formations.

Crossing boundaries and breaking the rules, as well as transformational transitions, alter the way that things are organized. As a trickster, he mediates or co-creates life-worldly configurations that are more complexified, colourful and vivacious, but also uncertain, questionable and indeterminate.

For him, being the liminal mythical character of a 'playfool' trickster, liminality is an original state of becoming. His transitional existence allows 'betwixing' and 'betweening' whom and what he relates to at different entry points, while flitting across borders at any time, penetrating the social structures at will. As we have seen before, the trickster Merlin is a personification of ambiguity (Radin, 1956: xxiii). Accordingly, he is a 'trans-former' who is de-constructing and re-creating, opening up for different kinds of values and practices. With his specific competencies and roles – like being an anomalous; trick-player; shape-shifter; situation-inverter or as a messenger, who is turning everything upside down or a bricoleur (Hynes, 1993) – the trickster Merlin functions as agent of change for society, communities and organizations. Hence, he is facilitating or provoking being creative in seeing things and handling issues from different, but relevant, points of view or from alternative perspectives or by different ways of doing.

As described in his role as wild man in the wood (see the next section), living in liminal times and places, Merlin withdraws from conventional social worlds, scrutinizing and reconsidering values and basic orientation of the culture from which he is marginalized. He not only lives on boundaries, but also redefines them. He sets traps, but also evades them, while taking the bait or taking the ways of others and adapts, thus surviving through protean, playful flexibility. Merlin's task as a trickster is to grab people from inside the circle and pull them out of their comfort zones, to

THE STORY OF MERLIN AS A TALE OF WISDOM

make people become outsiders or complicit of other life forms, showing that everything isn't really what it seems. For this to happen, he does not break rules, but much more reinterprets them or provides settings, where the rules are temporarily suspended. As he crosses lines, bends rules and undermines fixed positions and dualities, he is a polytropic figure, turning and twisting various ways (Hyde, 2008: 52). These ways include also performing roles as "creative idiot ... wise fool, the gray-haired baby, the cross-dresser, the speaker of sacred profanities ..." thus functioning as the "mythic embodiment of ambiguity and ambivalence, doubleness and duplicity, contradiction and paradox" (Hyde, 1998: 7). A shape-shifter who traffics in laughter, humour, and irony (Radin, 1956: x), the cry of Merlin lies in his deeper uplifting knowing about invisible connections that are an invitation to be expressed in playful and thus 'interplayfool' trans-formations (Küpers, 2017a).

However, he is more than and different from merely a mischievous misfit. Like the fire-stealing Prometheus and trading Hermes, Irish Leprechauns, Scandinavian Loki, Greek and other figures, he is also honoured as co-creator of creative cultures that help shape the world, who make it more hospitable and flourishing for all living beings. In his best moments he reveals ways of living that excite others to thought and action (Turner, 1982: 128–129).

He does this, by embodying "the human capacity to engage in abductive practices that bring forth new modes of being and acting from not-yet-articulated possibilities and create abductive expressions that disrupt culturally contrived or inscribed boundaries" (Kamberelis, 2003: 678).

Importantly, this Merlin acting as trickster figure is not a hero, but rather a marginal personage either by reason of social status or force of circumstance. While many heroic figures in mythology and literature are characters who develop, symbolize or reinforce the cultural norms of established order of society, thus being bound up in or associated with a particular cause, resolute position or fixated telos, tricksters are not. The trickster figure must be free to flaunt authority and thus remains partly outside the norms and socially different.

With all these trickster qualities, Merlin remains an equivocal and paradoxical character, an embodied spirit of disorder and underminer of boundaries, who tests the central beliefs and values of the predominant culture (Niditch, 1987), while subversively being part of the same. For a Merlinian trickster, good and evil are not opposites or mutually exclusive, but are overlapping and inseparable qualities of the same w/hole. Behaviours and events are seen by him as confused mixtures of both right and wrong, making available multiple opportunities or possibilities that have both positive and negative ramifications.

Merlin as Mad Wild Man – Return Forward to 'Nature-Culture' and Embodied Spirituality or Kinship Instead of Kingship

In contrast to the highly cultivated counsellor at the sophisticated court of Camelot, Merlin as Myrddin appears as a mad wild man. In many older legends and sagas,[19] the Myrddin is more a shaman and so-called 'horned one',[20] who is closely living in and with nature. Also as part of the later Arthurian dramatized story, he retreated to nature after a bloody battle he could not prevent from happening. Accordingly, he is both originally situated in nature and as one fleeing into the forest, where he is dwelling and communicating with 'other-than-human'. Being a Celtic shaman and druid, he served as a sacred man of nature (Markale, 1995), and keeper of uplifting deep, primordial knowledge, particularly of arcane secrets. In these realms, he lives in resonance with rhythms and cycles of nature and its living ecology.

Also conferring to Myrddinian tradition closer to his role as adviser and councillor, Merlin is said to have been driven mad by the loss of those dear to him, including some relatives and friends, and those ideals he aspired for in the Battle of Arderydd. Horrified by the scenes of slaughter, and being grief-stricken beyond words at the death of so many of his beloved, Merlin is overcome with madness[21] and runs away into solitude, evading capture and lamenting his fate.

Suffering such a violence-caused predicament,[22] and facing a kind of limit-experience, he withdraws from human society and returns to a primitive existence in companion with stones, plants and animals. In the wild, he is exposed to cycles of seasons and demanding circumstances. Living in self-chosen exile, traumatized and melancholic, he rejects what he has left behind, and is separated from the powerful and their heroic values and practices.

Accordingly, the wild Merlin appears embedded in a life-situation, where all reasonable insight, understanding, planning, decision-making, determination or good advice and wisdom cannot be mustered or where all those are given in vain or cannot find resonance in the world. As a kind of purposeful asceticism this retreat appears as a form of critique of secular power. In some ways, when Merlin turns from the court back into nature, he questions the established order with its warrior orientation. Instead he moves to unspoilt realms, resituating himself to attain an archaic pre-personal state of being. Here, the forest, itself as dark and impenetrable to the eye like deep water, represents the confronted contents and sphere of the subconscious, a milieu of the unknown and the mysterious.[23] Correspondingly, there exists a painting of Merlin as Wild Man of the Forest by Aubrey Beardsley (1893), who depicted him placed in nature, trapped in a round shaped frame.[24]

THE STORY OF MERLIN AS A TALE OF WISDOM

Figure 9.1 Merlin as Wild Man of the Forest.

As Jung and von Franz (1986) interpreted it, this 'natural-spiritual' retreat is:

> the decisive factor in Merlin's forest life (which) appears to have been his absolute surrender or *religio*, i.e., his painstaking attentiveness to the divine, through which he incarnated something of its knowledge and mystery within himself. The living reality of the unconscious was thereby enabled to manifest itself through him.
>
> (1986: 364–65).

As the wise old man in the forest, Merlin becomes a prime symbol for attention to the numinous (divine) in relation to nature, which emerges from being reinitiated to enter collective subconscious that can be used for transformation. Such transformational movement is full of tensions as it is situated – to use modern psychological terms – between states from neurosis to integration. In an extended sense, these transformative 'natural-spiritual' practices can be interpreted as vital, not only for individual health and healing, but also for the survival and flourishing of humanity and the world.

This 'contribution' appears even more valuable today as our world is countering an over-rational, one-sidedness of a Western, materialist culture, now globalized, and an ongoing splitting between body and mind, that cuts off culture and its members ever-diminishingly from nature and spiritual connections, purposes and meanings. Therefore, Merlin's reintegration in and with the natural-cum-spiritual and his 'human nature' (Shepard, 1992),[25] can be interpreted eco-psychologically. Such an approach rehabilitates being affected viscerally as well as becoming reconnected to a more sustainable form of living.

In the spirit of transpersonal studies and transpersonal ecology (Fox, 1990), with Merlin we can see that a revived identification or living resonance with 'nature-culture' can lead to greater respect for and engaging more wisely with the same.

However, the reference to the nexus of 'nature-&-culture' concerns the danger of a returning-back-to-nature move which is the so called "pre/trans fallacy" (Wilber, 1993). This fallacy refers to a confusion of transpersonal progression with pre-personal regression, manifesting a lack of differentiation. While the reductionist pre/trans fallacy is linked to the reduction of spiritual and transpersonal experiences to the pre-personal, devaluing transpersonal development or experiences, the elevationist pre/trans fallacy does the opposite. The elevation-oriented interrelation tends to be inclined to see the egoic stage of development as the lowest point in a 'fall' from pure spirit.

Being in contact with nature, and by enacting on dynamic grounds; a deep level of the unconscious with spiritual qualities, Merlin integrates the pre-personal stage of development as part of an embodied spirituality (Washburn, 2003a) that follows the principles and processes of a spiralling path.[26]

For Merlin, practicing this 'going back' is necessary before a higher 'going forth' can emerge. Thus, this move can be seen a deliberate regression that paves the way and serves for an 'immanent transcendence'. This understanding resonates with a revision of transpersonal theory, as developed by Jorge Ferrer (2001), who developed a more pluralistic and participatory perspective on spiritual and ontological dimensions.[27] Also for Merlin, the ocean of emancipation has many shores and thus different spiritual realizations and truths can be reached by arriving at different spiritual lands.

Following a participatory turn, Merlin also interprets earthly spiritual phenomena as co-creative events. These emerging events can occur not only in the locus of an individual, but also in a relationship, a community, a collective identity or a place (Ferrer, 2001; Ferrer & Sherman, 2008). This participatory knowing and interrelating is multi-dimensional, and includes all the powers of the human being (body/heart/soul). Such a vision embraced the features that embodied spiritual realities as plural and multiple, and its spiritual powers may co-create a wide, high and deep range of insightful revelations that in turn may be overlapping, or even incompatible.

Such a decentring and pluralizing motion is in contrast to an ascending, monopolar understanding of spirituality, operating via realization in consciousness. It underestimates or tends not to value, or ignores existences of immanent spiritual life or energy that is intimately connected to the vital world and arguably stores the most generative power of the mystery (see Ferrer, 2006, 2008a,b; Ferrer & Sherman, 2008). A fully embodied spirituality emerges from the creative interplay of both immanence *and* transcendence, including mind/body, feeling/thoughts, self/world, inside/outside, etc. Thus it is all about an incarnated spirit down to earth and up to heaven; or better to say entwined immanent and transcendent spiritual energies in in-dividuals and in-dividuations. These faithful to the earth embrace the fullness of deeply uplifting human experience, while remaining firmly grounded in body and earth, also as humans.[28]

Accordingly, Merlin lives an incarnational spiritual praxis (Ferrer, 2006, 2008a,b) as a multi-dimensional co-creative process. This process supports a participatory and performative enaction that seeks the creative transformation of the embodied person and the world, the spiritualization of matter and the sensuous grounding of Spirit.

Such undertaking is bringing together of earth and heaven (Ferrer, 2008a: 8–9; see also Ferrer et al., 2004).[29] It is sensitizing for the inner in(ter-)between in all its outer expressive ways and vice versa. Before these insights are related to body-mindfully practically wise leadership and organic-zations (Küpers, 2017a), we enter briefly an enfleshed wild be(com)ing.

Borne to be Wild?! Enfleshed Wild Be(com)ing

Merlin's being wild can be related to the wild being as part of Merleau-Ponty's late philosophy of flesh. Flesh was interpreted by him as an elemental carnality and post-dualistic formative medium, processed through foldings and chiasmic reversibilities (Küpers, 2015). This flesh generates an affective power through its intensive, libidinal decentred being that Merleau-Ponty qualifies as 'wild'. Specifically, Merleau-Ponty's notion of wildness, and the corresponding pre-reflective quality of wild meaning, indicates that the 'subject' and 'object' have not been tamed into discrete realms or separate categories or are put under regimes of control and mastery. Being a primordial energy of an over-spilling life that empowers intertwined being and acting, this fleshly being is a 'brute' fabric of meaning that is woven through all levels of experience. Merlin's existence as fissured, non-continuous, irreversible in 'chaosmic' forms of wild becoming triggers questions like: What does it mean that rupturing experiences of, for example, intoxication, exhaustion, illness, profound ennui, but also desires, orgasm or other affective states and further, odd or 'limit experiences' defy the relation of overlapping, reversible contact when the ground is raised and the form is shattered while rising to the surface, taking us unawares, carrying us off on a cyclonic wind over the horizon with creative lines of flight from territories (Deleuze, 1986, 1990)? By taking up and radicalizing Merleau-Ponty's wild being in this way it then becomes even wilder and more ferocious than yet approached; an even weirder collocation of forms, cracking fissures, 'under-lappings' and dissolutions that are all part of an expressive happening.

Importantly, Merlin not only knows about, but experiences itself the 'être sauvage' by being not only exposed, but elementally interrelated and interfolded with earthly flesh, as a cultural being. Crossing over, being chiasmically involved and folded, Merlin's sageious message is that there is a material-cultural continuity between self and world as we are bodies *in* and *of* this world. We are organs of this world, flesh of its flesh in a way that "the world is perceiving itself *through* us" (Abram, 1997: 68; see also Abram, 2007). Merlin reminds us to develop a carnal, sensorial empathy with the living that sustains us all.

What might a return *to* and different account *of* nature mean for us today? How can nature return to us and both nature and its human nature towards each other anew? How can we re-approach our own natureness, and re-conceive and re-evaluate nature, and our place within it (Sallis, 2016)?

There is a risk of anthropomorphising the flesh and dissolving all differences in nature which can lead to a retro-romanticism with regard to the embodied ecology of flesh.[30] Such orientation would collapse humanity and nature into a "predictable, continuous, and homogenous unity out of which we cannot make any distinctions, ethical or otherwise" (Brown & Toadvine, 2003: xvi). But any wise response to nature requires recognizing its unpredictable, non-homogenous and non-continuous character.

The flesh is less like a thing or animalistic substance, but more like a metaphorical fabric that is woven out of many threads – relations – of which the visible flesh is seen to represent a knot[31] or spiral, inspired by nature, which were and are used in Celtic patterns as shown in the following collection.

Merlin intuits that all beings in nature have both a 'quasi-subjective' capacity to sense, and being sensed, to feel and be felt, to be part of a pre-reflective 'intentional' becoming. The wild Merlin senses and makes sense of the creative potential of earthy fleshed nature and its 'inhuman

THE STORY OF MERLIN AS A TALE OF WISDOM

Figure 9.2 Nautilus, fern and Celtic knot and spiral patterns.
Source License: Creative Commons Attribution[36]

intentionality' and 'agencies' in relation to 'culture'. For him, nature, including humans as 'humanimals', is a kind of 'society' that has an intentional potentiality that could be actualized towards it, strives, thrives and 'wants' to express. In this way, Merlin is feeling in and through the flesh, for cultivating 'what could be' (Kirkpatrick, 2017).

Lesson and Guiding Questions for Leadership

As Merlin's practice illustrates, taking time for a retreat and connecting to cyclic and spiralling qualities of rhythms do help us to get back to the senses, for redeveloping living organs in the world and organizational life-world. Relating back to a 'pre-level' of wild being does not need to be retro-regressive, but can lead to re-connecting to forces of nature and thereby developing a co-creative relationship to culture again, differently.

Allowing one-Self to be 'wild', that is, to resonate radically with sensations, affects, emotions and passions, being vulnerable to deeper layers of one's 'nature', allows us to get out of one-sided frames and to move towards transformative experiences. This might involve embracing shadows, dark sides and the untamed, for a different, more integral becoming. This process of becoming is one that interrelates with the concrete material and living nexus of entwined nature-and-culture. This involves both material 'more-than-human' and socio-cultural fabrications that are all present in or affected by practices also of organizations and leadership.

Involvements with these phenomena in organizations imply also being with them on the move between an order and a disorder, between ambiguous 'immanent transcendence' and 'transcending immanence' towards different practices.

Living in age of an ecocidal Anthropocene and facing an ecological crisis, a 'anthro-decentred' orientation of wild becoming may guide leaders and organizations to develop genuine forms of responsive and responsible practices that are more in tune and sustainable, while rendering well-be(com)ing (Küpers, 2005) of stakeholders, including human-and-more-than-human, future generations, as well as potentialities to come.

For this to happen, a Merlinian approach towards an 'eco-scene' and corresponding genuine 'eco-nomics' aims at establishing and bringing the house 'in order', and governing it in an integrative way. Referring to Greek origin for '*οἶκος*' (house) and 'νόμος' ('nomos': custom or law), hence 'rules of the household', economics and its means are the use of knowledge about and shaping of sustainable practice of an appropriate 'house-hold' governance.

Merlin as Tragic Romantic Lover?

There are two quite different interpretations concerning what happened to Merlin at the end of his life. The most known, rather Christianized, antifeminist version involves the so called Lady of the Lake, also called Nimuë, Nymue, Nimueh, Ninianne, Nivian, Nyneve or Viviane, Vivien, Vivienne or Evienne, among other variations. In many tales, Merlin's downfall and final residence was at the hands of this lady, who was supposed to have seduced and entrapped him. Why and how did this happen? After Arthur has convinced Lady of the Lake to stay in his castle under Merlin's encouragement, and while getting to know her more closely, he falls in love with this beautiful, sensitive and intelligent wo-man. However, she fears Merlin will use his magical powers to take advantage of her. She swears that she will refuse to give him her love until he teaches her all of the secrets and magic he knows. Merlin agrees. Both of them depart to return to Northumberland, when they are called back to assist King Arthur. As they are returning, they stop to stay in a place with a cavity, where two lovers once died and were buried together. When Merlin falls asleep, Niviane places him under a spell, and entraps him within the tomb, where he became enframed. Thus, after having coaxed his magical secrets from him and turning her new powers against her master, she ensnared him in an enchanted prison, variously described as a cave, a large rock, a tree or hawthorn, an invisible tower, etc. where she comes to him every day or night. After enchanting Merlin she replaces him as Arthur's magician aide and adviser.

THE STORY OF MERLIN AS A TALE OF WISDOM

Merlin as Lover is depicted in various ways, for example by the British Pre-Raphaelite painter Burne-Jones in his famous "The Beguiling of *Merlin*" (1872–77), showing the infatuated Merlin trapped and defenseless in a hawthorn bush, recoiling as if under pressure, while Nimuë holds the book of spells away from her body and away from Merlin, emphasizing that she holds the power of enchantment and of motion.[32]

So, was he a tragic lady-friend, entranced by Nimuë, a tragic starry-eyed protagonist and doomed lover, or was he a faëry-ly lover, who accepted a boon that comes at just the right time and thus was willingly charmed by an individual and perhaps mutual bliss? Bliss here should be understood also as "that deep sense of being present, of doing what you absolutely must do to be yourself" (Campbell, 2004: xxiii) And following this bliss, he, and perhaps they, gained the possibility to live a "mythologically inspired life" (Campbell, 2003: 79). This is a darkness-embracing de-light of refreshing Ananda-ian rapture to be in touch with a lover and thus with bliss. The archetype of the wise man becomes that of the lover, bliss-full of appreciation, intimacy, ecstasy and serene joy. Correspondingly, to become a lover in his fullness, Merlin has had to learn to integrate the shadow sides of being an unfulfilled, addicted or impotent lover.

Thus, an alternative interpretation[33] does not see him as beguiled by the love-spell of a femme fatale, but as someone who consciously submitted and freely succumbed to his beloved one, who loved him in return.[34] In this version, this withdrawal from the humdrum world was a purposeful renunciation of worldly power and a deliberate entry into a world of 'real-virtual' real with its dream-streams. Being critical about a Christian moralizing and prejudicial animus that gives woman a kind of devilish status and treats them as seductive, this other reading would place them in a self-chosen fulfilling relationship. Perhaps both are adventurers and lovers together in their respectfully respective ways that is individuation seeking adventurer and unity seeking lover as a band of heroes bound by love for each other, sharing a higher cause but allowing one to be different on the common heroes' journey (Kostera, 2018).

Merlin is the one who follows "The Gleam" as expressed by Tennyson (1889) in his famous poem. Throughout the poem, Merlin is following various gleams: the floated, flitted and slided as well rested gleam, only then to again being clothed with and hovers gleams …

Over the margin,
After it, follow it,
Follow The Gleam

A poetic interpretation of Merlin and Vivien can be found in another poem by Tennyson (1859) with the very same name. In a Victorian spirit, here Vivien, unasked, followed Merlin all the way to the wild woods of Broceliande in Brittany, to which pursuits he first remained consentingly silent. Serving him, offering him worship and love, he feels that she breaks up his dark melancholic mood. But she seduces him to share his knowledge of magic, including a spell of self-closure of making invisible. Merlin, being old, tired and lonely, cannot help but find her pretended affection for him complimentary, holding and being held, boldly, while giving and fa(i)lling, in...

Merlin and 'Engaged Gelassenheit'

Merlin has learned not to possess or hold onto 'objects' or 'others', but to let them be and to resonate with and to witness their continued and discontinued becoming. This attitude manifests as comportment towards what could be called 'engaged releasement' or in German 'Gelassenheit' as a specific relational practice. This 'Gelassenheit', translated as serenity, composure or detachment, refers to a non-objectifying ethos of an active and ongoing passivity.

It is an accepting manner that implies an abandonment of habitual, representational and appropriating positioning, while suspending distorting projections and totalizing closures of enframing.

In this letting-be of things and phenomena, Merlin and others practicing it do not attempt to manipulate, master or compel things. Instead, he and they let things and issues be in the way they appear. Importantly, it does not involve following an unconcerned attitude of unresponsive indifference or lack of interest, but rather an 'engaged letting'. Entering the modus of this letting-be is realized by Merlin, and others following this path, through a receptive waiting and listening. Thus, it is more an 'active non-doing' rather than the willing and controlling business of heroic mastering. Specifically, it moves from a representational and calculative mode, via a presencing and meditative thinking or musing towards more poetic relations, as lived by Merlin Taliesin the poet, open to the promptings that come from the ontological depth of other beings and their irreducible otherness.

As a genuine and free relationship, practicing 'Gelassenheit' is accessibly open to being body-mindfully in the very presence of what appears with wonder.[35] At the same time, it is integrating a mindful living that can follow more non-instrumental, non-dominating, but intrinsic and aesthetical and ethical forms of relating and wisdom. An ethos of 'Gelassenheit' may then contribute to reconfiguring relationships for organizing in a more integrative way. By this proto-integral manner, those who are 'gelassen' embark towards unknown shores. On this journey or while landing, they then may contribute to 'alter-natives', that is, 'other-birthly' pathways and practices. Thereby, the spirit of releasement can release more responsive, responsible and thus sustainable presences and futures, in

Conclusion as Opening

Does Merlin fail at the end...? Does his fictional life end not only in let-down of love tragically, but overall? All kinds of human failures and disaster, irrational passions, lousy jealousy and insatiable greed, as well as various power-games can destroy his dreams and shatter all his ideals. This is captivatingly depicted in Tankred Dorst and Ursula Ehler's theatre play 'Merlin or the Wasteland' (1981; Dorst, 2001).

In this play, the dystopian finale shows not only the end of Merlin, and of the Arthurian Camelot and its ideals, but also the end of humankind and the planet earth, ruined by more than unkind, insane mankind that has lost all wisdom. Or on the contrary of such doomy imagination, are the stories of Merlin still at present and even more will they be time and again, offering in-spiring and enlivening tales, providing potential for learning and becoming wiser?

Is there an end of Merlin and his outdated legend, marking a passed past with no message anymore; or will there be with the Merlian stories new beginnings that mediate regenerating cycles towards sageness for this and the coming world? What would new ways of retelling and reinterpretations of Merlian tales be like? How will they resonate with whom, leading to what kind of effects? What qualities of Merlin's wisdom will become more important in the near future?

Any conclusion here renders more questions and investigations, thus is more an opening and a calling for inclusion. It is an invitation for considering what can be learned from Merlin's stories and its wisdom for us today and a future to come, in particular in relation to leadership and organization. Merlin haunts the landscape of history with ephemeral moments of light and then again opaque shades, new perspectives, and then again withdraws, only to reappear again, intricately patterned anew and in different shapes. So we will never catch him, but can enjoy re-entering the search of tracing his tales of wisdom and relating them to our time and forthcoming generations.

Over a thousand years since he stepped out of the mists of time, Merlin is still as powerful a figure as he ever was. The otherness of Merlin still may serve as a source for knowing and learning about ourselves, others and the world, all in a nexus. The enduring appeal of the myths of and around the shape-shifting sorcerer and the talent of those who iconized and revised it inadvertently invoked images and tales of wisdom for future Merlins and depictions of wizards. May the stories of Merlin, gracefully harnessed in compelling narrative forms, impact readers today and tomorrow in deeply profound and uplifting ways.

As we have seen, ranging from echoes of a preliterate Celtic tradition to post-modern vibrations, the stories of Merlin have eclipsed their original creations, and gained lives of their own, lasting and reaching into new ages. The Merlinian message can be one for our Millennium starting with the next years and decades to come.

As this chapter has tried to demonstrate, the old sage Merlin continous to offer new sagas on what it means become wise. Therefore, he and his accounts may serve, time and again, as critical repository of inspiration for wisdom in our unwise world, and possible tomorrows to emerge, differently.

His character and the inviting and challenging qualities of his messages still and will work into our current and future hearts and minds and hopefully also into organizational and leadership practices. These messages are not at all an escapism into a fancy world of yester-yesterday or idealistic utopia of 'never-no-where', but can serve for a living imagining in tune and astute reflexivity for co-creating different real-worldly 'scapes', acutely called for. The transformative moves towards these other worlds are journeys that involve a wayfaring travlleing of fluxes of 'inter-betweens', not only of individuals, but also socio-cultural groups and societal institutions and their relationships and practices.

This wayfaring is a storied touring and de-touring (Küpers, 2015) that moves along open(ing) lines and spirals as relational fields (Ingold, 2011: 69–70). These meshed fields are living con-textures of interwoven threads that are issuing along with multifarious things and paths in the very processes of their generation that is bringing forth a perpetual becoming (ibid.: 12) within an 'inter-world' (Merleau-Ponty, 2012: 373).

In this sense, and as we have seen in this retelling of his tale, the various mythical and narrative patterns underlying Merlin's pathways are quite unlike that of a linear route, but a transformational process unfolding by and through those embarking on this quest.

He is not only a hero with a thousand faces (Campbell, 2008), but consists of a series of a thousand and more 'heroic' and magical acts by one face (Spivack, 1994). Ambivalently, Merlin's face and what he faces will surprise, and call for being sparklingly alive in a whirring world, sometimes darkening sometimes delightful, putting up twists or taking bends, while moving through mazes also to amaze and teach us timely ways of living.

Even more, in a post-heroic sense, with Merlin we can see that there are not simple battles between good and evil. Tales of quests were and will never be easy or straight, but meandering. They are moving with subplots, turning points and often do not have happy endings. Inner and outer monsters and beasts, who the questers meet on the way, take always different forms and are difficult to recognize for what they are, while having stories of their own. Moreover, ambiguous experiences expressed in one tale keep

THE STORY OF MERLIN AS A TALE OF WISDOM

overlapping and blurring, as they mingle with many other stories, and there is no telling where any of them may lead to as a final destination.

Merlin's quest shows us how to search for relationships and knowing, also implicitly about things. Importantly these are not only those *within* the world, but its wisdom refers also to inter-relating to and knowing about our way *around* the world and thus 'worlding' of Earthlings. Moving in, through and around life-worlds with Merlin's trove of wisdom embraces what is not round, taking detouring indirect rounds through different times and places for learning about dealing and revealing roles in the co-evolutionary unfoldment of spiralling cycles of in(ter) betweening. ...

Notes

1 Following its etymological origin as *'monere'* = 'to warn', what do contemporary phenomena and fables of monsters of disembodied, occult (financial other) economies, markets and organizations warn us about; not only of what may happen but also of what is already happening? The sprawling monster of a hydra-headed menace of today's calamities is fed by neoliberal over-leveraged "Disaster Capitalism" (Klein, 2007), that – with its hubristic mind-set – is imploding. With its techno-scientific devising paws, this system monster colonizes and devours up the natural, socio-cultural and political life-worlds. It exploits those worlds of life by a strategic and instrumental rationality through an encroachment and pervasive hegemonic and homogenizing reduction of all spheres to the over-consuming economic logic and purpose-driven dominance.

2 Functional stupidity as inability and/or unwillingness to use reflective capacities, justification and substantive reasoning (Alvesson & Spicer, 2012) reigns not only in organizational and management contexts, but seems to have become systemic.

3 Fisher (2017) interprets *weird* as "that which does not belong" (p. 10) having the hybrid, the alien, the ancient; all these are potential sources of the weird and being typically grotesque, overwhelmingly shocking and even terrifying as the weird "exceeds our capacity to represent" (p. 61). By *eerie*, we designate "*a failure of absence* or ... a *failure of presence*. The sensation of the eerie occurs either when there is something present where there should be nothing, or there is nothing present when there should be something" (ibid.). Being born out of lack and something less overt than the weird, the eerie operates more by suggestion, by what is left unsaid. Weirdness makes itself known through an Escheresque array of doors, portals, entrances and exits, because it has to do with "that which lies beyond standard perception". To be confronted by the weird is to realize that "the concepts and frameworks which we have previously employed are now obsolete" when it comes to understanding the world. It is an exhilarating feeling of newness, not unlike revolution. Eeriness estranges us from the settlement we call reality or allows us to see it as temporary and changeable. For example, Stonehenge and the statues at Easter Island are eerie because we're not quite sure who made them and what set of beliefs made them meaningful at the time. This also invites "to speculate what the relics of our culture will look like when

the semiotic systems in which they are embedded have fallen away" (ibid.). For Fisher also "capital is at every level an eerie entity: conjured out of nothing, [it] exerts more influence than any allegedly substantial entity". As capital migrates across the world it leaves traces of the eerie, both in its abandoned factories and the new, post-modern forms it takes (ibid.). While the uncanny operates by "always processing the outside through the gaps and impasses of the inside" (ibid.: 10); the weird and the eerie "make the opposite move", that they "allow us to see the inside from the perspective of the outside" (ibid.: 10).

4 One main critique, raised against Jung and his concept of archetypes, is that of essentialism. The critique focuses on Jung's belief that the origins of archetypes (and their basis in the unifying collective unconscious) transcend the individual, in that they reflect an ancestral or universal 'essence' (Neher, 1996). Considering that Jung's belief in the genetic basis of certain unconscious content holds some promise, there is a needed modification in Jung's theory and concerning the kind of evidence required for its support. Seeing myths as universals tends to abstract them from the history of their actual creation, and their cultural context. Since archetypes are defined so vaguely and since archetypal images have been observed by many Jungians in a wide and essentially infinite variety of everyday phenomena, they are neither generalizable or specific in a way that may be researched or demarcated with any kind of rigor and systematic research and scientifically unfalsifiable (Hold, 2010). Jung was careful to distinguish between falsifiable, testable scientific hypotheses and data and the vast realm of experience in which these things are impossible and otherwise irrelevant. Thus he was trying to embrace both enlightenment tradition and self-critical reflexivity and a more intuitive approach following a gnostic ideology. Critically then "there are two Jungs, so to speak — the one with an open epistemology and Socratic ignorance who was constructionist and relational, and the other Jung who, following Gnostic epistemology, was, in fact, essentialist and universalist" (Papadopoulos, 2006: 48). Papadopoulos (2006) described Jung's gnostic epistemology as one that "provides readymade answers, offers proclamations and views phenomena with a closed system of belief" (p.46). While Jung's neo-Kantian epistemology was conscious, his gnostic epistemology was unconscious, perhaps a kind of *shadow epistemology* that lived below cultural consciousness – and possibly below Jung's consciousness too.

> Much like Nietzsche before him, Jung emphasises how on the one hand, modern consciousness has evolved in a specialised way thus enabling the greatest manipulation of the world humans have ever seen. On the other hand, however, neglect of the unconscious has resulted in great losses to humanity in the way that the creative potential of the psyche is, at best, ignored in favour of an assumption that progress may be achieved through the application of conscious rationality alone. At worst, this gives rise to great damage arising from neglect of the relationship between humans and the world and the failure to recognise the projections we place upon it. Thus, Jung's view of the unconscious offers a way of healing not only for the individual soul, but also for the 'soul' of twenty-first-century society in general.
>
> (Hauke, 2006: 71)

Importantly, archetypes are not personality types. Jung didn't think one could classify a person as a specific archetype. Rather, the archetypes are states of energies, patterns of feelings, thoughts and behaviour that can be found in all people in varying degrees.

5 Archetypes have been used to interpret organizational change management and the implications of psychodynamics for work organizations (Carr, 2002). Lalonde (2004) identified 'collectivists', 'integrators' and 'reactives' as Archetypes of Crisis Management. Also leadership has been explored as a holistic and value-laden process related to archetypes (e.g. de Vries, 2013) that comprise different activities in which ethics and responsibility play crucial roles (Kooskora & Isok, 2014). Illustrated by concrete examples of real leaders of today and from the past, Kooskora and Isok show how archetypal patterns of behaviour have strengths and weaknesses. For them leadership archetypes are powerful tools that, when accompanied by accountability and compassion, can be beneficial for leaders, for their organizations and for the common good. Kociatkiewicz and Kostera (2012) used an archetypical approach also for exploring the potential for morally sustainable leadership, i.e., leadership with an awareness of both light and dark sides contained in the role of the leader.

6 To become a magician in his fullness, Merlin himself needs to integrate his shadows, especially those of being a detached cynical manipulator or a denying 'innocent' disengaged one (see also Moore & Gillette, 1990).

7 Similar with Yeats, for Merlinian magic: (1) the borders of our mind are ever shifting, and that many minds can flow into on another, as it were, and create or reveal a single mind, a single energy; (2) the borders of our memories are as shifting, and that our memoirs are a part of one great memory, the memory of Nature herself; as well as (3) this great mind and great memory can be evoked by symbols (1901/1980: 28).

8 There are recent attempts to trace the origins of the Arthurian wizard Merlin to a northern Scottish figure (Clarkson, 2016).

9 As Knight has shown (2009), various reinterpretations of Merlin positioned him from wild man and wizard to national prophet and counsellor. For Knight there are four main stages or formations of the Merlin myth: Wisdom (early Celtic British), Advice (medieval European), Cleverness (early modern English) and Education (worldwide since the nineteenth century). Accordingly, for Knight, each of these topical forms corresponds broadly to a different historical period and geographic distribution of the Merlin literature, from ancient Britain through medieval Europe to early modern England and finally the contemporary global scene. For Knight, in all his guises and reformations, Merlin represents a (dialectic) conflict basic to Western societies – the clash between knowledge and power – and as such embodies the contentious duality and ambivalence between the two, inherent to organized societies. He reconstructs the generic figure of Merlin as one who is developing, possessing (or being possessed by) and deploying, multiple possibilities of knowledge, full of value, potencies, advisory qualities, taking control, sometimes fated or poetic; and with all this, in complex, mutual and recurring, recurrently varied transformational relation with power and the powerful. Regardless of the era in which he appears or the form he takes, Merlin "[will use] knowledge on behalf of those

in power, and so in some way, and ultimately in an unacceptable way, expose the limits of the power of the powerful" (xii). Throughout the book Knight argues for the subversive potential of Merlin's knowledge, however sometimes it may be used for affirming the status quo suiting specific political or cultural agendas. Refracting to the worlds of its creation, Merlin has been adapted to specific, given contexts, asserting the challenges that knowledge (beset by pressure) should advise and admonish power, rather than serving it (41). "Each identifiable context seems to start again with the Merlin story, picking some pieces from the past but relocating them in improbable but apparently comforting ways" (xxii). Accordingly, knowledge and its relationship to power and the powerful is shown as being a socially contingent phenomenon, imagined and cocreated in each new context as immanently transcendent, but always very much the product of historico-socio-cultural processes. As Merlin embodies the nexus of knowledge and power in every incarnation, he provides an invaluable window onto the construction of the same over time.

10 For example: Black Book of Carmarthen, the Red Book of Hergest, the White Book of Rhydderch.

11 The figure of Merlin, in particular as fool and wise man, has consistently exerted influences on popular culture. For example, recent popular phenomena are used to support or build up new interpretations on the legacy of Merlin in culture (Petrovskaia, 2017).

12 With the historian of religion, Mircea Eliade, Merlin can be interpreted as man of an archaic primordial and mythic society that is able to "detach himself from profane time and magically re-enters the Great Time, the sacred time" (Eliade, 1976: 23). The figure of Merlin resonates with the "*coincidentia oppositorum*" that presents a reconciliation of opposites and the unification of diversity "to reach a perspective in which the contraries are abolished, the Spirit of Evil reveals itself as a stimulant of Good, and Demons appear as the night aspect of the Gods" (Eliade, 1976: 440). Eliade has been critiqued for being essentialist, gnostic and history escaping nostalgia and even proto-fascist and reactionary political positioning as well as being accused of making over-generalizations and having no empirical support (Ellwood, 1999; Guilford, 1977).

13 https://ztevetevans.wordpress.com/2017/07/05/the-prophecy-of-merlin-the-two-dragons/; http://faculty.arts.ubc.ca/sechard/merlin.htm; www.alamongordo.com/prophecies_and_predictions_of_Merlin_Myrddin.html

14 There exists a fifteenth century work that shows Merlin revealing to King Vortigern visions of wars between the Britons and the Saxons, symbolized by the red and white dragons: Source *Wikimedia Commons* https://commons.wikimedia.org/wiki/File:Vortigern-Dragons.jpg: Lawrence-Mathers, 83; See English School, Ms.6, f.43v The Battle of the Red and White Dragons with the King and Merlin Looking on, Illustration from St Alban's Chronicle, Illumination of 15th manuscript of Historia Regum Britanniae, Lambeth Palace Library, London, Bridgeman Images, image no. LAM140291.

15 In books like "The Merlin Factor" (Smith, 1995) and "Navigating From the Future" (Smith, 2009), Merlin is used for developing visionary and transformational leadership that is acting in the present as envisioning ambassadors of a different future. This is related to the aforementioned feature

THE STORY OF MERLIN AS A TALE OF WISDOM

of Merlin as one who lives in a different relationship with regard to temporality, specifically moving backwards in time. Accordingly, he was born in the future and aged as he proceeded into the past, influencing events by drawing on his foreknowledge of their destined outcomes. Smith links this different orientation to leadership practices, as exceptional leaders cultivate the Merlin-like habit of acting in the present moment as ambassadors of a radically different future, in order to imbue their organizations with a breakthrough vision of what it is possible to achieve. The Merlin Factor is the process whereby leaders transform themselves and the culture of their organizations through a creative commitment to a radically different future. ... Leaders who employ the Merlin Factor are engaged in a continual process of unconcealment of the desired future in the competitive opportunities of the present (ibid.). Smith substantiates this idea by quotes from interviews with successful visionary leaders whose commitment to future achievements that seem 'impossible' by past standards are producing extraordinary results in the present. These first-hand accounts illustrate what the author identified as the three action phases of the Merlin Factor: Invention, Ignition and Implementation.

While, according to Smith (1995), in the first stage, Intervention, the vision of the future is refined and formulated as a strategic intent, in the stage of Ignition the proposed stragtegic intent functions to inspire commitment and enrolment from others, and in the Implementation stage the new initiatives are designed to move from the status quo to the envisioned future including external and internal challenges. Smith (1994) formulated these stages as Co-Invention, Engagement and Practice.

> The first stage is Co-Invention—the stage at which the leadership's vision of the future is formulated as a strategic intent. Co-Invention is essentially a revolution in the thinking and the shared commitment among leadership. The second stage is Engagement—the stage in which the entire organization is engaged to participate with a strategic intent based on their own commitments. The effects are enrollment, ignition, and a platform for support for change and development activities. Finally, there is a stage of Practice—the stage when rigor and discipline are brought to the organization so it can on-goingly learn by having its actions be consistent with values and a shared future. It is a state change from how people were doing things to what they can do and how they can be in the future. It involves the development of change agents and champions for the new culture.
>
> (Smith, 1994: 69)

All of these phases and the strategic intent require re-visiting from time to time. For keeping aware of emerging development an ongoing dialogue is essential. A Merlinian inspired transformation is even more called for today as narratives of an open and different nature – as time-yet-to-come – are not part of most conventional leadership practices for which 'business as usual' still reigns (Berg Johansen & de Cock, 2018). Even the more, what is needed is Merlinian inspired leadership that is trans-formative which involved embodied, emotional and importantly aesthetic dimensions of leader- and followership (Küpers, 2011b), as part of the genuine art of wise leadership (Küpers, 2013a).

16 The Round Table was interpreted not as a table but as a Tabled Round that is a structure built in the round, a Rotunda (see Goodrich, 1988).

17 In the Jungian tradition it is interpreted as an underground or undercurrent mystical tradition compensating for certain one-sided developments in Christianity that endeavour to fill in those lacunae which the tension of the opposites in Christianity had left wide open.

18 Morgana (a.k.a. Morgan Le Fay) and the treasonous Mordred (originally, Medraut) often appear in Arthurian legends as antagonists that were driven to evil by a confluence of inner desires and external influences. They were evil for a reason of complex simplicity. Morgana, as half-sister of Arthur, was originally a healer, an enchantress, a good kind of sorceress and vibrant lover of life. Later, she is caught in one of many trysts with a knight and the king, publicly reviled by Guinevere, the wife of Arthur and banished. Being shamed in public and cast out by one hiding the same sin, ignited in her fiery furnaces that made her, becoming a revenge-seeking sorceress of deadly intrigues. Mordred, being Morgana's nephew and Arthur's son as child of incest is acting as treacherous throne stealer, liege killer and queen seducer. Both join for murderous betrayals usurping the throne, while Arthur is off fighting somewhere else. Morgana twists Mordred – a classic tale of "the throne should be yours not his." Both seem to be triumphant, right up until Arthur finds out and comes home with an army. Battle ensues, and as Merlin's prophecy would have it, Mordred is destined to bring Arthur to his grave. Accordingly, in the final fight he mortally wounds his father in the same moment that Arthur kills him. In a twist, tradition has it that Morgana is one of four enchantresses that carry Arthur to his final resting place on Avalon, 'the isle of apples', as an act of remorse that shows the true nature of Morgana. Yes, she was evil, but only because the hidden sins and hypocrisy of others drove her to be so. Regardless, it is clear that the fire from Morgana's hatred is extinguished after the death of Arthur and she fades away into legend. For one like her, obscurity is greater than death and yet also a relief from the pressures of public disgrace; all because of Love and Sin.

19 Different to Merlin Ambrosius, who served as trusted teacher, mentor and advisor of the prince and later king Arthur, he featured here as *Myrddin*, as a wild man of the woods. This role appears as original, old characterization, described very early in Celtic poetry from the sixth century. In particular, Merlin had been identified by the Welsh fictional bard named Myrddin of the late sixth century in the Welsh poem called *Afallenau* and several other poems, preserved in the manuscript known as the *Black Book of Carmarthen*, c. 1250.

20 The horned one or cernuous is related to Celtic myth symbolizing a fluctuating halfway state between this world and the Otherworld, thus decentring the centre of gravity. As the "Horned one", Merlin becomes the "guardian, healer, and shapeshifter who mediates the world of the objective psyche. He is the elusive, transformative substance of the psyche itself – the adversary ... and the saviour ..." (Salman, 1986: 7). This mediational role of the horned stag God serves to protect the mysteries from destructive influences and, with

THE STORY OF MERLIN AS A TALE OF WISDOM

the Other, protects the human psyche from contact with what it cannot bear. Encountering him means to confront the objective psyche or human limitations, that serves as an essential task of healing and psychotherapy (ibid.: 7). According to Salman, if integrated this figure gives a man an effective masculine ego in possession of its own destructiveness (ibid.: 16).

21 This state of been overwhelmed refers also to Promethean and Faustian modes of humans, who are of oracular inspiration, being possessed by forces and nonrational knowledge. Goodrich (1994/2004, 2002) described the figure of the mad scientist as (anti-)Merlin, manifesting what a white wizard can become when the demons within him are released through the complex alchemical interaction of divine knowledge, demonic ambition and human fallibility, which also re-expulse them from human companionship.

22 Nikolai Tolstoy (1985) relates this suffering of the original pagan Merlin as a chief druid (also being project manager and custodians of Stonehenge) in relation to the newly triumphant Christianity in Britain.

23 The folkloric motif of the 'wild man in the woods' is ancient and universal; referring to those who inhabited the unsettled, uncultivated woodlands beyond the villages and towns of 'civilized' society, thus represented an escape from civilization's 'corrupting' influence through a rejection of its social values and its technology, and a reversion to primitivism or 'radical archaism', proto-Rousseauist 'Back-to-Nature-ism'.

24 https://commons.wikimedia.org/wiki/File:Merlin_by_Aubreybeardsley_1893.jpg

25 Psycho-historically, Shepard explores four successive epochs of civilized life: the first domestication or agricultural society, the monotheistic time of the desert fathers, the puritanical experience of pre-industrial Europeans and the era of modern city-dwelling people. Each of these eras and the idea of 'progress' deformed healthy human ontogeny in unique but cumulative and increasingly far-reaching ways.

According to him we have not grown up in a world that we could love as our own grounding. This causes our failure to treat the world as something living, numinous, animate, something with which to enter into a relationship marked by reciprocity and respect. "In this dark shadow of adult youthfulness is an enduring grief, a tentative feeling about the universe as though it were an incompetent parent, and a thin love of nature over deep fears. What agriculture discovered was not only that plants and animals could be subordinated, but that large numbers of men could be centrally controlled by manipulating these stresses, perpetuating their timorous search for protection, their dependence, their impulses of omnipotence and helplessness, irrational surges of adulation and hate, submission to authority, and fear of the strange."

26 For concept of a spiral-dynamic, see Washburn, 2003b.

27 With Ferrer, we can question three major limiting and problematic presuppositions, or frameworks for interpretation, that have been dominant in transpersonal studies. Specifically, these refer to approaches of individual-based *experientalism* (the transpersonal understood as an individual inner experience); inner *empiricism* (the study of transpersonal phenomena according to the standards of empiricist science) and *perennialism* or perennial philosophy (the legacy of the perennial philosophy in transpersonal studies).

Alternatively, he focuses upon the great variety, or pluralism, of spiritual insights and spiritual worlds that can be disclosed by transpersonal inquiry, especially for exploring a "dynamic and indeterminate spiritual power" (Ferrer, 2001).

28 In this, he resonates with Val Plumwood, whose *Feminism and the Mastery of Nature* (1993) argued also for a non-dualistic conception of nature in a way that accounts for both continuity between humanity and the rest of nature and the distinctiveness of the various forms of life and inanimate beings that comprise nature.

29 For Ferrer (2008a: 2), a fully embodied spirituality is engaging the body and its vital/primary energies for spiritual transformation. This transformation: "emerges from the creative interplay of both immanent and transcendent spiritual energies in complete individuals who embrace the fullness of human experience while remaining firmly grounded in body and earth and creative exploration of expanded forms of spiritual freedom" (Ferrer, 2008a: 2) and who cooperate in solidarity with others in the spiritual transformation of self, community, and world, while being "firmly grounded in Spirit-Within, fully open to Spirit-Beyond, and in transformative communion with Spirit In-Between ..." (ibid.: 8). Accordingly, a living spirituality is an embodied co-creation and enactment of the space between via an 'inter-embodiment' (Todres, 2007: 31; see also Todres, 2000) and an aesthetic communication and sharing. Based on and mediated through attunement, movement and rhythm, metaphorically expressed, being spiritual is like an embodied intuitive and creative dance with the now as and in a 'soulful space', a living encounter of embodied co-presences. Poetically expressed, being rooted in the bodily way, we can fly between sky and earth on the wings of "the angel of the between" (Todres, 2007: 18).

30 Merleau-Ponty's critique against Cartesian dualism – which separates subjects and objects, culture and nature, mind and matter – and his continuous emphasis on the relational Flesh of the world seems to suggest a revived romantic holism. Such holistic orientation appears similar to what some deep-ecology approaches follow when they favour an all-encompassing identification of self with other species. The theory of the all-inclusive Flesh and of its intensive, libidinal, decentred 'wild being' with its primacy of the elemental and feminine earth seems to lend towards a pre-philosophical, mythological notion of the 'Great Earth Mother/Nature', which is the foundational principle of numerous religions. As such, it may be opposed to a dominating spirit as the masculine realm of high-altitude thinking. In contrast to female receptivities and sensibilities, such abstracting orientations attempt to categorize and reduce the world to its essential structures or forms of availability and thus to forego the entire existential significance of the lived-body. But not only do the symbols of the earth, mother and Flesh signify an original differential a-structure of libidinal investment, they also symbolize the limit and the ultimate negation of the symbolic register. Insofar as an earth symbolism is all-encompassing, and therefore subsumes all contradictions, it denies symbolic efficacy. Moreover, this denial of symbolic efficacy disavows the possibility of the oppositional structures, whereby signs obtain their meaning

within a system (Weiss, 1981: 92). As much as Merleau-Ponty's idea of Flesh is founded upon and reverberates with the ontologization of the phenomenological notion of the lived-body, it is not a new philosophical monism. Rather, it refers to an open processual becoming without end or closures. Being a nexus of historico-cultural and natural processes, Flesh serves as a medium of structures of significant exchange and involvement. As such, it is encompassing though not isolated or distant as it is simultaneously 'before' us, and thus it is not foundational or transcendent of consciousness (Weiss, 1981: 95) or of other materialist or idealist principles. Merleau-Ponty's form of advanced phenomenology and relational ontology of inter-becoming shares the well-founded criticisms concerning retro-romantic approaches of a questionable re-enchantment. These can be problematized as a single-boundary fallacy concerning the status of the somatic body (Wilber, 1995: 697, 708). Conversely, phenomenological and ontological approaches, in the spirit of Merleau-Ponty, do not take the somatic-sensory body to mean experience in general, nor to mean only a pre-conventional body. Thereby, it is not descending into a one-sidedness or sliding towards regressive fallacies, such as those that aim at re-contacting to a body-id as in Gaia-approaches (Roszak et al., 1995) or as other harmony-seeking re-enchanting eco-philosophies tend to do. While understandable as a yearning for returning to a pre-reflective unity for the disembodied, alienated humans in late modernity or as fragmented as relativistic post-modernism consciousness appears, there is no nostalgic way back to a retro-regressive coincidence with nature or supposed pre-existing given 'Truths'. Because the reversibility of being is always imminent and never realized in fact 'the coincidence eclipses at the moment of realisation' (Merleau-Ponty, 1995: 147); relations to nature and to the body are always already culturally mediated as much as culture is 'natural' and embodied. Merleau-Ponty looks neither forwards nor backwards for a time or space more plentiful than the present. Rather, with him we can understand Flesh as a process of endless creative differentiation, integration and re-differentiation that finds richness and depth in the fullness of the present (McCann, 2011: 506) and in a future to come. The Flesh's communal nature invites us to perceive the surrounding world alongside the multiple viewpoints of co-perceivers. It facilitates negotiated, co-authoritative, social and political 'constructs' that accommodate differences, integrations and de-differentiations. This radical openness joined with an acknowledgement of relational excess is far from being nostalgic or ignoring the critical significance of contingencies or exchanges with unforeseeable alterities (McCann, 2011: 506). As Kirby (2006: 132) notes:

> By recasting the question of subjectivity as 'the flesh,' that is, as the world's becoming itself, Merleau-Ponty is suggesting that there can be no final arrival any more than there can be a single beginning ... Rather, the world, by implication, would always have been in the process of discovering, exploring, redefining, and reinventing the nature of its humanity.

Even more, the interrogative nature of the Flesh, in which it builds self-understanding through encountering alterity, encourages political interaction that welcomes different voices and enables us to construct a political land-scape that reflects "the energies, torsions, contrasts, and tensions of [the Flesh's] non-coincidence" (Kirby, 2006: 133). Rejecting any absolute claims of a specific, supposedly pure and authentic relation with 'nature', Merleau-Ponty's phenomenology encourages an 'a-romantic' orientation and perspec-tive on what nature and the body each is and together are, mean(s) and can become. This does not exclude using Merleau-Ponty's phenomenology for investigating concrete, emotional and spiritual experiences that people can have in relation to the natural embodied world, unbiased by either romantic or dualistic worldviews. Merleau-Pontyian ontology and epistemology pro-vides indirect directions and approaches – for example, into the structures of relations between animals and humans that go beyond abstract divisions or mere utilitarian transactions. Accordingly, with Merleau-Ponty it is pos-sible to discover many more ways and levels in which natural, social, cultural and 'spiritual' dimensions and worlds are interrelated than traditional science could approach or describe.

31 In the final words of 'Phenomenology of Perception', Merleau-Ponty quotes Saint-Exupéry in saying that "Man is a knot of relations, and relations alone count for man" (2012: 483).

32 See www.lookandlearn.com/history-images/A011881_Edward_Burne-Jones and http://d.lib.rochester.edu/camelot/image/dore-vivien-and-merlin-repose; see also: "Look and Learn No. 520" The Prophets: Merlin, Master of Magic. Merlin and Vivian, the fairy Lady of the Lake. Original artwork from Look and Learn no. 520 (1 January 1972).

33 Such interpretation is one that is following a critical feminist reflection about the status of women and gender in these conventional gendered stories (Boyd, 2012). A further gender critical interpretation was developed in relation to the homosocial context of the 'bromance' relationship between Merlin and Arthur in the recent BBC series; not a love story but a story about love (Semper, 2015).

34 In Mary Stewart's novel 'The Last Enchantment', the story of Merlin and Niniane, is also interpreted radical differently, as it is not referring to the malicious ideas of seduction and treachery as expressed in traditional ver-sions. In her novel, Merlin takes Niniane on as an apprentice, that appears at first disguised as a boy, to whom he willingly teaches his magic. Despite their age difference, they both fall in love for each other. As he voluntary shares his secrets and capabilities and how to control them, he seems to lose them himself which Merlin accepts. Then in a depleted condition of vulner-ability, he takes falls into a coma, and is believed to be dead. Niniane has him buried within his crystal cave, where he awakes some time later. He escapes after a few weeks, through a combination of chance luck and ingenious plan-ning, and travels incognito to let Arthur know he is still alive. Niniane takes Merlin's place as the court wizard-seer, while Merlin retires to the crystal cave and lives a quiet and happy life as a hermit.

35 With Merlin we can re-discover the qualities and value of wonder-ing and the wondrous as part of exploring a critical minded re-enchantment (Curry, 2017). Being in wonder, Merlin was fascinated and moved by something that is beyond his understanding. In this state, he opens up his vulnerability.

Interestingly the very term 'wonder', from the Old English 'wundor', might be cognate with the German 'Wunde' or 'wound'. Wonder is an attitude also of longing as well as belonging to what is not appropriated or in control. Being in a wondering mode motivated him for response patterns that do not fit with standard accounts of functions. While questioning what is and can be, wonder allowed the indeterminate, unthinkable and impossible to happen. He knew that a hospitality to wonder can open "to the possibility of the transformative" (Rubenstein, 2008: 189).

36 www.craftsmanspace.com/free-patterns/celtic-patterns.html

References

Abram, D. (1997). The Spell of the Sensuous. In: Perception and Language in a More-than-Human World. New York: Vintage Books.

Abram, D. (2007). Earth in Eclipse: An Essay on the Philosophy of Science and Ethics. New York: State University of New York Press.

Alloa, E. & Michalet, J. (2017). Differences in Becoming Gilbert Simondon and Gilles Deleuze on Individuation, *Philosophy Today*, 61(3): 475–502.

Alvesson, M. & Spicer, A. (2012). A Stupidity Base Theory of Organization, *Journal of Management Studies*, 49(7): 1194–1220.

Antonacopoulou, E. P. & Bento, R. (2018). From Laurels to Learning: Leadership with Virtue, *Journal of Management Development*, Special Issue. 37(8): 624–633.

Bannon, B. E. (2011). Flesh and Nature: Understanding Merleau-Ponty's Relational Ontology, *Research in Phenomenology* (41): 327–357.

Bathurst, R. & Monin, N. (2010). Shaping Leadership for Today: Mary Parker Follett's Aesthetic. *Leadership*, 6(2): 115–131.

Bell, C. R. (2000). The Mentor as Partner, *Training and Development*, 54(2): 52–56.

Berg Johansen, C. & de Cock, C. (2018). Ideologies of Time: How Elite Corporate Actors Engage the Future, *Organization*, 25(2), published online.

Bowles, M. L. (1993). The gods and Goddesses: Personifying Social Life in the Age of Organization, Organization Studies, 14: 395–418.

Boyd, W. (1998). Armadillo. New York: Knopf.

Boyd, T. (2012). Merlin's Faery Mistress, www.sacredthreads.net/www.sacredthreads.net/merlins_fairy_mistress.html

Brown, C. S. & Toadvine, T. (2003). Eco-Phenomenology: An Introduction. In: Eco-Phenomenology: Back to the Earth Itself. Eds. Charles S. Brown and Ted Toadvine. Albany: SUNY Press.

Bush, T. (2013). Distributed Leadership: The Model of Choice in the 21st Century, *Educational Management Administration & Leadership*, 41(5): 543–544.

Calabretta, G., Gemser, G. & Wijnberg, N. M. (2017). The Interplay Between Intuition and Rationality in Strategic Decision Making: A Paradox Perspective, *Organization Studies*, 38(3–4): 365–401.

Campbell, J. (2003). The Hero's Journey: Joseph Campbell on His Life and Work. Novato: New World Library.

Campbell, J. (2004). Pathways to Bliss: Mythology and Personal Transformation. Novato: New World Library.

Campbell, J. (2008). The Hero With a Thousand Faces (3rd ed.). Novato: New World Library.

Casey, E. (1974). Toward an Archetypal Imagination, Spring: An Annual of Archetypal Psychology and Jungian Thought, 1–32.

Campbell, J. & Moyers, B. (1988). The Power of Myth. Ed. Betty Sue Flowers. New York: Doubleday.

Carr, A. (2002). Jung, Archetypes and Mirroring in Organizational Change Management, *Journal of Organizational Change Management*, 15(5): 477–490.

Casey, E. (2000). Imagining: A Phenomenological Study. Indiana: Indiana University Press.

Clarkson, T. (2016). Scotland's Merlin: A Medieval Legend and its Dark Age Origins. Edinburgh: John Donald.

Connolly, W. (2013). The Fragility of Things: Self-Organizing Processes, Neoliberal Fantasies and Democratic Activism. Durham, NC: Duke University Press.

Cunliffe, A. L. & Eriksen, M. (2011). Relational Leadership, *Human Relations*, 64(11), 1425–1449.

Curry, P. (2017). The Enchantment of Learning and 'The Fate of our Times' For 'Re-Enchanting the Academy'. In: Re-Enchanting the Academy. Eds. Angela Voss and Simon Wilson, pp. 33–51. Aukland/Seattle: Rubedo Press.

de Vries, M. (2013). The Eight Archetypes of Leadership, *Harvard Business Review Digital Articles*, 12(19): 2–4.

Deleuze, G. (1986). Cinema 1: The Movement-Image. Translated by H. Tomlinson and B. Habberjam. Minneapolis: University of Minnesota Press.

Deleuze, G. (1990). Logic of Sense. New York: Columbia University Press.

Deleuze, G. (2005). Difference and Repetition. New York: Continuum.

Denis, J-L., Langley, A. & Sergi, V. (2012). Leadership in the Plural, *The Academy of Management Annals*, 6(1): 211–283.

Dorst, T. (2001). Merlins Zauber. Frankfurt: Suhrkamp.

Dorst, T. & Ehlers, U. (1981). Merlin oder Das wüste Land; Uraufführung am Düsseldorfer Schauspielhaus. Regie: J. Chundela, Duesseldorf.

During, S. (2002). Modern Enchantments: The Cultural Power of Secular Magic. Boston: HUP.

Eliade, M. (1961). The Sacred and the Profane: The Nature of Religion. Translated by Willard R. Trask. New York: Harper Torchbooks.

Eliade, M. (1976). Myths, Rites, Symbols: A Mircea Eliade Reader, Vol. 2. Eds. Wendell C. Beane and William G. Doty. New York: Harper Colophon.

Ellwood, R. (1999). The Politics of Myth: A Study of C. G. Jung, Mircea Eliade, and Joseph Campbell. Albany: State University of New York Press.

Ferrer, J. (2001). Revisioning Transpersonal Theory. A Participatory Vision of Human Spirituality. Albany, NY: SUNY Press.

Ferrer, J. N. (2006). Embodied Spirituality: Now and Then. Tikkun: Culture, Spirituality, Politics, 41–45.53-64.

Ferrer, J. (2008a). What Does It Really Mean to Live a Fully Embodied Spiritual Life? *International Journal of Transpersonal Studies*, 27, 1–11.

Ferrer, J. (2008b). Spiritual Knowing as Participatory Enaction: An Answer to the Question of Religious Pluralism. In The Participatory Turn: Spirituality, Mysticism, Religious Studies. Eds. J. N. Ferrer and J. H. Sherman, pp. 135–169. Albany, NY: SUNY.

Ferrer, J. & Sherman, J. Eds. (2008). The Participatory Turn: Spirituality, Mysticism, Religious Studies. Albany, NY: SUNY Press.

Ferrer, J., Albareda, R. V. & Romero, M. T. (2004). *Embodied Participation in the Mystery*: Implications for the Individual, Interpersonal Relationships, and Society, *Re Vision: A Journal of Consciousness and Transformation*, 27(1): 10–17.

Fisher, M. (2017). The Weird and the Eerie. London: Repeater Books.

Fox, W. (1990). Transpersonal Ecology: 'Psychologising' Ecophilosophy, *Journal of Transpersonal Psychology*, 22(1): 59–96.

Gollnick, J. (1990). The Merlin Archetype and the Transformation of the Self, *Studies in Religion/Sciences Religieuses*, 19: 319–329.

Goodrich, N. L. (1988). Merlin. New York: Franklin Watts.

Goodrich P. (2002). Merlin in the Twenty-First Century. In New Directions in Arthurian Studies. Ed. A. Lupack, 51, 49–62.

Goodrich, P. (1994/2004). The Lineage of Mad Scientists: Anti-types of Merlin. In Dionysus in Literature: Essays on Literary Madness. Ed. Branimir M. Rieger, pp. 71–88. Bowling Green, Ohio: Bowling Green State University Press.

Goodrich, P. H. & Thompson, R. H. (2001/2003). Merlin: A Casebook. New York: Routledge.

Guilford, D. (1977). Religion on Trial: Mircea Eliade & His Critics. Philadelphia: Temple University Press.

Harris, A. (2013a). Distributed Leadership Matters: Potential, Practicalities and Possibilities. Thousand Oaks, CA: Corwin Press.

Harris, A. (2013b). Distributed Leadership: Friend or Foe, *Educational Management Administration & Leadership*, 41(5): 545–554.

Hatch, M. J., Koźmiński, A. K. & Kostera, M. (2006). The Three Faces of Leadership: Manager, Artist, Priest, *Organizational Dynamics*, 4: 7–21.

Hauke, C. (2006). The Unconscious: Personal and Collective. In: The Handbook of Jungian Psychology Theory, Practice and Applications. Ed. R. Papadopoulos. London and New York: Routledge.

Holt, D. (2010). Cultural Strategy. Oxford: Oxford University Press.

Hyde, L. (1998). Trickster Makes This World: Mischief, Myth, and Art. New York: Farrar.

Hyde, L. (2008). Trickster Makes This World: How Disruptive Imagination Creates Culture. Edinburgh: Canongate Books.

Hynes, W. J. (1993). Mapping the Characteristics of Mythic Tricksters: A Heuristic Guide. In Mythical Trickster Figures. Eds. W. J. Hynes and W. G. Doty, pp. 33–45. Tuscaloosa: University of Alabama Press.

Ingold, T. (2011). Being Alive: Essays on Movement, Knowledge and Description. London: Routledge.

Jung, C. G. (1953–78). The Collected Works of C.G. Jung. Eds. H. Read, M. Fordham and G. Adler. London: Routledge.

Jung, C. (1954). On the Nature of the Psyche, in CW 8: pars. 343–442 in Herbert Read, Michael Fordham and Gerhard Adler (1983). The Collected Works of C.G. Jung. London: Routledge.

Jung, C. (1975). The Archetypes and the Collective Unconscious. Princeton: Princeton UP.

Jung, C. G. (2003). The Spirit in Man, Art and Literature. Translated by R. F. C. Hull. London: Routledge.

Jung, E. & von Franz, M. L. (1960). Die Graalslegende in psychologischer Sicht. Zürich: Rascher.

Jung, E. & von Franz, M. L. (1986). The Grail Legend. Boston: Sigo, pp. 364–365.

Kamberelis, G. (2003). Ingestion, Elimination, Sex, and Song: Trickster as Premodern Avatar of Postmodern Research Practice, *Qualitative Inquiry*, 9: 673–704.

Kemmis, S. (2012). Phronēsis, Experience, and the Primacy of Prâxis, in Phronesis as Professional Knowledge: Practical Wisdom in the Professions. Eds. E. A. Kinsella and A. Pitman. Rotterdam: Sense, pp. 147–162.

Kemmis, S. & Smith, T. (2008). Prâxis and Prâxis Development. In: Enabling Prâxis: Challenges for Education. Eds. S. Kemmis and T. Smith, pp. 3–13. Rotterdam: Sense.

Kirby, V. (2006). Culpability and the Double Cross: Irigaray with Merleau-Ponty. In: Feminist Interpretations of Maurice Merleau-Ponty. Eds. D. Olkowski and G. Weiss, pp. 127–146. University Park: The Pennsylvania State University Press.

Kirkpatrick, A. (2017). Feeling in the Flesh: Approaching an Ecological Ethic Through Whitehead and Merleau-Ponty, *Parrhesia: A Journal of Critical Philosophy*, 28: 176–196.

Klein, N. (2007). The Shock Doctrine: The Rise of Disaster Capitalism. New York: Metropolitan Books/Henry Holt.

Knight, S. (2009). Merlin: Knowledge and Power through the Ages. Ithaca: Cornell University Press.

Kociatkiewicz, J. (2008). The Cosmogonic Duel. In: Organizational Epics and Sagas: Tales of Organizations. Ed. M. Kostera, pp. 142–155. London: Palgrave.

Kociatkiewicz, J. & Kostera, M. (2012). The Good Manager: An Archetypical Quest for Morally Sustainable Leadership, *Organization Studies*, 33(7): 861–878.

Kooskora, M. & Isok, P. (2014). Ethical Leadership and Different Leadership Archetypes, *International Leadership Journal*. Fall, 6(3): 30–52.

Kostera, M. (2018). Adventurers and Lovers: Organizational Heroines and Heroes for a New Time, In the Hero's Journey. A *Tribute* to *Joseph Campbell* and *his 30th Anniversary* of *Death*, Special Issue, *Journal of Genius and Eminence*: 116–126.

Küpers, W. (2005). Phenomenology and Integral Pheno-Practice of Embodied Well-Be(com)ing in Organizations, *Culture and Organization*, 11(3): 221–231.

Küpers, W. (2011a). Dancing on the Limen – Embodied and Creative Inter-place as Thresholds of Be(com)ing: Phenomenological Perspectives on Liminality and Transitional Spaces in Organisations, Tamara, Journal for Critical Organization, 9(3–4): 45–59.

Küpers, W. (2011b). Trans-+-Form – Transforming Transformational Leadership for a Creative Change Practice, *Leadership & Organization Development Journal*, 32(1): 20–40.

Küpers, W. (2011c). Integral Responsibilities for a Responsive and Sustainable Practice in Organizations and Management, *Corporate Social Responsibility and Environmental Management Journal*, 18(3): 137–150.

Küpers, W. (2012a). Integral Response-abilities for Organising and Managing Sustainability. In: Business and Sustainability: Concepts, Strategies and Changes, Critical Studies on Corporate Responsibility, Governance and Sustainability. Eds. Gabriel Eweje and Michael Perry, Volume 3, pp. 25–58. London: Emerald.

Küpers, W. (2012b). Embodied Transformative Metaphors and Narratives in Organisational Life-Worlds of Change, *Journal of Organizational Change Management*, 26(3): 494–528.

Küpers, W. (2012c). Inter-Communicating – Phenomenological Perspectives on Embodied Communication and Con-Textuality in Organisation, *Journal for Communication and Culture*, 2(2): 114–138.

Küpers, W. (2013a). Between the Visible and the Invisible in Organisations. In: The Routledge Companion to Visual Organization. Eds. Emma Bell, Samantha Warren and Jonathan E. Schroeder, pp. 19–32. London: Routledge.

Küpers, W. (2013b). The Art of Practical Wisdom ~ Phenomenology of an Embodied, Wise Inter-practice in Organisation and Leadership. In: A Handbook of Practical Wisdom. Leadership, Organization and Integral Business Practice. Eds. W. Küpers and D. Pauleen, pp. 19–45. London: Ashgate Gower.

Küpers, W. (2015). De-+-Touring through 'Inter-Place'. In: Touring Consumption, Series Management-Culture-Interpretation. Eds. S. Sonnenburg and D. Wee, pp. 133–160. Heidelberg: Springer.

Küpers, W. (2017a). The Embodied Inter-Be(com)ing of Spirituality. The In-between as Spiritual Sphere in Practically Wise Organizations. In: Managing VUCA by an Integrative Self-Managed way: Enhancing Integrating Simplification Theory. Ed. Sharda Nandram, pp. 229–247. London: Springer.

Küpers, W. (2017b). Inter-Play(ing) – Embodied Possibilities of Serious Play at Work, *Journal of Organisation and Change Management*, 30(7): 993–1014.

Küpers, W. (2019). Reintegrating Práxis, Practices, Phrónêsis & Sustainable Action for Processing Systemic Constraints in the Business and Society Relationship. *Society and Business Review* (forthcoming).

Küpers, W. & Gunnlaugson, O. (2017). Wisdom Learning: Perspectives on Wising-up Business and Management Education. New York: Routledge.

Küpers , W. & Pauleen, D. (2013). A Handbook of Practical Wisdom: Leadership, Organization and Integral Business Practice. London: Ashgate Gower.

Küpers, W. & Weibler, J. (2008). Inter-Leadership – Why and How to Think Leader- and Followership Integrally, *Leadership*, 4(4): 443–447.

Lalonde, C. (2004). In Search of Archetypes in Crisis Management, *Journal of Contingencies & Crisis Management*, June, 12(2): 76–88.

Landes, D. (2018). The Art of Character: Between Repetition and Creation in Bergson and Merleau-Ponty. Karen Burke Memorial Lecture Stony Brook.

Landes, D. A., & Cruz-Pierre, A. Eds. (2013). Exploring the Work of Edward S. Casey: Giving Voice to Place, Memory, and Imagination. New York & London: Bloomsbury.

Lawrence-Mathers, A. (2012). The True History of Merlin the Magician. New Haven and London: Yale University Press.

Markale, J. (1995). Merlin: Priest of Nature. Richmond, VT: Inner Traditions.

Matthews, J. (2004). Merlin: Shaman, Prophet, Magician. London: Mitchell Beazley.

McCann, R. (2011). A Sensuous Ethics of Difference. *Hypatia*, 26(3): 497–517.

McGuire, W. & Hull, R. F. C. Eds. (1977). C.G. Jung Speaking: Interviews and Encounters. Princeton, NJ: Princeton University Press.

McNally, D. (2011). Monsters of the Market: Zombies, Vampires and Global Capitalism. Boston: Brill.

Mendenhall, M. E. & Marsh, W. J. (2010). Voices From the Past: Mary Parker Follett and Joseph Smith on Collaborative Leadership, *Journal of Management Inquiry*, 19(4): 284–303.

Merleau-Ponty, M. (1995). The Visible and the Invisible. Evanston: Northwestern University Press.

Merleau-Ponty, M. (2012). Phenomenology of Perception. London: Routledge.

Moore, R. L. & Gillette, D. (1990). King, Warrior, Magician, Lover: Rediscovering the Archetypes of the Mature Masculine. San Francisco: Harper.

Neher, A. (1996). Jung's Theory of Archetypes: A Critique, *Journal of Humanistic Psychology*, 36(2): 61–91.

Niditch, S. (1987). Underdogs and Tricksters. New York: Harper Collins.

Owen, A. (2004). The Place of Enchantment. Chicago: University of Chicago Press.

Painter, M. G. (2016). The Idea of Merlin: Artistic Depictions of Merlin and their Inspirations, Proceedings of the National Conference on Undergraduate Research (NCUR) 2016, University of North Carolina Asheville Asheville, North Carolina, April 7–9.

Papadopoulos, R. K. (2006). Jung's Epistemology and Methodology. In: The Handbook of Jungian Psychology: Theory, Practice and Applications. Ed. R. K. Papadopoulos, pp. 7–53. London: Routledge.

Parse, R. R. (1998). The Human Becoming School of Thought. Thousand Oaks, CA: Sage.

Parse, R. R. (2002). Mentoring Moments, *Nursing Science Quarterly*, 15: 97.

Petrovskaia, N. (2017). The Fool and the Wise Man: The Legacy of the Two Merlins in Modern Culture, *The Legacy of Courtly Literature*: 175–205

Plumwood, V. (1993). Feminism and the Mastery of Nature. New York: Routledge.

Radin, P. (1956). The Trickster: A Study in American Indian Mythology. New York: Bell.

Rego, A., Cunha, M. P. & Clegg, S. (2012). The Virtues of Leadership: Contemporary Challenge for Global Managers. Oxford: Oxford University Press.

Rooney, D., McKenna, B. & Liesch, P. (2010). Wisdom and Management in the Knowledge Economy. London: Routledge.

Rosanvallon, P. (2011). Democratic Legitimacy: Impartiality, Reflexivity, Proximity. Princeton: Princeton University Press.

Roszak, T., Gomes, M. E. & Kanner, A. D. (Eds) (1995). Ecopsychology: Restoring the Earth, Healing the Mind. San Francisco, CA: Sierra Club Books.

Rubenstein, M.-J. (2008). Strange *Wonder*: The Closure of Metaphysics and the Opening of Awe. New York: Columbia University Press.

Sallis, J. (2016). The Return of Nature. Bloomington, IN: Indiana University Press.

Salman, S. (1986). The Horned God: Masculine Dynamics of Power and Soul, *Quadrant*, 19(2): 7–25.

Scherer, A. G. & Palazzo, G. (2007). Towards a Political Conception of Corporate Responsibility. Business and Society Seen From a Habermasian Perspective, *Academy of Management Review*, 32(4): 1096–1120.

THE STORY OF MERLIN AS A TALE OF WISDOM

Semper, P. (2015). 'Camelot Must Come Before all Else': Fantasy and Family in the BBC Merlin. In: Ashton Medieval Afterlives in Contemporary Culture, pp. 115–123. New York: Bloomsbury.

Shepard, P. (1992). Nature and Madness. San Francisco: Sierra Club.

Simondon, G. (1995). L'individu et sa genèse physico-biologique (l'individuation à la lumière des notions de forme et d'information). Paris: PUF.

Simondon, G. (2007). L'individuation psychique et collective. Paris: Aubier.

Smith, C. (1994). The Merlin Factor: Leadership and Strategic Intent, Business Strategy Review, 5(1): 67–83.

Smith, C. (1995). The Merlin Factor: Keys to Corporate Kingdom. London: Gower.

Smith, C. (2009). Navigating From the Future: A Primer for Sustainable Transformation. POD BookSurge Publishing.

Spivack, Ch. (1994). Merlin: A Thousand Heroes with One Face. New York: The Edwin.

Stevens, A. (2006). The Archetypes. In: The Handbook of Jungian Psychology Theory, Practice and Applications. Ed. R. Papadopoulos, pp. 74–93. London and New York: Routledge.

Steward, R. J. (1986). MERLIN: The Prophetic Vision and The Mystic Life. London: Arkana.

Stewart, R. J. (1986). The Prophetic Vision and Mystical Life of Merlin. London: Arkana.

Stewart, R. J. Ed. (1987). The Book of Merlin. Poole, Dorset: Blandford Press.

Stewart, R. J. & Matthews, J. Eds. (1995). Merlin Through the Ages: A Chronological Anthology and Source Book. London: Blandford.

Tennyson, A. (1859). Merlin and Vivien, in Idylls of the King. London: Edward Moxon & Co.

Tennyson, A. (1889). Merlin and the Gleam. In: Demeter and Other Poems, pp. 132–141. London: Macmillan.

Todres, L. A. (2000). Embracing Ambiguity: Transpersonal Development and the Phenomenological Tradition, Journal of Religion and Health, 39(3): 227–237.

Todres, L. (2007). Embodied Enquiry: Phenomenological Touchstones for Research, Psychotherapy and Spirituality. Hampshire & New York: Palgrave.

Tolstoy, N. (1985). The Quest for Merlin. London: Hamilton.

Turner, V. (1982). From Ritual to Theatre: The Human Seriousness of Play. New York: Berghahn.

Uhl-Bien, M. (2006). Relational Leadership Theory: Exploring the Social Processes of Leadership and Organizing, The Leadership Quarterly, 17: 654–676.

Washburn, M. (2003a). Embodied Spirituality in a Sacred World. Albany, NY: SUNY Press.

Washburn, M. (2003b). Transpersonal Dialogue: A New Direction, The Journal of Transpersonal Psychology, 35(1): 1–19.

Weiss, G. (Ed.) (2008). Intertwinings: Interdisciplinary Encounters with Merleau-Ponty. Albany, NY: State University of New York Press.

Weiss, G. (2000). Écart: The Space of Corporeal Difference. In: Chiasms. Merleau-Ponty's Notion of Flesh. Eds. F. Evans & L. Lawlor, pp. 203–218. Albany, NY: State University of New York Press.

Whitney G. J., Tesone, D. & Buchalski, R. (2000). The Leader as Mentor, Journal of Leadership Studies, 7(3): 56–67.

Wilber, K. (1993). The Pre/Trans Fallacy. In: Paths Beyond Ego. Eds. R. Walsh and F. Vaughan, pp. 124–129. New York: JP Tarcher/Putnam.

Wilber, K. (1995). Sex, Ecology, Spirituality: The Spirit of Evolution. Boston: Shambhala.

Wood, M. (2005). The Fallacy of Misplaced Leadership, *Journal of Management Studies*, 42(6): 1101–1121.

Yeats, W. B. (1901/1980). Magic, in Essays and Introductions. London: Macmillan.

Ying-hsiu, Lu (2014). Magic as Gendered Knowledge in Merlin's Rise and Fall: A Discourse on Male Homosocial Bonding NCUE, *Journal of Humanities*, 9: 83–100.

INDEX

Note: Page locators in *italic* refer to figures or photographs.

Aeneid 136, 137–147, 150–151, 155–157
aesthetics and leadership 173–174
Ah-Ah 6–7, 116–122; ambush of hope 119–120, 126–127; arrow of uncertainty 120–122, 127–129; implication for management and leadership education 129–132; interpretation 122–129; museum show experiment 129–130; poison of arrogance 118, 122–124; trap of doubt 118–119, 124–126
alternative economic organisations 90–91
amor fati 170–171
animal allegories and metaphors 1–2, 36–43
Anthropocene Age 1–2, 3, 4, 5, 7, 8, 9, 168–169; attunement with natural rhythms 174–175; leadership and hope 11–35; leadership as collective action 174–176; leadership as non-doing 176–177; leadership requirements 14; wild becoming and leadership 207–208
archetypes: critique of Jungian 182, 214–215n4; Merlin as 180–182; Merlin as magician and wise man 182–185; Merlin as trickster 200–201; in relation to organisation and management 182, 187, 215n5
Ardelt, M. 19, 25n4
Aristotle 13, 56–57, 123, 165, 166
Armstrong, Louis 161, 166
arrogance, poison of 118, 122–124

art: division of media 147–151, 154; as propaganda, crowding out truth 150–151; as separate from leadership and management of affairs 150, 157–158
Arthur, Merlin as counselling adviser to King 188–192
Attali, Jacques 159
Aurelius, Marcus 72
"Autobiography in Five Short Chapters" 70–71

Bakhtin, Mikhail 29n8
Bauman, Zygmunt 86, 87, 88
Beardsley, Aubrey 202, *203*
Benjamin, W. 19, 25–26n5
Blake, William 136, 151–155, *152*, 158–159
Braybrooke, D. 128
Bruya, B. 19, 25n4
burdens, carrying our: approach to suffering 64–65; assessing our capacity for 71–73; assessing the burden 70–71; choosing with wisdom 3, 63–64, 65–67, 68–69, 73–75; joy in 67, 68; in leadership roles 68–73, 75–78, 79–81; Picking a Cross folktale 3–4, 62–63; search for happiness 65–66, 67, 68
Burne-Jones, Edward 209

Carnegie Foundation for Excellence in Teaching 19
charismatic leadership 125
Choepel, Gedun 121, 129

INDEX

choices, making wise 3, 63–64, 65–67, 68–69, 73–75
collective leadership 91, 174–176, 193–194
collectivism 40–41
colonial culture 110
common good 14, 19, 194, 196; cooperating in nature for 1, 38, 42; practical wisdom for 13, 56, 57, 65, 70
communication of a message 112–113
compassion 70, 75, 80–81, 197
competition: animal fable an allegory for business 1–2, 36–43; monster of 77
confidence 50; over- 48, 49, 50, 53–54, 56
control over events 66–67; monster of need for 77–78
corporate: culture 107–108, 109, 113–115; psychopaths 91
cross, picking a *see* Picking a Cross
cultural: control, narratives a mechanism of 16; diversity, visitors navigating 106, 108, 109–110; heritage 130–131; superiority 108–111, 114
culture: colonial 110; conflicting versions of 130–131; within an organisation 107–108, 109, 113–115; tolerance for change 111, 114, 115
cunning 147, 154–155, 156, 158

Dædalus and Icarus myth 2–3, 48–49, 51–53; hubris and hubristic leadership 49–51; hubrists of recent times 57–58; interpretation 53–54, 56, 57; mitigating hubristic leadership 55–57; re-storying 54–55; sensemaking 54
David-Neel, Alexandra 124
Davidson, J. 49
death: affirmative attitudes to 170–173; cut down in prime 166–167; fear of 78, 170, 172; inevitability of 166–169; living and facing 169–173; narratives of 168–169
democracy 87, 90–91
digital storytelling 16

disconnection of leadership from people and land: alternative forms of leadership 90–91; in the interregnum 86–88; 'ivory tower syndrome' 89; Legend of King Popiel 4–5, 83–86; losing legitimacy 88–89; post-lie leadership 94–95; relevance of Legend of King Popiel for leadership practice 91–93
disruptive innovators 41
distributed leadership 193–194
Dorst, Tankred 211
doubt, trap of 118–119, 124–126
Douglas, M. 124
Dreiser, Theodore 38
Dutton, J. 70, 80
"The Dyin' Crapshooter's Blues" 169, 171–172

eco-eschatology 24n1
Ehler, Ursula 211
embodied spirituality 204–205, 220n29
emotion 46–47, 57
emulation exemplars 21–22
engaged Gelassenheit 210–211, 222–223n35
engraving, Laocoön as 151–155, 158–159
Epictetus 72
ethical behaviour 190
experiential processing 46–47, 57
expertise 127–129; dealing with the 'utterly unexpected' 131–132; questioning official sources of 129–131

fake news 104
falsehoods and truth 104–105
fear: 'be not afraid' 79–80; of death 78, 170, 172; monsters of 78; of suffering, overcoming 65, 66–67, 74
Ferrari, M. 18, 20, 21, 25n3
Ferrer, Jorge 204, 205, 219–220n27, 220n29
Ferry, David 144
The Financier 38
Fisher-King 195, 196
Fisher, M. 15, 180, 213–214n3
flesh, philosophy of 205–207, 220–222n30
Flyvbjerg, B. 124, 128, 129

232

INDEX

Follett, Mary Parker 193
Four Zoas 155
Frankl, Victor 63, 70, 73, 74
Franz, M.L. von 203
friendship 165
Fuld, Richard 57–58
fundamentalism 109
future: burdens 71; managerial imperative of looking to 89; prophecies and visions of 186–187, 188, 216–218n15, 217

"Gambler's Blues" 170
Gawande, Atul 170
Gelassenheit 210–211, 222–223n35
general wisdom 21
Gesar of Ling, King 117, 121, 122, 129
gifts of learning 76–78
"The Gleam" 209
good life, living the 163–166
Grail Quest 194–198; lessons for leadership 198–199
Gramsci, Antonio 86, 87
Grant Study 165
greed, tale of 39
Greek myths: Muses 173–174; Ovid and Greek 47–49; Phaethon 53–54; Prometheus 11–12 *see also* Dædalus and Icarus myth
Gulliver's Travels 5–6, 98–103; allure of pride 111–115; falsehoods 104–105; fitting in 109–110; *Gulliver's Gate* 99, 105–108, *107, 110, 114*; Houyhnhnms 98, 100, 101, 102–103, 108–109; Lilliputians 98, 101, 105, 110; navigating cultural diversity 106, 108, 109–110; paradise in land of Houyhnhnms 98, 108–109; Projectors 110–111; reinterpretations 106; return to England 109, 111–112, 114; superiority and distorted morality 108–111, 114; Yahoos 98, 103, 108, 109
Guthrie, Graeme 131

happiness: Grant Study 165; as hubris 147; living the good life 163–166; searching for 65–66, 67, 68
Hauke, C. 214n4

heritage sites 130–131
hero worship 112
heterogeneous leadership 94–95
heteroglossia 24, 29n8
Hirschman, A.O. 125, 129
history, multiple versions of 130–131
hope, ambush of 119–120, 126–127
hubris 49–51, 53, 112, 147
'hubris syndrome' 49–50
hubristic leadership: Dædalus and Icarus myth and lessons for 2–3, 48–49, 51–54; destructive nature of 45; examples 49, 54–55, 57–58; and hubris 49–51; practical wisdom for mitigating 55–57; re-storying 54–55; sensemaking 54; use of myth in relation to 2–3, 44–45, 53–54

Icarus *see* Dædalus and Icarus myth
'The Icarus Paradox' 49
ideologies, narratives and reinforcing of 16
individualism 40
information received, evaluating 105
inner work in leadership development 79–80
innovation: disruptive 41; excessive 98, 110–111; fear stifling 78
insecurity, monster of 76–77
interregnum 86–88
'ivory tower syndrome' 89

jazz funeral 174–175
joy 67, 68, 171–172
Jung, Carl 181–182, 203; critique of 214–215n4

Kagemusha, Shadow Warrior 127
Kirby, V. 221, 222
Knight, S. 184, 215–216n9
Kurosawa, Akura 127

Lady of the Lake 208
Landman, T. 129
Laocoön 7–8; as montage 151–155, *152, 158–159*; as parrhesiast 146–147; as sculpture 147–151, *148, 152–153, 157–158*; as text 137–147, 150–151, 155–157; in three different tales 136; wisdom and leadership 155–159

233

INDEX

leaders-as-learners 75–78, 79, 80, 189
leadership from within 75–78, 79, 80–81
legacy, leaving a 192
Legend of King Popiel 4–5, 83–86, 91–92; consequences of disconnected leadership 86–88; implications for development of more responsible leadership practices 94–95; morale of story 88–89; personal resonances 89–91; relevance for leadership practice 91–93
Lessing, Gotthold Ephraim 136, 147–151, 157, 160n2
Lindblom, C.E. 128
living cross of wisdom 69–73

MacIntyre, A. 18
Markowicz, A. 116
McGuinn, Roger 170
McTell, Willie 169
meaning, search for 65–66, 73–75, 76
media: art as separate from leadership 150, 157; division of artistic 147–151, 154
mentoring 188–192
Merleau-Ponty, M. 180, 195, 205, 206, 212, 220–222n30
Merlin 9–10; advice to King Vortigern 186–187; as archetype 180–182; embodied spirituality 204–205, 220n29; enduring appeal 211–213; enfleshed wild being 205–207, 220–222n30; engaged Gelassenheit 210–211, 222–223n35; Grail Quest 194–198; Grail Quest and lessons for leadership 198–199; lessons for leadership and organisation 187–188, 198–199, 207–208; as mad wild man 202–205, 218n19, 218n20; as magician and wise man 182–185; many representations and interpretations 183–185, 215–216n9, 216n12; as mentor and counselling adviser to King Arthur 188–192; moving backwards in time 188, 217; moving between visible and invisible 187; origin and destiny 185–187; prophecies and visions of future 186–187, 188, 216–218n15, 217; reasons to

study 178–180; and Round Table 192–194; as tragic romantic lover 208–210, 222n34; as trickster 200–201; virtues, enacting of 191–192
"The Merlin Factor" 188, 217
'Merlin or the Wasteland' 211
Metamorphoses 44, 47–49, 53
 see also Dædalus and Icarus myth
middle way, keeping to 53–54, 56, 57
Mitchell, W.T. 149, 150, 151
monsters in learning to lead from within 76–78
montage, Laocoön as 151–155, 158–159
Montaigne, M. 166–167, 169, 172
Morgana and Mordred 195, 218n18
Morvan, F. 116, 130
Muses 173–174
music and leadership 173–174
Myrddin 183–184, 202, 218n19
mystification, narratives as mechanisms of 16–17
myths 44, 45–47; Muses and Greek 173–174; Ovid and Greek 47–49; Phaethon 53–54; Prometheus 11–12; use in relation to hubristic leadership 2–3, 44–45, 53–54
 see also Dædalus and Icarus myth

narcissism 50, 89
narrative: co-creating 22–24; contributing to education of wise leaders 18–22; emulation 21–22; meaning 15–18; simulations 20–21; wisdom and 2–18
nature: animal fable of competition in 1–2, 36–43; attunement with 174–175; contact with 87, 88, 90; Merlin as wild man in 202–205, 220–222n30; re-conceiving and re-evaluating 206–207; wild being and lessons for leadership 207–208
Nelson, Portia 70–71
Nietzsche, F.W. 170–171, 175
Niniane 222n34
noise 159
non-doing, leadership as 176–177
Nussbaum, Martha 19, 28–29n7

order, creating new 124–125
over-ambition 49, 50, 53–54, 56, 57

234

INDEX

over-confidence 48, 49, 50, 53–54, 56
Ovid 44, 47–49, 51–54, 56
Owen, D. 49, 51, 187

paideia 64, 69
Palmer, Parker 75–78, 79–80
Pandora's box 11
parrhesiasts 146–147
Parse, R.R. 189
Parsifal 195–197
Pascal, B. 126–127
past: learning from 70–71; multiple versions of 130–131
Pausch, R. 22
personal growth, struggle as integral to 3, 63–64, 64–65, 66–67
personal wisdom 21
Phaethon 53–54
phronesis 13, 56, 64, 65, 69, 70, 74, 123–124; prototypes 22
Picking a Cross 3–4, 62–63; choosing wisely 63–64; implications for development of leaders 75–78; implications for development of more responsible leadership practices 79–81; moral of story 64–67; personal relevance 67–68; relevance for leadership practice 68–73; search for meaning 73–75
pluralizing leadership 193–194
poetry, medium of 147, 148–149
policy making, synoptic ideal of 128
Popiel, King *see* Legend of King Popiel
post-lie leadership 94–95
power: illusion of 126–127; intoxication of 49–50, 52; relationships, narratives legitimising 16
practical wisdom: associated with leadership 14; Laocoön, leadership and 155–159; meaning 13–15; for mitigating hubristic leadership 55–57; relation between narrative and 18, 19, 25–26n5, 26–28n6, 28–29n7; for strategic decision-making 128–129, 131–132
praxis 193, 198, 199, 205
pre/trans fallacy 204
Prisoner's Dilemma 40
Prometheus 11–12
prototypes 22
psychopaths, corporate 91
public institutions 130–131

Rake *see* The Unfortunate Rake
Rancière, J. 149, 150, 153, 157, 158
re-storying 54–55
reason: deadening forces of 154–155; helping people to exert practical 130–131; orders of 153, 158–159
relationships, interpersonal 165
responsible and sustainable leadership practices, developing 79–81, 94–95
Ricoeur, Paul 19, 26–28n6
Round Table 192–194

The Sandpiper and the Clam Struggle 1–2, 36; as a battle for survival 38; fisherman as disruptive innovator 41; interpretation 37–41; as a Prisoner's Dilemma about trust 39–41; as a tale of greed 39
satire 112–113
Schram, S. 129
sculpture, Laocoön as 147–151, *148*, 152–153, 157–158
Segalen, Victor 123
self-belief, inflated 50–51
self-esteem 56
sensemaking 20, 44–45, 54
'sentence image' 153
Serenity Prayer 69–70, 71, 73
Shepard, P. 204, 219n25
simulations, narrative 20–21
situational leadership 193
skills: building practical 128; development of new 124–125
Smith, C. 216–217n15
social media 66, 104
somatic body 221
sorcerer, song of 116
spirituality, embodied 204–205, 220n29
"St. James Infirmary" 161, 166
Stevens, A. 181, 182
stoicism 66–67, 72
stories 15–18; co-creating 22–24; contributing to education of wise leaders 18–22, 44 *see also* narrative storytelling 25–26n5, 113; digital 16
Strathern, Marilyn 127
success: business school students' definitions 163–165; images of 162–166
suffering: approaching with wisdom 63–64, 64–65; being worthy of our

235

INDEX

73; in leadership education 80–81; overcoming fear of 65, 66–67, 74; search for meaning through 73–74, 76; stoic approach to 72
survival, tale of a battle for 38
sustainable and responsible leadership practices, developing 79–81, 94–95
Swift, Jonathan 98, 99–103, 112
synoptic ideal of policy making 128

Taylor, Mark 171
Tennyson, Alfred 184, 209
Theoi 173
"This is Water" 41
transpersonal studies 204, 219–220n27
trickster archetype 122, 131, 200–201
Troy, siege of 136, 137–147, 155–157
trust, tale of 39–41
truth: failure in persuading others of 156–157; and lies 94–95, 104–105; parrhesiasts and telling of 146–147; questioning official sources of 129–131
Twitter 66, 104

uncertainty, arrow of 120–122, 127–129
unexpected, dealing with 123, 128, 131–132
The Unfortunate Rake 8–9; affirmative attitudes to death 170–173; ambivalent figure 162–163; cut down in prime 166–167; history 161; inevitability of death 166–169; life facing death 169–173; living the good life 163–166; musical cultural tradition 173–174; relevance to leadership scholars 173–177
Urizen 155

Virgil 136, 137–144
virtue ethics 56
virtues 191–192, 194, 196, 198
visionary leadership 91–92, 188, 216–218n15, 217
Vivien 209–210
Vortigern, King 186–187

Wallace, David Foster 41
Worline, M. 70, 80

Zundel, M. 15, 24–25n2, 147